WISE HER STILL

Copyright

info@tiffanykameni.com

ISBN-10: 0-9854106-7-1
ISBN-13: 978-0-9854106-7-4

Contributors:
Tiffany Buckner- Kameni (Author)
Iris L. Jones (Editor)
Lynette Wallace (Editor)
B. Davinia Gordon (Proofreader)

Anointed Fire Christian Publishing

Disclaimer

This book is designed to provide information and motivation to our readers. It is sold with the understanding that the publisher is not engaged to render any type of psychological, legal, or any other kind of professional advice. No warranties or guarantees are expressed or implied by the author, since every man has his own measure of faith. The individual author(s) shall not be liable for any physical, psychological, emotional, financial, or commercial damages, including, but not limited to, special, incidental, consequential or other damages. Our views and rights are the same: You are responsible for your own choices, actions, and results.

The stories in this book are fictional. Names, characters, businesses, places, events and incidents are either the products of the author's imagination or used in a fictitious manner. Any resemblance to actual persons, living or dead, or actual events is purely coincidental.

Table of Contents

Note From The Author

Thank you so much for your continued support.

When we exit a chapter in our lives, if we get in GOD and stay there, HE explains to us what it was that we went through and why we went through it. In other words, HE shows us the lesson in it, if we'll only listen.

If this book blesses you, be sure to tell your friends and family. As you're reading it, I am sure some of the stories will hit home for you. Maybe it's your sister, your cousin, your friend or yourself that you can relate one or more of these stories to. Either way, be sure to spread the word and encourage them to go and get it...or get it for them. But, don't give them your copy because when one of life's lessons is upon you, you may want your copy for sharpening. And when one of life's lessons is upon them, they may want to get your copy again for sharpening.

And please, don't just look for the familiarity in the stories, but look for the meat of revelation. Thanks again and I love you much!

Sincerely,
Tiffany Kameni
www.tiffanykameni.com

INTRODUCTION

"Now the serpent was more subtle than any beast of the field which the LORD God had made. And he said unto the woman, Yea, has God said, you shall not eat of every tree of the garden? And the woman said unto the serpent, We may eat of the fruit of the trees of the garden: But of the fruit of the tree which is in the midst of the garden, God has said, You shall not eat of it, neither shall you touch it, lest you die. And the serpent said unto the woman, You shall not surely die: For God does know that in the day you eat thereof, then your eyes shall be opened, and you shall be as gods, knowing good and evil. And when the woman saw that the tree was good for food, and that it was pleasant to the eyes, and a tree to be desired to make one wise, she took of the fruit thereof, and did eat, and gave also unto her husband with her; and he did eat. And the eyes of them both were opened, and they knew that they were naked; and they sewed fig leaves together, and made themselves aprons." (Genesis 3:1-7)

In the beginning of mankind, there were no questions asked. GOD created Adam; the first man to ever walk the earth, and HE formed Eve from Adam's rib. HE gave the pair a few instructions to live by, and they did as they were told. However, something was introduced to Eve that would change the face of mankind forever. What was introduced to Eve? Doubt. Genesis 3:1 reads: ***Now the serpent was more subtil than any beast of the field which the LORD God had made. And he said unto the woman, Yea, <u>hath God said, Ye shall not eat of every tree of the garden?</u>***

The serpent simply planted a seed. He knew that by planting a seed of doubt in the woman, he could cause her to question the very words of GOD. He introduced her to an alternative to GOD'S instruction, and that alternative was independence. She didn't have to listen to GOD; she could be like GOD! She began to consider what the serpent said against what GOD said (confusion); she looked at the tree and saw that the fruit was pleasant (temptation), and the tree could make her wise like GOD (envy). Therefore, temptation, confusion and envy first entered mankind through woman! After the devil lied to Eve; she took of the fruit and gave some to her husband.

Nowadays, women still wrestle with question marks. Women still wrestle with temptation; even using their bodies and their beauty as vessels of temptation to seduce men into sin. Women still wrestle with confusion, and this confusion triggers our heightened emotions. When a woman is sure of herself, her relationship, her job and her finances; she is at peace. But, when a woman begins to consider the alternative to what GOD has said; confusion always wakes up and dances with fear. This is why women tend to panic and become extremely emotional during times of confusion. No matter what GOD has said; women often consider the alternatives and panic. Women still wrestle with envy. A woman can see another woman and decide that she doesn't like her, or that she wants to be just like her. These sins are strongest in the woman because they first entered mankind through the woman.

Nevertheless, women see men as stubborn creatures; and they are. But, why is that? Because men tend to make decisions and finalize them without considering the alternatives. This makes them great leaders, but for a woman spun by fear; this makes him a liability. For example, a man can walk into a store looking for a pair of pants to wear to an event. Once he sees the one that he likes, if the size is right and the price is right; he's sold. He then heads to the cash register to make his purchase and leave. His shopping trip could take less than 15 minutes. But, a woman, on the other hand, could go into that same store on that same mission and spend hours trying to decide between several pairs of pants. Because the curiosity of a woman is triggered when she has an alternative. This is why GOD gave man the position as head over the woman. It wasn't because the man was made first; it was because the woman was tempted first and temptation would now be a part of her make up. This is why you will find that it is very hard for women to stay friends with other women. Because when a woman is confused, she does like Eve and carries the fruit of their confusion to anyone that she has access to, and we hate that.

'Wise Her Still' is a unique teaching device that answers many of the questions that the enemy has presented to women. Questions designed to birth doubt and send us on undercover missions outside of the protective walls of truth. Questions about relationships are at the top of our lists. Why did he cheat? Why do women envy one another? What are the symptoms of envy? Is GOD'S Word true?

In this book, you will find several stories that you may relate to. These stories are created to teach, inspire and diffuse that deadly question mark that has poisoned so many women today. In 'Wise Her Still,' you will find the stories of more than 25 women who took the alternative routes and you will witness what happened to these women as a result. Their failures don't have to be your failures. Let their lessons be your blessings!

Loyalty Invokes Blessings

"Dedication Not Medication."

As the world spirals away from GOD, medication is quickly becoming an alternative. More believers believe in the power of medication versus the power of GOD. Believers are quick to say, "Well, I'll pray that the LORD heals me through this medication," or "I'm praying over my medication." That's fine if that's how high your faith can jump, but dedication to learning the WORD of GOD will benefit you more than medicating yourself or your children. Medication is the world's version of power. Sometimes it works; sometimes it doesn't. But, GOD'S WORD works always.

Why are more people turning to medication? Because there aren't many who take the time to study the WORD daily and pray to GOD daily. People are becoming seasonal prayers; praying only when they find themselves in a storm, but ignoring the LORD through sunny weather.

Chasity is a troubled young woman. She goes to church every Sunday, pays her tithes and tries to live a life that is pleasing to GOD, but Chasity, like everyone else, has an issue. She was diagnosed with bipolar disorder and schizophrenia some years ago. Rather than rebuke the spirit behind her condition, Chasity medicates herself every day to keep from climbing the 'highs' and dropping into the 'lows' of her condition. Chasity also recently left her church and joined another one. It turns out, the pastor (Patrick Turner) at her old church gave a sermon about demons being behind most illnesses and psychological disorders and Chasity just does not believe this. After all, her doctor is the educated one, and he gave her a reasonable sounding explanation as to why she has this condition. Her pastor had been getting on her nerves anyway. Chasity always felt like he was referring to her during service and his Facebook posts, she felt, always seemed to be targeting her. In addition, Pastor Turner would always ask the congregation to come to the altar, so he could pray over them, but when he did so, Chasity would get up and leave. She believed that he was looking for an excuse to touch her.

One day, while at the supermarket, Chasity meets another woman. Not knowing that this woman is a pastor, Chasity strikes up a conversation with her as they wait in the backed-up lines. They began to talk about church and the LORD. Chasity tells Pastor Rhonda about her diagnosis and why she has decided to look for another church. Pastor Rhonda agrees and says to Chasity that she too believes that bipolar disorder, schizophrenia and many psychological issues occur as a result of a chemical imbalance in the brain and not as the result of a demon. Chasity is overtaken with joy. She believes that GOD has sent her this woman to be her pastor and best friend! So, the next Sunday, she attends Rhonda's church and joins immediately.

Every Sunday, Chasity goes to church for service and leaves fulfilled. Her new pastor doesn't bother her at all. As a matter of fact, she wants to ordain Chasity as an Evangelist.

Explanation:

This is very common. Chasity chose medicating herself over simply dedicating herself to the WORD of GOD. Pastor Turner was telling the truth in his sermons, but Chasity, like many believers, did not understand that the truth will cut any flesh that is not under subjection to the WORD of GOD. If it's not dead, you will feel its sting. Nor did Chasity turn to her Bible to study and show herself approved. She trusted more in man's findings than she did in GOD'S WORD. So when the tests came her way, of course, she failed them because she was trying to take a spiritual test with a natural pencil. She looked for someone who would pacify the demons in her, rather than cast them out. Pastor Turner had been making altar calls, but this intimidating fear would come over Chasity, and she began to reason in her infected thinking that he was after her. Because Chasity's mind was under siege and she was used to it being there, she didn't like the sound of any keys that threatened to set her free. Nope. She was comfortable in her bondage. GOD gave us a sound mind; a mind of peace and not disorder. Anytime chaos is present; Satan is present.

There are many leaders out today who will preach to the flesh because they believe two doctrines. They partly believe the WORD of GOD, and they wholly believe in man's findings. Of course, this won't change a life or a mind; it'll only pacify the flesh and put that person's demon at ease. This helps some leaders to keep the numbers up in their churches or followers, and at the same time; they don't have to tap into faith that they don't have, trying to deliver these people. All they have to do is give them man's report and let them learn to co-exist with their demons. They reason with man and try to combine natural doctrine with spiritual doctrine and forge GOD'S Name to it. Their words don't match GOD'S WORD! Read it! That's why it is important to consult with the LORD before you get up and go into anybody's church building or eat food from anybody's table. This food I refer to is whatever information they are serving you.

Pastor Rhonda knew a lot of scriptures, but she did not know the

WORD, and the WORD was not found in her. Instead, she memorized scriptures. Now, this is not to say that every leader that gives misguided information is not of the LORD because many of them are. Sometimes they are simply in the wrong season trying to feed people with their understanding when it has not yet yielded its fruit. Then again, many are simply not HIS.

"For God has not given us the spirit of fear; but of power, and of love, and of a sound mind." (2 Timothy 1:7)

If a sound mind is from the LORD, where do you think an unstable one comes from? GOD is definitely not a double agent and since HE told us in ***Ephesians 6:12, "For we wrestle not against flesh and blood, but against principalities, against powers, against the rulers of the darkness of this world, against spiritual wickedness in heavenly places,"*** we can only draw the conclusion that anything that wrestles against our sanity is of the devil.

If someone doesn't have the faith to be healed, by all means, recommend medication, therapy, surgery and whatever treatment they can get. But, remember this: JESUS healed a boy with epilepsy. Speak with a non-believing leader and he/she will try to discredit even the very works of the LORD.

PREPAID PROSTITUTION

"Some men will spend a little bit of money a little bit of time for a whole lot of you"

"Trust in the LORD with all your heart; and lean not unto your own understanding. In all your ways acknowledge him, and he shall direct your paths" (Proverbs 3:5-6)

There are so many women within the church that are still bound by fornication. Fornication is not only a sin against GOD, but it is a sin against the body. It goes without saying, most women in fornication, who know that it is wrong, are hoping to come out of it. In the majority of these cases, the women believe that sex would convince the men in their sights that they are marriage material because they are still bound by a worldly way of thinking. They believe that without sex, a man won't marry them. And in many cases, some of the women are demonically infected with what has manifested as a sexual addiction. No matter how we chop it up and explain it, it's wrong.

But, even worse than those are the women who believe that they have it all figured out because the man that's sleeping with them is paying their bills or helping to pay their bills. When I was in the world, I can remember hearing women boast about how their boyfriends or sex partners would, for example, pay their car

> notes. They looked down on the women who got little or nothing for their crimes against GOD. My question to you: Is the price of fornication worth allowing a man who is not your husband to park his soul in your soul and then leave your remains for another man to ravish? And then still have hell to pay for it? Whether he pays your rent or buys you a house, there is no price high enough for your soul. And cash is not the accepted currency in hell.

Camille went to church twice a week. She was also the Bible Study Teacher for the little girls, ages 10-17, and she sang in the choir. She knew what was right, and she knew what was wrong. Nevertheless, Camille was leading a double life. On one hand, she was this "church" girl as many would label her. On the other hand, she was an active fornicator.

Her boyfriend, Dexter really liked her. He called it love, but love leads no man to sin; love only leads to repentance. Therefore, what Dexter had for Camille was lust coupled with his obsession with Camille's physical appearance. Camille looked like she was torn from the pages of an exotic magazine. Camille was a unique mixture of races. Her dad was Japanese, and her mother was biracial; Indian and African American. So, Camille had a uniqueness about her. Her skin looked like smooth peanut butter, and her eyes were a light golden brown that seemed to blend perfectly with her skin. Her hair was dark and cut into a bob hairstyle that framed her beautiful oval face. Dexter just could never get enough of looking at her, and he was determined to have her for life. And he paid good money to make sure she would never feel compelled to look outside of him.

Dexter was a cardiovascular surgeon, so he made really good money, and he wasn't ashamed to flaunt it. He had the great career, the trophy girlfriend and a huge house. Plus, he enjoyed the perks of having multiple women, but Camille was his "main trophy." Nevertheless, he loved his freedom, so he opted to purchase another home and let Camille stay there. He also bought her a brand-new BMW and kept her up by buying her clothes, regular visits to the salon and so on. Camille pretty much knew about Dexter's other female interests, but she prided herself in being the one and only one that he spent large amounts of money on. She believed herself to be the "one" that he'd chosen as the future Mrs., and if not, at least she'd gotten a house, a car and a whole lot of cash out of it. She didn't care that Dexter liked to snort cocaine and loved to frequent strip clubs in search of women. She was the main girl and she knew it.

Camille also knew her lifestyle was wrong, but to stop it meant she would have to move back home with her mother and father and finish college. She would have to turn down the monthly $5,000 allowance that Dexter gave her. Wrong or no wrong, Camille believed that if she continued to look the part and act the part that eventually she would be Mrs. Dexter Palmer. After all, she was the most "exotic" and best looking of all the candidates.

And Camille did what was expected of her. She didn't try to trap him with a baby or pressure him into commitment. Instead, she made it a point to keep Dexter smiling at all times. No matter what Dexter wanted from her, she gave it to him. But, what GOD wanted, she ignored.

Three years after their relationship began; Dexter came down with pneumonia and was hospitalized. There, he learned that he was HIV-positive, and he had to notify all of the women that he'd been intimate with. It turns out, of all the women he had an ongoing sexual relationship with; Camille was the only woman that he slept with without using a condom. He liked her that much. But, he didn't catch HIV from Camille. He'd met a woman some eight months ago at a party. He snorted cocaine and wound up having unprotected sex with this woman. And it was she that gave him HIV.

Dexter had given Camille a lot. He gave her a house, a car, furniture, clothing, jewelry, tons of cash and HIV. The women whom she'd laughed at for accepting little or nothing were all negative of the disease because, again, Dexter always wore condoms while having intercourse with them.

Explanation:

Now, I know you are probably saddened that this story couldn't end better. We all love a happy ending! But, often in life, we have to come face to face with reality. This story isn't designed to make you feel all warm inside. It's to inform you that Satan will pay top dollar for your life. But, CHRIST paid the highest price to be paid and that was HIS life. You put yourself on clearance when you accept Satan's offer to buy you with the things of this world. Many women have paid for their choices with their own lives because they chose to auction themselves off to the highest bidder.

Having sex with a man for gain is prepaid prostitution. If you're giving him your body for money, a place to stay, or the chance to one day be his wife; you are paying for him with your body, and he is paying for you with material things, lies, and promises. No matter how much this woman sleeps with that man and gets nothing for it, she is still no more evil than the woman who sleeps with men with hope of gain. And many men will pay you upfront for a chance to one-day roll in the bed with you. Study prostitution and you will find that all prostitutes don't cost the same; even the ones who walk the streets. The crack addicted, older and the least attractive ones are the cheapest. They have to offer competitive prices so that they could compete with the younger, prettier ones who aren't on drugs. The prettiest ones get the most money per client. Then there are the call girls or escorts. Often times, they are better dressed and can earn thousands of dollars for spending the day with one man, whereas a street prostitute may get less than one hundred dollars per man and have to take on several a day. At the same time, many of them are not paid with money; they are paid with drugs and places to stay. But, in reality...think about it. Could the call girl brag of being the better woman because she sleeps with one or two men in a day and earns more money? I guess, here on Earth, she could. But, hell doesn't accept cash, Visa, MasterCard, American Express or Discover Card. Beauty amounts to nothing there. I mean, who's pretty after being dipped in fire and brimstone?

You have to come into the realization that your soul is invaluable to GOD. No man, no matter what he gives you, is worth death or an eternity in hell. One thing about the husband who GOD has reserved for you is the fact that he will give you far more in a day than sleeping around would have paid you in a lifetime. Money couldn't save Camille. But, had she followed the instructions as noted in the Bible (our instruction guide), she would have been rewarded for her servitude. Being beautiful doesn't grant us leniency or an extended stay here on Earth because disease, death and hell are all blind.

Envy's Poison

"There's only one you and only one me, so no one else can successfully be who you were called to be"

Two of the most common issues that women deal with in relation to other women is jealousy and envy. Many women opt not to have other women as friends because they have dealt with backbiting, gossip and worst of them all, envy. Jealousy is coveting what a woman or man has, but envy is coveting the life of someone else. Someone who is jealous of you could easily hurt or kill you, but someone who envies you has already killed you in their heart.

Ailani spent her entire life acting stand-offish. She didn't like being around too many people, and she only had one or two people that she associated with on a regular basis. She liked it that way. Ailani was like her mother; a private, but outgoing woman. Ailani was very active in her community, and she owned a gym, a spa, and was in the process of purchasing some land to build her boutique on.

Ailani was a very nice girl, by all accounts. But, despite her outgoing personality, she preferred the comforts of home and seclusion over gatherings. And she would often vocalize this to her two closest friends, Lela and Candice. Every time they heard another story of betrayal, they would call one another and speak on it. They were all proud of the fact that they were reclusive and didn't need the validation of many friends. They had each other and that was enough.

However, there was a problem brewing in paradise. Ailani and Candice were both successful and climbing the ladder of success to greater heights. Like Ailani, Candice owned a gym, had a spa in development and was looking into other venues. Lela, on the other hand, was more of a dreamer. She planned to do much, but never seemed to have the energy or the know-how to get started. So, Lela started an online clothing boutique at the urgency of her friends, but Lela's heart wasn't into entrepreneurship at that time. Lela worked at a clinic as a registered nurse and fancied herself as someone to come to for advice. She loved sharing the wisdom that was in her with others, but being the friend of two professional women could be challenging at times because she felt pressured to launch into business ownership. Therefore, she found herself avoiding Ailani and Candice's calls more and more. Lela felt that the two women had gotten beside themselves, and Lela opted for more humble friendships with a few co-workers.

One day, Ailani got a call from an organization that had been sponsoring a few of her charities. Ailani had seven charities and three of them were targeting low-income children. The call came as a surprise to her. The organization was notifying her that, after the end of the month, they would no longer be funding her organization. When pressed as to why they'd come to their decision, the woman on the other end said that they'd received a couple of calls from an anonymous woman claiming that Ailani had been using the funds to open more businesses. Ailani was hurt and angered that the sponsor didn't take the time out to try to verify or discredit the claim; nevertheless, she asked if she could send in evidence to show how she'd been distributing the funds. The operator accepted her offer, but warned her that if she had been misusing the funds that she could face jail time.

Later, that evening, Lela returned Ailani's call. Ailani had called her over a week ago, but Lela had been avoiding her calls. When Ailani answered, she could feel that there was some negative energy between her and Lela. Lela didn't seem like her usual perky self. As a matter of fact, for the last six months or more, Lela seemed dry; only answering Ailani's questions and trying to send subliminal messages by making random comments like, "Some people pretend to be friends when, in reality, they couldn't care less." Ailani proceeded with asking her the usual questions. "How are you doing? Why haven't you been calling me or returning my calls? What's wrong?" Lela responded in a low, less than friendly tone, "I'm fine. I've been busy. That's all."

Ailani didn't want to believe that something was wrong, so she proceeded to tell Lela about her anonymous enemy. Who'd want to destroy her charities? And what about the bomb threats that the gym received on Tuesday? Ailani was in tears as she went down the list of strange occurrences that had taken place in her businesses and charities. After she was done talking, Lela seemed to yawn before she replied, "Goodness. Hey, let me call you back." Ailani paused. What was going on? What was this? She politely agreed and hung up the phone. And it was after hanging up that Ailani began to ponder on Lela's timeline. It has been about six months since Lela started acting strange, and it has been about six months since she began having these anonymous calls to her businesses and charity sponsors. Could it be Lela?! No! That seemed too far fetched, but it did make sense.

As she was pondering these things, Candice called. Candice had been having problems too. It seems someone had been calling and placing bomb threats to her gym, and someone had gone so far as to spray paint a vulgar word on the side of one of her businesses. Candice also informed Ailani that Lela had finally returned her call and seemed very short and dry with her. But, unlike Ailani, Candice is more outspoken and has trouble holding her feelings in. Previously, she'd confronted Lela about her distancing herself and her noticeably negative attitude. At this, she said, Lela had yelled, "Okay, I won't hold it back, since you want to hear it. I don't want to be around you nor do I want to be around Ailani anymore. The both of you are not my friends! You run around here thinking you got it all and everyone who doesn't have what you have is beneath you. And quite frankly, I'm tired of being your self esteem boost! Always remember, Candice, what goes up, must come down!" After this, she'd hung up.

As Candice shared this with Ailani, they both agreed that Lela had been harboring some venom towards them for a while and more than likely, Lela was behind the bomb threats, vandalism, and all of the sabotage attempts against their businesses and charities. And they decided to meet at noon the next day for lunch and a little shopping to discuss the issue further and develop a counter-strategy to stop Lela's envy from going any further in their lives.

The next day, Ailani sat down to eat in a new restaurant that she'd been eager to try. The restaurant was in the downtown shopping district, so she'd chosen it because it was conveniently located and new. Candice was five minutes late, but she arrived looking beautiful as always. A little overdressed, but that's how Candice was. Candice was wearing an olive-green overcoat, tan heels, and carrying a tan handbag. After removing her coat, her beautiful dressed was revealed. It was crème, brown, and olive green. Each color looked as if it had been sown onto the dress in patches, nevertheless, the dress was classy and fit Candice as if it was made just for her. Her dark-brown eyes were accentuated by her olive-green eye shadow and sandy colored hair.

As they sat down, Ailani complimented her friend as always, and they didn't waste any time jumping into the conversation about Lela. And the discussion revealed a lot that neither girl was aware of. For example, Ailani didn't know that Lela had attempted to speak ill of her to Candice, just as Candice didn't know that Lela had told Ailani that Candice wasn't anyone's friend. Both women were hurt, but laughed as they compared their stories.

After dinner, they went over to a dress shop next to the restaurant. It was a new dress shop. As they were shopping, Ailani went over to look at a section of dresses as Candice followed, still talking about Lela. By this time, Ailani was done with the discussion and just wanted to enjoy the rest of the day. She'd finally reconciled with her decision to let Lela be and to move on, but Candice seemed more infuriated by what she'd heard and wanted to speak on it further. Ailani attempted to shift the conversation by asking Candice about a dress that she thought was beautiful. "What do you think about this dress? I was thinking it would look good with my blue shoes, and I could wear it to the church banquet on Sunday." Candice looked and picked up the dress. She turned it and asked her friend, "Tell me again, why do you like this dress?"
Ailani: What? You don't like it?
Candice: Well, not really. It looks like it would have been cute if they hadn't tried to do too much with it.
Ailani: What do you mean? It looks simple to me. Just a crème colored dress with a crème and blue jacket. What's busy about that?
Candice: I'm not really sure what it is, but it just doesn't sit right with me.

Trusting her friend's judgment, Ailani tried the dress on, but decided against it. After shopping for about 30 minutes, the only thing that Ailani bought was two necklaces and a pair of shoes. It seemed like she had bad taste because "Mrs. Fashionable"

Candice wasn't into much of what she picked up. They continued their day like this with Ailani finally settling on a dress from a small boutique that she wasn't really crazy about, but Candice had talked her into getting it; promising to come by before the banquet to help her accessorize it.

The next day, another bomb threat came into Ailani's gym, but this time, the police managed to track the location of the caller. It looks like Lela was at it again! Police discovered that the call was made from a prepaid cellular phone that pinged off a cell tower near the shopping area where Candice and Ailani had gone shopping the previous day. However, they were unable to find the assailant. At this, Ailani decided to call and confront Lela. Lela lived about 30 minutes away, but she loved to shop those boutiques in that area as well. As the phone rang, Ailani paced back and forward, biting her lips, and trying to contain her anger. And, like always, Lela didn't answer, so Ailani left her a voice message. Her voice quivered with anger as she spoke the words she'd never thought she'd say to someone she considered such a dear friend. "Listen, Lela! I don't know what your problem is, but what I do know is you'd better stop calling and placing bomb threats to my gym! You'd better stop all of this nonsense! Don't you remember that no weapon formed against me shall prosper?! I don't know what I've done to you, but I do know that I'm not going to stand by while you call my sponsors, threaten my businesses, and run your mouth about me! I'm going to tell you this one time, and I pray you heed the warning! If you don't want to be friends with me, that's fine! If I'm the self-serving arrogant goody-two shoes that you told Candice I was, that's fine! You don't have to deal with me! But, call my businesses or charity sponsors one more time, and I'm headed your way! Try me, Lela!" At this, she hung up; collapsing into her office chair and sobbing. Lela had been such a good friend. What happened? Was envy so powerful that it could divide a friendship so bitterly?

Ailani wanted answers, but she continued to focus on work and prepping for the upcoming banquet.

On Saturday, the day of the banquet, Ailani called Candice to see where she'd be parking. She didn't know that Candice had called her twice that day because her phone was on silent all day. When Candice answered, she seemed upset, but talkative. She expressed her disappointment with Ailani not answering her phone, but Ailani expressed to her that she'd been at the beauty shop for a few hours and didn't know her phone was on silent.
Candice: Beauty shop? You didn't tell me that you were getting your hair done!
Ailani: Ha! That's because I don't have to tell you everything, silly! And why didn't you come over to help me accessorize this dress like you'd promised?
Candice: Girl, today was so stressful and rough that I forgot. But, how did it come out?
Ailani: I wouldn't know. I went and bought another dress today.
Candice: What? After all that shopping.......
Ailani: Yeah, yeah....I just didn't like it. I went back downtown after I left the beauty shop and found a beautiful dress that I thought was perfect for the event. I actually like it better than the blue one you talked me out of.
Candice: Uh-oh. I'm worried, because I know the kind of dresses you like. I hope you don't come in there looking like a well-dressed tarp.
Ailani: Oh, hush! No. I prayed on it and was reminded that you are you, and I am me; therefore, even if I don't look so hot to others, if I like it, that's all that matters.
Candice: Whatever. Take a picture with your phone and send it to me, so I can see it.
Ailani: Why? You'll see me in an hour. Besides, I want it to be a surprise.
Candice: That's not right, but okay. I have a surprise for you too.

Oh, and I think Lela is coming; so beware.
Ailani: I'm not worried about Lela. Lela better be worried about me.

They end the call so that they could prepare to meet up at the event.

As usual, Ailani arrived early, but Candice wasn't there yet. Ailani decided to go into the building, so she could help out and about 30 minutes after the event began; Candice still wasn't there. The building was full and Ailani felt happy and comfortable with the dress she'd worn. Without warning, she felt a tap on her shoulder. She turned and was surprised to see Lela standing there. "May I talk with you in private?" Fearing that Lela could be up to something, Ailani suggested that they go to the front of the banquet hall, where no one was standing. They'd sectioned off an area for the banquet, but Ailani and Lela decided to go under the ribbon and go into the other area where it wasn't so noisy.

Lela: First off, let me say this. I'm not even mad at you about your voicemail. I listened to it and at first I was very upset. Then I thought about it. You were led to believe what you believe and I know the culprit behind your thinking that way.
Ailani: Lela, you and I were friends and I thought the world of you. When I was pushing you to go into business for yourself, it was because I love you, and I wanted to see you prosper. I tried to teach you everything I knew because it hurt me to see you have to get up and go into a job that was frustrating you. I wasn't trying to act as if I was better than you. I was trying to be a friend and for that, you turn on me? I don't get it. I thought so highly of you.
Lela: Like I said. You got me all wrong and I can't be mad at you for that. I should have come to you long ago, but I didn't

want to be a gossip or a back-stabber. I'm not the one calling your businesses nor have I ever called anyone about your charities. I distanced myself from you because you were hanging out with a she-devil and that she-devil is Candice.

Ailani: Candice? Lela, please don't...

Lela: No, listen. You think I envy you? It's not me that envies you; it's Candice. Didn't you notice how when you got a gym, she had to have a gym? When you opened a spa, she wanted a spa? Everything you do she does, but she tries to do it better. You can't be that blind, Ailani.

Ailani: I just figured that I had shared so much with her about the business opportunities and income potential with gyms and whatever else that she'd decided to come aboard. That did not intimidate me at all. After all, I'm her friend, and I want to see her prosper.

Lela: Yeah, you're quote-on-quote her friend, but your friendship is a one-way street. Candice called me one day and started trying to talk about you. She said that you were a self-serving goody-two shoes that needed to be humbled. I told her that I didn't agree and I made it clear that I saw what she was doing. She was trying so hard to be you and then turn around and tear you down; it was all too obvious to me that she envied you. And I asked her if she felt that way about you; why she didn't tell you? She got mad at me and we exchanged some words. And that was the last time I talked to Candice.

Ailani: According to Candice, you were the one that said those things about me. And didn't she call you last week going off, or something?

Lela: Girl, no! Candice knows not to call me with that. Every since you've known me; you have never heard me speak about Candice or gossip about anyone. Even now, I am not gossiping; I'm putting the truth out there so that you can finally see what's going on. I distanced myself because I got tired of seeing you walking around as if you don't see Candice mimicking everything

that you do. She always tells you not to do this or that, and you listen. Then, she goes out and does it. For example, you remember that weight set that you wanted to order that Candice talked you out of?
Ailani: Yeah.
Lela: Obviously, you haven't been to Candice's gym. She went and took a loan out just to buy that weight set, and now it's sitting in her gym!
Ailani: What?!
Lela: But, wait...there's more! Do you remember that guy you were dating? What's his name again? Mark, I think? Do you remember how Candice kept telling you that you could do better than that and how she'd seen Mark out with another girl?
Ailani: Yeah, I broke it off with him because of that.
Lela: Yeah and did you know that right after you broke up with him, Candice started going over to his house talking about she was consoling him, since he was so heartbroken?
Ailani: Stop, Lela...
Lela: No. I think it's time that you found out the truth. Candice told me that she tried to sleep with him, but he turned her down. She wouldn't have told me that if one of my co-workers, who happens to be Mark's neighbor, didn't see Candice being put out of Mark's house creating a scene. He had to call the police to have her removed from his property. Where have you been, Ailani? Asleep?
Ailani: To tell you the truth, that makes perfect sense. I remember Mark called me one day, but I didn't answer his call and he called me for three days and I would never answer his calls. I thought he was trying to reconcile. I didn't even listen to his voice messages. I kept hitting the number seven to delete the messages before he got a sentence out, but I did hear him on one of the messages saying, "Ailani, Candice came...," but, I'd already pressed the button to delete the message. Whoa. I think I need to sit down for the rest of this.

Lela: I stopped coming around, and I was wrong in how I handled it. Plus, I know that you and Candice have been friends for almost all of your lives. Should I have said something to you, who would you have believed? Her, I'm sure! I should have handled it better, and I'm not asking you to go back and play back what I said. What I'll say is this. Pay close attention. Those bomb threats and every bad thing that's happening is coming from your best-buddy Candice. And believe me, no one is threatening her businesses. She told you that as a rouse to keep you from seeing her forked tongue. Candice is jealous of you. No, wait. Candice envies you.
Ailani: But, why would she envy me? Candice's gym has more exercise equipment than mine. She seems to have more money than me. She has no reason to be jealous or to envy me.
Lela: Ailani...Ailani...Ailani! That's because you pay for your equipment out of your pocket, but Candice gets everything on credit! If you get two new machines, Candice will go out and finance four! Pay attention. Remember this. All of the ideas that GOD gives you; don't hand them to someone else. I didn't like being pushed into starting a business because, Ailani, I am a business owner in spirit, even if you don't see a building yet. I don't want to be Ailani. I love and respect you enough to let you be you, and I'm trying to find myself and who I am; but I'm in no rush. GOD controls the seasons. If I ran out and started a business, the only knowledge I could boast of was your knowledge and that's murder! For me to be you, you'd have to not exist anymore. I've been through that before and I wouldn't take anyone through that.

The talk lasted for over an hour and even though Ailani was comforted knowing that her and Lela were still friends; she was truly heartbroken about Candice. They'd been friends almost all of their lives, whereas Lela had come into the picture six years ago. After they'd concluded talking, Lela excused herself back to her table and promised to call her more. Ailani stayed at the front, hiding herself, so that no one could see her crying. How could Candice do this? She would have given Candice everything she had. How could Candice go so many years, even giving to her when she needed it, and still harbor envy towards her? As she stood up to collect herself, she saw the rear door open and in came a woman wearing the crème and blue dress that she'd initially thought of getting. It was Candice! She was even wearing blue shoes similar to the ones that Ailani had. It all began to make sense. But, they were at a church banquet and Ailani reasoned within herself to keep it all in and pretend that all was well until the next day. She made her way back into the banquet area as Candice approached her. Candice looked her up and down.

Candice: Well, you look half-way decent.
Ailani: And you look like I would have looked had you not talked me out of buying that dress. Thank you for the warning.
Candice: Oh girl, I couldn't find anything else. I went back and saw a girl try it on, and it was actually cute <u>on her.</u> So, I decided to get it.
Ailani: Yeah, you do seem to like the things that you talk me out of getting. Funny. If I didn't know any better, I'd swear those were my blue shoes too, but mine are open toe, so you get a pass.
Candice: *(Laughs)* No. I bought these shoes the other day. Anyway, let's go sit down. My feet are killing me! And what's wrong with you? I know you're not mad about a dress!
Ailani: No. Let's just go sit down.

After the banquet was over, Ailani decided to go straight home. Initially, she and Candice had planned to go re-paint some of the rooms in Ailani's gym, but Ailani excused herself claiming that she wasn't feeling too good. She wanted to go home and lay down. Candice, knowing something was wrong, nodded and wished her well. After she left, Candice stayed around greeting some of the people there, and it was then that she spotted Lela. Lela had been sitting at a table right behind her, but because her back was turned, she didn't initially see her. As Lela got up to leave, Candice attempted to greet her, but Lela countered with, "I'm praying for you."

Candice's thoughts got the best of her. Had Lela and Ailani talked? Her stomach began to churn as she considered the possibilities. She looked for her cell phone, but couldn't find it. She'd laid it next to her at the banquet. She wanted to call Ailani to put her fears to rest, but where was that cell phone?
What she didn't know was that Ailani had taken the cell phone to the police department. Candice, in her brazen attempts to keep people from sitting next to her, had placed her bag and cell phone on the seat next to her. She looked high and low, but she didn't see that cell phone. Then she remembered. She couldn't call Ailani from that particular phone anyway. The phone that she'd used to call Ailani with was the one in her purse. Maybe she'd left the other phone at home. She went into her purse and got out her main cell phone and called Ailani, but there was no answer. Ailani was at the police department trying to see if this was the phone that had been used to make those bomb threats. She knew that because it was in her possession, she could look like a possible suspect. So, she wiped her fingerprints from the phone and placed it in an envelope. Having worked at the police department before, she knew where the cameras were, so she avoided them. She placed the brown envelope near the side entrance with a typed note that read, "Are you looking for this phone?"

The next day, Ailani got a call from the police department. Her heart fluttered. What if they'd changed the position of the cameras and she'd been caught on camera planting the phone?

What if someone saw and recognized her? The possibilities were endless. But, the investigator on the other end wanted to inform her that they'd made an arrest in connection with the bomb threats that had been placed to her businesses. He seemed to wait too long to reveal who it was, but Ailani knew already. It was Candice! Her cell phone had all the information the police needed to make an arrest!

Explanation:

Ladies, there are several lessons to be learned here.

1. One is, be careful who you hang around. Sometimes, we count years and not incidents. Sometimes, it's the little things that we need to pay attention to. Envy never comes out and declares its own name!

2. Please know that whatever a person is fed; they become. When a woman is fed wisdom; she becomes a wise woman. When a woman is fed foolishness; she becomes a foolish woman. When she is fed 'you;' she becomes you. When you talk to people too often, and you are no longer feeding them wisdom, but you start to feed them with stories from your life, your wants, your dreams and your ambitions, they can't help, but to start morphing into you. Especially if your dreams are bigger than theirs or your blessings are manifest, and theirs haven't manifested yet. Be careful what you share with your friends. Some things are to be kept between you and the LORD. If you feel the need to talk to someone, ask the LORD to send someone who shares those same ambitions so that the two of you could share your stories; someone mature enough to pray for you, and you pray for them. Someone who is so busy walking down her own path that she does not entertain the thoughts of trying on your shoes. She's too busy walking in her own! Never tell a woman, or any person who

does not fully understand who they are, who you are. Tell them who GOD is and feed them wisdom. However, feeding them with your testimonies behind your testimonies only entices them to want to be who you are. People want the testimonies, but do not understand that you had to go through the tests to get to them!

3. The next lesson is obvious. Let GOD be GOD. Sometimes we get so anxious to have something, do something and be something that we try to take on the role and responsibility of GOD. We try to push others into their seasons of success, when they are supposed to be in a season of sowing or watering.

4. Be who you are and love your friends as they are. Your path is not lit for a reason. You have to walk it in faith and not by sight. Sure you see her blessings but you may have greater blessings awaiting your arrival. You will never push someone else out of being who they are and find success in it. Instead, what you are doing when you try is murdering a person in your heart, and at the same time, saying to GOD that you don't trust HIM. Remember this, if you live by the sword, you die by the sword. You say, "Well, I haven't killed anyone." If you are operating in envy, you have committed the sin in your heart; just as if a man looks upon a woman and lusts after her, he has committed adultery in his heart. On "her" path, your feet will touch the cancer of envy, and because you have murdered "her" in your heart, the sword will brandish itself against you. That's why you see so many people who die earlier than expected because they were in the wrong place at the wrong time. Understand that on her path, there are tests reserved for her that she is called to survive, but when you step on that path and walk into that test, you were not called to survive it because you were not called to go through it. But, you entered it anyway. Be who you are and do not murder your sister! You have a purpose, but it takes you to go through your own tests to draw it out of you.

5. Envy is like cancer. It can grow up all of a sudden. I have seen it happen too many times. Friends were friends for years, but all of a sudden, one day; one of the friends began to exhibit symptoms of envy, but the other friend doesn't recognize it because she just doesn't want to believe that her friend could envy her. As we grow up in HIM, there are friendships that we absolutely have to end to keep going forward. Sure, you don't want to. Who does? But, if envy or jealousy has entered the equation, then GOD is not in the midst of that friendship. If the two of you are not gathered in GOD'S Name; the Devil is in the midst of that friendship. You have to be willing to go in order to grow.

6. When a friend puts you down, it isn't because she loves you. Often women belittle other women to tear one another down and build themselves up in their places. And sometimes, they do it out of hurt and insecurity. If she has torn you down to where she is; she can now relate to the new and ruined you. Sure, a good friend will tell you if your shoes are embarrassing, but if you find that your friend never seems to compliment you, but always has something negative to say, you are witnessing one of the symptoms of envy. Or, if your friend simply never compliments you at all; pay attention. Just like a doctor can identify a disease by its symptoms, many demons and demonic mindsets can be identified by the symptoms and behaviors that their host exhibits. Don't look at what you believe someone to be. Look at the fruit!

7. Pray always. Ask the LORD to deliver you from evil communications and relationships that were not established by HIM. Ask HIM to deliver you from relationships that have run past their seasons. Every time you're in the wrong place, you're missing out on the right things.

8. Don't ignore your internal alarm. When something evil is in someone for us, GOD warns us from the inside, but all too often, we turn off HIS voice to hear her voice. This is when you will find yourself going through unnecessary attacks and offenses.

9. Pay attention to how you feel. It is better to humble yourself than to be humbled by GOD. If you feel envy or jealousy rising up in you; cast it out! Don't entertain demons! She is who she is and you are who you are because GOD made you that way! Keep your hands clean and your heart pure! GOD will never place a blessing in dirty hands, nor will HE reside in an impure heart. Remember, HE said to cast down evil imagination!

10. Know when your season is up. When things that are not of GOD enter the friendship; it's time for you to make your exit. If you sense envy (again, trust your alarm and be prayerful if doubt arises), jealousy or a disdain for you; you must know that nothing good will come of your continued relationship with her. You stick around because you're still trying to fit into man's definition of friend, when often times, man calls his worst enemy-his best-friend until GOD shows him otherwise. Remember, offense comes into the friendship when GOD has left it.

Friendly Enemies

"It is better for someone to mourn your success than to celebrate your failure"

Just as some women live their lives trying to be you, there are many women who dedicate their lives to trying to stop you from arriving in who you are ordained to become. Now, I would say "arriving in success," but as you arrive in "you" (your parking space in CHRIST) or who you were called to be; success is just one of your attributes. Health, wealth and a sound mind is found in you; but sickness, poverty and an unstable mind is found in sin. You are not sin, but when you enter sin, you become one with sin. This is why you have to repent because GOD cannot look upon sin.

There are many who will never reach their blessed place of ever knowing who they are, and they don't intend to even try to get there. Too much work! So, they dedicate their lives to trying to keep you and others from getting there. They wake up in the morning and their adopted purpose is by their bedside. They have taken on the evil assignment of assassinating the women of GOD. Their first attempt to assassinate you starts with them impersonating themselves as your friend. They will try to connect to you. Let me explain through an example.

Erin is an accountant. She makes decent money, lives on her own and has one child. Now, Erin is a woman of GOD, but she wasn't always saved. She had her baby girl at a young age, but as Erin got older, she matured. She then gave her life to CHRIST, passed many of her tests, and she is now living in a state called 'testimony.'

Shelly sees Erin. Shelly works at the accountant's office as well, but she is a desk clerk. She desires to be an accountant one day, but what fascinates her so much with Erin is that she has a house, a car and is a great mother. Erin is always using her lunch breaks to either go by the school and check on her daughter, or she'll call to make sure that all is well with her. Erin also seems very happy and unlike the other ladies that work in the office, Erin is a loner. She isn't into gossip or large crowds. The men at the office seem to be in love with Erin, but she pays them no attention; even though many of the women there are all over these guys, who in turn, pay them no attention. Sure, some of the men have had flings with the women in the office, but Erin is untouchable. She's single and content that way.

Shelly just admires Erin. She wants to be cool, content and collected like Erin. So, every time she sees Erin, she stops and compliments her. One day in the lounge, Shelly hears some of the other girls talking badly about Erin. She knows that it is envy that is driving them, but she does not realize the fact that envy is driving her because in them, it manifests itself as obvious envy; whereas in Shelly, it masquerades itself as admiration. Shelly stops Erin the next day and says to her, "Hey Erin. I think you are a really nice person and I'm not a gossip, but I just wanted to warn you. I heard Brenda, Sharon and Gertrude in the lounge saying this and that about you. I know you're not like that and it just disgusted me, so I wanted to let you know to be careful." Erin thanks Shelly and goes on her way. She already knew that the women there didn't like her and it did not bother her. You see, Erin is saved and her blessed walk is a ranking where many

5/6/2020
Father God, forgive me for everytime I have envied any one in Jesus name I ask amen.

When we Know our rank in Christ or our "blessed walk is a ranking!" then we will realize that those devils that are in other who envies us are low level devils, and they don't rank high enough to get our attention."

women never get to, and those devils that are in her co-workers are low level devils, so they just don't rank high enough to get her attention. It's like sharing a sidewalk with an ant. If you don't look down; you won't see it and even if it bites you, it can't kill you.

Anyhow, one day Shelly comes to work and just hands Erin a new shirt in a bag. "I bought this yesterday at the mall and thought it would look cute on you." Erin thanks her and begins to see Shelly as a sweetheart. It starts off with brief conversations and graduates to them calling one another, hanging out for lunch and a year later, they are the best of friends.

Erin is promoted to office manager and transferred to another office, but she and Shelly still remain friends. Shelly continues to watch as Erin is just blessed on every side and even admires how she handles adversity. She never seems too bothered by trials. One day, Erin announces to Shelly that her goal is to start her own accounting firm eventually. She has been pricing some buildings to rent or possibly purchase, and has saved a few thousand dollars to go towards her goal, plus she tells her about a pastor that has been pursuing her for a few years. His name is Christopher and he pastors the church over on Triangle Road. Erin knows that PC, as she calls him, is different from any other man. Anytime she sees him, her heart races, and she hurriedly excuses herself from his presence. She believes that he could see how nervous she is in his presence. Erin pretty much knows that this is the man sent to be her husband. He didn't tell her that, she saw it in a dream; plus it was confirmed by two people who didn't really know him or her. Nevertheless, she's been running from him and the more she runs, the more he chases. His eyes are fixated on her, and he knows that she is his other rib, his wife and the "one-day-to-be" mother of his children. So, he is unrelenting.

Anyhow, at telling Shelly all of this, she watches as Shelly's countenance is hardened. She looks at Erin and says, "First off; you you make enough money doing what you are doing as it is, plus you just got promoted. Why would you even think about throwing that away to chase dreams of owning your own business? I know a guy named Wayne, who did the same thing, and he wound up quitting his job and renting a building. In one year, he got three clients. He wound up having to close his business and start back at the bottom. GOD blessed you to come this far, so don't be greedy. I'm happy to hear about your love interest and all, but you have to consider the fact that you have a daughter. You can't just be assuming that this man is your husband just because you had a dream, and some people called themselves prophesying to you. That man may be the devil incarnate. Plus, I hear that a lot of those pastors are some of the biggest womanizers out there. I remember hearing one girl talk about a pastor called Chris. She had been sleeping with him, and he made her feel like she was the one, but one day he just up and broke it off. She later found out that he was getting married to another girl. I wonder if he's the same pastor that you are talking about. Let me look into it and see; I bet it's him. I just don't want to see you ruin your life, girl."

Now, Shelly's argument, to the untrained ear, sounds justifiable and wise, right? But, to someone with discernment, you can hear the phlegm of envy rattling in her lungs. Erin has an anointing to own businesses, properties and to prosper. The man who is anointed for Erin had to exceed her height, and that's why Erin wasn't distracted by all of those other men, but PC has gotten her attention.

Erin takes Shelly's advice into consideration, not paying attention to the fact that Shelly seemed almost agitated about her news. After praying on it, Erin discovers that GOD has called her to purchase a building on Triangle Road, not far from the pastor's church. By this time, she hasn't seen PC in months, and he happens to come into the building one January morning to seek some accounting advice. When he sees Erin sitting behind the desk, he grins and approaches her. "I came in here for one reason, but I believe that I was sent in here for another," he says. Erin's usually serious face softens, and she smiles softly as he continues. "Erin, you are a beautiful and virtuous woman of GOD, and I have been chasing you for years. I don't want to make you uncomfortable, and if you say no, I'll understand; but I will never stop chasing the woman who GOD has anointed the eyes of my heart to see. Please let me take you out with your daughter, just as a friend...for now. We don't have to ride in the same car, if you're not comfortable. I heard about a nice restaurant on 8th Street, and I have been wanting to try it out. Will you accompany me this Saturday at five p.m. just for dinner and discussion?" Erin finally agrees and the pastor leaves, forgetting what he'd initially come in for.

Later that day, Erin calls Shelly and tells her what happens, but the line is quiet. Erin had pulled away from Shelly, for the most part, because when she'd purchased the building, Shelly took it personal and was offended that Erin did not listen to her. But, in her moment of joy, she calls Shelly. Then she hears Shelly's voice, after a long pause. "Congratulations. I have to go. Later." She knows what this is. Shelly is envious and Erin immediately begins to pray over herself and her plans because she suspects that Shelly is speaking all manner of evil against her. She instantly regrets making the call.

Saturday comes and Erin prepares herself and her daughter. They leave and meet the pastor at the restaurant. He's already there, seated. Over dinner, they discuss their lives and find that they both have a lot in common and share the same beliefs. In addition, Erin's daughter seemed to take an instant liking to the pastor and he just adores her.

They continue to go out together for seven months and one day, he proposes to Erin, and she accepts. "When a woman is anointed to be your wife," he says, "you don't need two and three years to see this. I just know who you are because you fit so well into my life, and I have loved you since the day I saw you. You are my missing rib, Erin and I thank GOD that I found you because it hurts to not have you by my side."

At this point in her life, Erin has completely disassociated herself from Shelly. She sees her around from time to time, but Shelly doesn't even speak to her.

After the wedding, Erin and PC are having a discussion one day. He tells her about the time he almost had second thoughts about her, but GOD had corrected him and reassured him that Erin was his wife. The story goes like this:
He was at the church one Saturday morning cleaning up. It was already nice and neat, but he always had to add his own touch to it. Anyhow, in walks a woman. She was about 5'4, slim, dark-brown eyes and fair skinned. He'd seen her a few times before outside of the church. She was always waving at him and grinning, but he could see the devil on that girl. This woman says to him, "I know you don't know me, but I just came in here to warn you. I think you are a nice man, and I don't want to see anything happen that compromises your ministry. Anyway, there is a girl named Erin, who has her eyes on you, but Erin is what some would call "loose." She loves to date men of GOD and then seduce them into sin. Before you know it, she has robbed you blind and destroyed your good name. I just thought I would warn you because I think you are a nice man." At this, the pastor immediately asked her to leave the building and says to her, "I don't entertain gossip. You don't need to tell me anything because

GOD is with me, and HE would have told me that. I hear HIM, you know. Please leave." Embarrassed, the woman leaves, but she's comforted by the fact that she has just sown a seed.

That same day, while out at the store, PC had seen Erin talking with another pastor that he knew. She was smiling, and they were so into their conversation that they didn't see him, and he left. Heartbroken, he went into prayer. "GOD, you told me that she was my wife. Did I not hear you correctly?" Three days later, he sees the pastor that Erin had been talking to (Pastor Ulysses). Pastor Ulysses stops him and says, "Hey brother Chris, how are you? I have to tell you that you've been on my mind. The other day, I had a dream that you married this local girl named Erin. She is a beautiful woman of GOD, and I would love you to meet her. Anyhow, I just saw her the other day, and I was telling her about this dream. She grinned and told me that she'd had the same dream. Let me tell you about Erin. She used to go to my church, and she is really focused on the LORD. I always said she would make some man a Proverbs 31 wife one day, but it has been revealed to me that you are that man. So, even before you see it, I want to say congratulations, man!" PC is shocked, teary eyed and just lifts up the praise to GOD.

This story is one that touches Erin's heart, and she begins to cry, but she can't get her mind away from this fair complexioned girl with dark-brown eyes. That sounds like....no, it couldn't be. "What was this girl's name; do you remember?" PC answers, "I think she said Shay or Shell or something like that." Erin interrupts, "Shelly?" He confirms this and suddenly, everything that Shelly has ever done begins to flood the thoughts of Erin. It was all beginning to make sense now. The whole time, she thought she had a friend, when she was hanging out with a friendly enemy.

Explanation:

Envy doesn't always look like envy. We have a tendency to associate envy with negative behavior, when envy sometimes and many times does mask itself. Envy is patient. A person that envies you can buy groceries for your house when you need it, give blood when you need it, take you to work if you don't have a car, fight others on your behalf and be there for you in some of the hardest times.
Why? Because they are investing in who they want to be. They are simply spies looking for your weakest points. In Shelly's case, she didn't realize that she envied Erin. She saw herself as a friend, and she believed that the fall of their friendship was due to Erin's greed. So, while Erin's focused on GOD, Shelly is focused on Erin.

Take this truth with you. A person that focuses on you and what you have is not focused on GOD. Anybody that focuses on you will go after you. Often times, I have found that the warning signs were there from the beginning. Sometimes when someone says that they admire you, they are toying with envy. It doesn't seem like it, but admiration often leads the heart into some pretty dark places because the motive for their friendship is seeking the foundation; the substance, and the covering of what it is about you that they admire. Once they have gotten to this part of you, they will toss you away or try to tear you down. Why is that? Think about a man. If a man can have all of you, there is nothing left for him to pursue and he will lose interest. A husband will spend a life time trying to figure out the mystery that is his wife. As he finds clues and makes discoveries about you, he will rejoice at every find, however, every time he thinks that he has arrived at the whole you, he discovers that there is more about you that has to be discovered. But, when a woman comes and gives herself wholly to a man, he will lose interest, because a man's purpose is wrapped up in his journey. On a journey, he is always searching and seeking, but if there is nothing left for him to seek out, he dies to purpose and lives in depression. This is when you see a man become restless, depressed and many turn to substance abuse and violent tendencies. Because he is not on his path of purpose anymore, he had to find something or someone to occupy his time and give him a sense of purpose. A man is like blood in the veins; he has to keep circulating in purpose, otherwise, his heart goes out. Motives act the same way. A motive is one's desire to reach the knowledge or obtain the substance of something. Once that thing has been accomplished, it is no longer of use. When the person that admires you has nothing else to admire about you, that's when character assassination and many other strife-filled attacks will follow. Now, if someone is inspired by you, that can be a good thing, just as long as she doesn't get lost in trying to be you or place her feet on the path that GOD created for you. If they are inspired to do their own thing....that's good, but envy always wants to wear your shoes and envy will always justify doing so.

You are going to meet many women, in your purpose-filled heights, that will come up to you and just try to attach to you. Beware! They may be babes in CHRIST or adult devils. Anything that is not attached by GOD is attached by the enemy of GOD, and anyone that comes in illegally to your life cannot celebrate your success. They will, however, push for your failure. If you fail, they will celebrate your fall. When GOD sends people into your life, they will come through the door at the appointed season; and at the same time, be wise enough to go out that door when their season with you is up. Even after their season in your life has ended, they will still love you and be there for you. They will understand that their absence in your life does not mean the friendship has ended, but it could mean that you are both walking different paths leading to GOD. Anyone the enemy sends into your life will always come through the window because the door is not opened. Anyone who enters through the window is a thief! Any woman who comes in as a thief is there to not just steal your joy, but your purpose. She's there to siphon the anointing oil out of you. Even though it was fuel created for you, and she won't get far on it; she doesn't understand, know, or believe that. She has seen you prosper, and she wants your oil. If you let her in, in your disobedience, you won't get far either.

Pray about any and everyone that enters or attempts to enter your life. Some trials aren't trials; they are tribulations and you wouldn't have to go through them, if you would have just let GOD be LORD of your life.

Close Isn't Close Enough

"If you want to be married, you must first master being single"

I minister to a lot of single women, and the ones who are not considered by men to be marriage material (as of yet), have one thing in common: They don't know how to be single. Many of them are beautiful to look upon, but they don't think like a wife; act like a wife, or look like a wife. They believe that being able to cook, have a decent conversation; not to mention, be intimate with a man sets them at the top of the list of women to be considered for wife-material. There are many women who can cook; some better than others, just as there are many women who know their way around a bedroom. And they spend their lives going from relationship to relationship, always feeling like they are getting closer to being a wife. She knows something new today that she didn't know yesterday. 2012's guy is so much better than the one from 2011.

There are many women who have learned to look sexually appealing, but they don't understand that short skirts and belly rings does nothing more than make them look like they are walking about town in lingerie. So, when men meet them, they pursue the chance to bed them; some men being more patient than others.

Many single women keep on getting broke down on the road of 'Close Enough.' But, they never arrive at a level of maturity where they can truly say that they understand what it is to be a wife and consequentially, they are never taken down the aisle. Instead, they are taken down the hallways of motels and hotels. Men shack up with them, leasing them for six months, six years and so on; but never marry them. Some even make it to an actual engagement before they are thrown back into the raffle hat. Then, there are the ones that do get married, but they forgot to invite GOD to their weddings and as a result, happiness avoids them. They thought marriage would equal happiness, when in truth, it only brought on a whole new set of problems that they weren't equipped to handle.

Leslie dated Darrin back in 2004. They had a three-year relationship, and a son was born to their union. They broke up in early 2007. In late 2007, Leslie met Reuben. Reuben was so very different from Darrin. He was a hard-working man who seemed to have it all together. He was buying his home and worked as a Paramedic. Not to mention, he was an Inventor; creating several items that were sold in some of the major department stores. Leslie was very excited about Reuben to the point where she'd told every one of her friends about him. She was hoping he would be the one. He had to be! Leslie and Reuben carried on for seven and a half months before he broke it off without explanation. Truth is, he'd just had his fill of her.

It took Leslie three months to start the healing process after the breakup with Reuben, but once she did; she met Minister Albert Erickson. Albert was different. He was an ordained minister, and he talked a lot about the LORD. Leslie's friends were sure he was the one. He was mature, said he loved the LORD, and said he didn't have time for girlfriend/boyfriend relationships; he was looking for his wife. Leslie pretty much began to plan her life with Albert because he was so serious about her. Even after they had several intimate encounters, he didn't show a change, but instead, seemed to draw closer to her; even acting like a parental figure to her son. Seven months after meeting, Leslie and Albert moved in together and not long after that, they had a child together. After their son was born, the relationship seemed to go sour. They were always fighting because Albert was addicted to pornography. (Hey, if the man is willing to fornicate with you, what makes you think he's a follower of CHRIST? His title? *(Go to the corner.)* They finally split when their son was two months old.

After Leslie and Albert's split, she decided to concentrate more on the LORD and stay away from men. This didn't last long when she met Louis. Louis was a good man, by all accounts. He'd just split from his wife and was going through a divorce. By Louis's account, his marriage ended due to his wife's violent temper and infidelities. Leslie felt like she'd struck gold. Finally! An honest, faithful man who does not like porn and does not cheat! Three months into their relationship, Louis broke it off with Leslie because he and his wife decided to reconcile. Leslie had held out a whole three months before finally feeling comfortable enough for intimacy with Louis and a week later, he announces that he and his wife are an item again?! Bummer! But, that's okay. Because a local plumber named Stephen had been flirting with her. And Leslie just knew he was the one. Leslie Dukes. Yeah. That had a great ring to it.

Stephen was very humble and a great listener. Plus, he seemed to be really into Leslie and her kids. He had never been married, had no children and shared the same life goals as Leslie. Stephen was 15 years older than Leslie, but that could only mean he'd be more mature...or so she thought. And two months into the relationship, Stephen asked Leslie to move into his home with him. Yay! Finally! So, this is what it took? Obviously, all the men who were Leslie's age were immature. And here is this man who wants to provide for Leslie and her kids and does not want her to work. He just wanted her to sit at home and be his. Five months into the relationship, Stephen proposed and Leslie accepted. Leslie began mentoring her friends about relationships. “Girl, you have to get an older one who is more mature. Young men don't know what they want. That's why Stephen, and I get along so well.”

But, Stephen had a dark side. He was bothered by Leslie's connections to people. He wanted her to disassociate herself from her friends and family. He seemed to find something wrong with all of them. Leslie was head strong though. After all those men, she'd been with, she'd learned to roll with the best of them. So, she wouldn't listen and one day it came. The first push. Thankfully, her sons were at school, but not long after this, the pushes turned into slaps, and the slaps turned into punches. Leslie's family wanted her to get out of the relationship, but he was such a good provider that Leslie tried to stay in it and avoid angering him. That day was unavoidable, however. The day that she knew she had to walk out on him.

That day came on a Saturday. Leslie's oldest son, Caleb, wanted to call his dad to wish him a happy birthday. He hadn't talked with his dad in eight months. Leslie was all for it, but Stephen was against it. “I'm his dad! That deadbeat hasn't even called his son and now that ungrateful bast....I mean boy wants to call him and disrespect me?!” Leslie could not believe what she was hearing. So, she began to pack up the children's clothing. While packing, she felt a blow and found herself on the floor being drug by her hair. Her sons looked on crying as Stephen beat their mother and told her how he'd kill her before he would let her leave. Caleb tried to defend his mother, but was pushed into the wall. The youngest son, Drew, stood there frozen and frantic; begging Stephen to stop.

That following Monday, when Stephen went to work, Leslie called the police and had them to stand there while she moved her things out of Stephen's home. She also pressed charges for the assault and moved back to Washington, DC to live with her mother for a while.

Leslie told her friends, "I have learned my lesson finally! The next man I'm with will be my husband. No more premarital sex. No more shacking."

Four months later, Leslie met Mao, a Chinese immigrant from Beijing through a mutual friend. Mao was nothing like any man she'd ever met. His accent made him difficult to understand, but his eyes weren't. He looked at Leslie with such a deep affection, and she just couldn't resist his charm. He didn't want to live together, and he didn't talk about marriage. He just took her and her kids out often. Leslie told all of her friends how horrible American men were and how much better a foreign man was. The only problem with Mao was that he was Buddhist, but that's fixable, right? Leslie felt that maybe after marriage, she could introduce Mao to Christianity and he'd see the light. This day never came. Six months into the relationship, Leslie went to Mao's apartment to check in on him. She hadn't heard from him in two days and he wasn't answering his phone. Concerned, she went to his apartment and began ringing the doorbell. With no answer, she decided to look in through one of the windows. Hopefully, he wasn't hurt, or worse...dead. The blinds were gone, but the curtains were still up. Leslie found a slight opening in the curtains and could see that the apartment appeared empty. Maybe he'd been robbed and hurt! Maybe he was scammed and forced to move! Leslie was horrified. Her sons loved Mao and so did she. She was even trying to learn to speak Chinese, hoping to impress his family the day she would meet them. Suddenly, a voice came

from behind her. “Who are you looking for?!” It was a scruffy looking older guy who could surely use a bath. Maybe he was Mao's kidnapper! “Mao,” Leslie replied and the old guy responded, “The Asian guy? He went back to China a couple of days ago. He was only supposed to be here six months conducting a study for some company, but he ended up staying eight months and missed the birth of his daughter. Now, he's back home with his wife and their daughter is doing fine from what I heard.”
Wife? Daughter?

Yep. Mao was married and Leslie was his American concubine. Leslie was heartbroken and went back to her car stone-faced. She tried to hold back the tears. How could he not be the one? They'd never even argued. Everything was so perfect. How was she going to break it to her children that another man has walked out of their lives?

All of these failed relationships took a toll on Leslie's thinking. She'd tried men of different races, faiths, older men, younger men and now a foreigner. But, it all ended the same. Mao could have at least left a note.

As time went on, Leslie tried to cope with life, being without Mao. She couldn't completely forget him because she was pregnant. She just didn't know how to reach him to tell him that he had fathered a child with her.

Ten months later, Leslie got an email from Mao. “I coming to Washington on Saturday. I want to see you.” The nerve of him. But Leslie, now in another relationship responds, “Good. This way you can meet your daughter, Maya. She's almost two months old and looks just like you. See you Saturday.” When Mao saw that he'd gotten a response from Leslie, he was happy, but once he opened the email, he was devastated. Daughter?! Daughter?! What daughter?! He decided not to respond in hopes that Leslie would just go away, but it didn't work. Leslie called the company that Mao had conducted his studies with and found what hotel he'd be staying in. She told them that she was his old landlord, and that he'd left some belongings in his previous residence and had contacted her and asked her to bring them to him on Saturday. Saturday came, and Leslie was at the Hampton in the lobby with her new daughter; waiting for Mao. She could see him approaching the desk, but she sat in the lobby out of sight. She wanted him to finish the sign in process and hopefully follow him to his room to discuss their daughter. After he'd gotten his key, Mao went to the elevator and held the door for Leslie as she approached. He didn't recognize her since she'd cut her hair, died her hair black and was wearing sun glasses. But, as soon as she entered the elevator, and he saw the baby; his heart began to flutter. "Leslie, I don't want trouble," he said. "Me neither," replied Leslie. "I just want you to meet your daughter and possibly have a relationship with her. I won't tell your wife a thing, but I won't let Maya be ignored." No matter what Leslie said, Mao kept repeating the same thing, "Leslie, I don't want trouble." He refused to let her come into his room, and he refused to discuss Maya. He didn't even want to look at her.

Leslie called her now fiance, Roger. Roger offered to come up and teach Mao a lesson, but Leslie told him no, fearing that Roger would lose the fight. Roger and Leslie had been dating for six months and Leslie knew he was the one. I mean, what man would take you while you're pregnant with another man's baby? This was her line of reasoning. They didn't live together, but Roger spent the night at her apartment at least five nights a week and helped her pay rent. Roger was a computer geek. A man who was socially retarded, meaning he didn't know how to function in the real world. That was okay. He loved Leslie and she could feel it. All was fine until Leslie discovered that Roger was "off his rocker." He'd first told Leslie that he'd worked for the CIA and she believed him. According to Roger, he'd done a lot of secret covert operations in Russia, China and Japan. He was discharged when he got hurt during an undercover sting. Now, the CIA still contacted him to do a little work for them here and there. Well, this was according to Roger anyway.

Truthfully, his stories got weirder by the day. He was always checking her apartment for cameras, evidence of phone tappings and spies. He even believed that some form of super-mutant insect was being placed in his apartment, and this is why he spent so many nights at Leslie's apartment. Those roaches weren't normal, according to Roger. They were too big, and he believed that they were allegedly micro-chipped and purposely placed there to spy on him. So, he didn't kill them; he talked to them.

One day, while at work, Leslie called Roger to see if they could meet for lunch. While talking with Leslie on the phone, Roger began to hear a clicking sound on her phone. From then on, he accused Leslie of being an undercover spy. He even added Mao to the plot, saying that he'd followed him back from China. Schizophrenia! It hit Leslie suddenly. Roger was schizophrenic!

Explanation:

We'll stop the story there because we all know how it ends. Leslie would spend her best years being tossed around from man to man until she woke up one day old, alone, bitter and telling young women that all men were no good. Her sons would never learn how to be men of GOD, and her daughter was set up to follow the steps that her mother taught her.

Satan loves to play on a woman's desire to be married. To be married; however, the purifying fire of GOD has to come upon her and cleanse all of that woman out of her and reveal her as a wife, but Leslie never stayed still long enough. She was jumping between wanting to serve GOD to actually serving herself. She was like a leaf in the wind. Whatever she thought would work; she did. As she got older and older, her beauty began to fade, her parts began to sag, and her attitude got more and more sour. She was never short on getting a date, but she never got the date she wanted... a wedding date.

Some women leave this pattern, but many stay in this mindset, believing every lie Satan tells them. They look for the differences in a man and not the differences in themselves. They believe that the last call was so close that the next one is a sure-fire wedding ceremony. Many make it down the altar to marry the wrong man, while the majority spend their lives refusing to do it GOD'S way. Satan always takes them down the roads of 'Close, Closer....and finally Closed.' It was a dead end. Any woman can be found by a man, but it takes a GOD-fearing and obedient wife of GOD to be found by her husband.

Problem nowadays is that a lot of ladies have their priorities all wrong. For them, it's get a man first, seek GOD later. Or they want to give a man all that they are and give GOD what's left of them. Then, they're hurt and abandoned again and again to the point where many women begin to settle for anything that is labeled a man.

Many begin to take on men who are unattractive to them, believing that he would appreciate them more, since they are labeled "out of his league." Then, that man goes out and has a bigger field day cheating on them than the men they thought were in their league.

GOD said we are to be changed by the renewing of our minds.

GOD said that we are to seek first the Kingdom of GOD and all its righteousness and everything else will be added to us. GOD said to lean not to our own understanding. GOD said that if you love HIM, you are to keep HIS commandments. GOD said that if we asked for something, and believed HIM for it with faith at least the size of a mustard seed, we will have whatever we asked for. Solomon was wise enough to ask for wisdom first.

Many women ask for husbands, but they do not understand that in order to have a good marriage, wisdom must live in the hearts of both parties. Again, ladies, many of you are getting close...closer and then the door closes in your face...again and again. When will you realize that you are running in a circle? Will you risk your soul because you want a man so bad that you dedicated your life to finding him when GOD was saying all along that HE wants and loves you? Why do you break HIS heart? All FATHER asks is that you seek HIM out and have a relationship with HIM first, and HE will take care of the rest. But, when you are out laying with this guy and that guy, what's going to happen is you will watch the women around you get married and live happily ever after while you're at their weddings wearing a mini-skirt and tons of makeup. You'll still be casting out your line for the next opportunity, hoping to reel in your husband there. Twenty-five guys later, the light just might come on. This is to say to you in love....there is no other way, no alternate route; JESUS is the only way, the Truth and the Light. You don't have to keep walking in darkness, being led by Satan's lies, brushing up against death, disease and destruction, when GOD has a fool-proof plan that is designed to protect you, bless you and prepare you for the husband HE custom built just for you!

Next time Satan reminds you that your last encounter was close, say to him, “Yeah, that was close, but it wasn't close enough.” GOD has a plan for you that will outshine your best plans for yourself, but you have to trust HIM. Remember, HIS promises are 'Yea' and 'Amen.' Rest in HIM and ask HIM for peace.

Life Responds To Our Choices

"Every action results in a reaction"

The consequences of our choices do follow us. We know this. Nobody has to tell us this, even though most people have heard that said religiously and to them, it is nothing more than a quote. GOD has designed the earth and everything in it to respond to every word we say and every thing we do.

Rachelle is just an ordinary woman from a small town in Alabama. She has three sisters and two brothers and both of her parents were still alive and doing well.

Rachelle is going through a divorce, so she moved back in with her parents. The divorce is weighing heavily on Rachelle. She has a three-year-old daughter with her husband, and she just does not understand how everything could add up over time and equal a divorce. She thought all was well. That is, until one day when Rachelle's husband Bob left for work and forgot to take his cell phone with him. Normally, Rachelle doesn't answer his phone, but after noticing it, she decides to keep it near her just in case he gets to another phone and calls her to verify that it was at home.

Thirty minutes later, the phone rings. The caller identification reads, 'Bridgette.' Assuming that her husband was using one of his co-worker's phones, she answers and the conversation went

like this:
Rachelle: Hello?
Bridgette: *(Pauses)* I must have the wrong number. *(Hangs up.)*

This call bothers Rachelle, but she dismisses it until it rings again and this time, it's her husband calling from one of the office phones.
Rachelle: Hello?
Bob: Hey sweetness! Great! So I did leave my phone there! I'm coming home on my break to get it. Do me a favor; if it rings, don't answer it. Some of my bosses call me on that line and may think that I'm monkeying around at work.
Rachelle: Bob, who is Bridgette?
Bob: *(Pauses)* Why...why do you ask? You been answering my phone, Rachelle? Did she call?
(Rachelle decides to test Bob, so she lies to him.)
Rachelle: Yeah, she asked to speak with you and told me that you were her boyfriend.
Bob: That woman is crazy. No, baby. Can we talk about this when I get home?
Rachelle: No, I need to know, otherwise I won't be able to work today.
Bob: *(Sighs)* I wish this could wait. Well, I have known Bridgette for some years now. We went to school together. I ran into her at the market one day, and I helped to load some dog food into her car. She gave me her business card, and I was planning to throw it away; but when she left the parking lot, I saw that she had left some kitty litter at the bottom of the basket. So, I called the number on the business card and told her. She came back and got the litter, and she got my number off her caller I.D. She tried to hit on me, but I told her I was happily married with a daughter, and she kept calling me anyway. I will handle it, don't worry.

Rachelle is beside herself and just hangs up the phone. At this,

she calls Bridgette back from Bob's phone.
Bridgette answers.
Bridgette: Hey babes. Is she still around?
Rachelle: Yes, I'm still around. Bob told me about how you are stalking him. Bob is married; spell-it-out! Don't call him anymore.
Bridgette hangs up, and that's that. When Bob comes home, he claims to have already handled the issue despite Rachelle's request that he call Bridgette in her presence.

Weeks go by, and Rachelle has now been paying more attention to Bob's behavior. He seems to guard his cell phone more; even going so far as to leave it in his car and password protect it. His trips to the store can take over an hour, even though the store is just 10 minutes away. Sex? That's now a thing of the past because Bob is now saying that his job is wearing him out, and when they do engage in intercourse; it's different. There's no passion in it anymore. It's just monotone, reminiscent of riding a bike down a bumpy dirt road.

Rachelle questions Bob often. "Baby, please tell me the truth. Please. I won't get mad. Are you having an affair?" Every time this question is posed, Bob gets extremely defensive and would lash out by saying, "My grandmother always said if you keep accusing a man of doing something, he's going to go out and do it!"

Tired, Rachelle decides to take matters in her own hands. The cell phone account is in her name, so she decides to order detailed billing and have the bill go to her parent's house. This way, Bob won't see what she's been up to.

When the bill arrives, Rachelle is sick with fear. She can't wait to get home; she has to open it and now! She retreats to her car and begins to look at the bill. Anger overwhelms her, and tears begin to flow non- stop as she sees Bridgette's number overpowering the sheet in addition to all of the calls that Bob has been making to Bridgette. She can't hold her pain, and she can't contain her rage; so she drives up to Bob's job, knowing he should be getting off work at any minute.

When she arrives, she could already see many of the employees getting into their vehicles to leave, but Bob's truck is still there. So, she waits. She scans the faces of every woman who leaves the building, trying to figure out if one of those women could be the infamous Bridgette. One woman captures her attention because she looks like Bob's type. She's short, pretty, slender and wears her hair long. And she looks like a Bridgette! Rachelle keeps her eye on this petite potential home wrecker, wondering if this was her competitor. She was so focused on this woman that she didn't see Bob come out and get into his truck. But, when it cranks up, Rachelle's eyes immediately goes to the truck, and she begins to put her car in drive to pursue Bob. Maybe, just maybe he'll go to Bridgette's house. After all, he doesn't always come directly home. And she's right. Bob turns off and drives five minutes down the highway before making a left turn. He doesn't see his wife behind him because there's too much traffic on the highway and people are driving frantically to prepare for the upcoming Christmas holiday. Rachelle turns behind him and watches as he pulls into the driveway of this small white house. Rachelle parks a few yards away so he won't see her. Bob doesn't knock on the door. Instead, he unlocks it with a key and goes in. At this moment, Rachelle can feel all of her internal organs in operation. Her heart is beating so loudly that she can hear it. She can hear the activity going on in her stomach, and everything seems to be going in slow motion.

Rachelle gets out of the car and approaches the house. She knows what to expect, but that doesn't soothe the horrible pain and fear that has taken refuge in her. Numb, she knocks on the door. No answer. She knocks again and a few seconds later, she could hear Bob's voice saying, “One minute!” He opens the door and is stunned to see his wife there. “Baby, who is that?” The voice comes from Bob's mistress as she peeks around the corner, revealing the strap of bra that has now fallen or been pulled over her arms. When she sees Rachelle standing there crying, she knows immediately who Rachelle is. So, she runs back into the bedroom and locks the door. After a long silence, Bob says, “I don't know what to say.”

Explanation:

We can end this story here, but first let me ask you this question. You are probably saying that Bob is a bad man, and his wife was right all along. And you're right. Bob was an adulterer, but what you don't know is that Rachelle met Bob when he was married, and she was his mistress. For three years, she played the fiddle, and now she is having to dance to the music that she made someone else dance to. She had her share of the destruction of Bob's first marriage. That's why she was so suspicious and just couldn't trust him. Because she knew Bob and was afraid that she would suffer the same fate as his first wife. And now, here she was standing there feeling the pain that she'd enjoyed watching another woman go through. And Bob, cold as ice, shuts the door and tries to figure out how to get to the house and get his clothes out without a fight.

Bob is an adulterer. That's what he is. A cat is a cat; a pig is a pig, and a duck is a duck. Go out and marry a cat, and he won't become a duck. He'll still be a cat after the vows and meows are said. Again, Bob **is an adulterer**. So, when Rachelle was enjoying the perks of being the 'other woman,' she saw his wife as the problem in the marriage. Bob had told her so many evil things that were not true about his wife. She enjoyed toying with his wife. She enjoyed the attention from Bob. She enjoyed feeling like the pick of the litter. Now, as she stands there no longer the one holding the sword, but as the one penetrated by the sword, she realizes just how much it hurts. An adulterer commits adultery against his wife. When the woman is the other woman, she's safe from his adultery because she is the person that he is committing adultery with, but not the one that he is committing adultery against. But, once she becomes the wife; he does as an adulterer does and commits adultery! So now, he no longer works with her; he works against her. Any man that will do something evil with you will one day do it against you. Guaranteed.

This is life's reaction to Rachelle's choice. Of course, Bob will get his and Bridgette will get hers, just as Rachelle got hers. Life is designed to play for us what we play for others. To bless us as we bless others; to render upon us the wages that we have worked for.

Sometimes, people stop and talk about how this person has done them or that person has done them, but they never take the time to ask themselves if what they are going through is the response from something they put out.

Another example of life's reactions to our actions is evidenced in Simone's story. Simone is a gossip. She talks about everybody and everything at every time. Her evil tongue is a reflection of her evil heart, but she just can't stop. She loves how it feels to talk about this and that person and their issues. It just makes her day and takes her mind off her own issues.

One day, Simone goes to the doctor and is diagnosed with lung cancer. She's heartbroken and afraid. She doesn't want to die. She's too young. She doesn't smoke, so how did she get lung cancer?

Simone goes through chemotherapy and the cancer goes into remission. The doctors are surprised. They thought that the cancer was too aggressive and had spread too much, but they did the chemo just to look like they were making an effort to save Simone, but in truth, they had given up on Simone. Nevertheless, Simone slowly healed, to their surprise.

Months later, Simone is back at work and sees Mrs. Betty standing in the lounge talking on the phone to her husband. Mrs. Betty is an older woman. She's quiet and keeps to herself. She's always smiling and always has a warmness about her. Many went to her when they were troubled, and she would listen to their problems and advise them according to the WORD of GOD. For others, they felt like she was acting as if she never had a problem. So, when Simone saw her looking distressed in the lounge and talking on her cell, Simone hid on the other side of the wall and listened.

"What do you mean you're leaving?" Mrs. Betty asks her husband. "I have done everything you have asked of me, Troy. I cooked; I cleaned up, and I even helped take care of your mother, and now you want to announce to me, when I get to work that you're leaving? What am I supposed to do now?"

Simone is overjoyed at the news. She can't wait to tell her crew. She's not happy that Mrs. Betty's husband is leaving, she's excited because she has something to talk about. Mrs. Betty's life isn't so perfect after all.
Lunch time comes, and Simone spots the pack of vultures (gossips) sitting down ready to feast on the latest gossip, and Simone can't contain herself. The conversation starts. Simone comes into the lounge; mouth already open. "Did y'all hear that Ms. Betty's husband is leaving her? I heard her talking today to him, and she was begging him to stay! Kept telling him how

she's been there for him; she's cooked for him and took care of his mother! I believe he's leaving her for another woman because, remember I told you that I saw him in Wal-Mart two weeks ago with some younger girl, and they were all hugged up. And guess what? The girl was pregnant! Looks like Mrs. Betty might need the counseling this time!" At this, they all laugh and continue to feast on Mrs. Betty's name.

After the gossip feast; the word spreads. Mrs. Betty's husband is leaving her for another woman; a younger woman. It gets back around to Mrs. Betty, who laughs it off and never takes the time to say what was really going on. She understands that she does not owe these people an explanation about what is going on in her life or her marriage. She comes to work one day not feeling so good, and it spreads that she is going through the motions.

Months later, Simone goes to the doctor to get the results of her last check-up. Her doctor had called her to tell her to come in. She thought this was odd, but she went. When she arrived at the office, she could see the downtrodden look on her doctor's face. "The cancer is back and I don't know if we can stop it this time." At this, Simone breaks down crying and praying. She reminds the LORD that HE said HE would never leave or forsake her. Why was this happening? She goes on crying, going so far as to loudly rebuke the devil.

A few weeks later, Simone is hospitalized because she'd collapsed at work. The cancer had spread quickly and vigorously. Upon waking up, she finds Mrs. Betty by her side, holding her hand. No one else was there, but Mrs. Betty. Then she opens her mouth and begins to tell Mrs. Betty the agony she's been going through.

Simone: Mrs. Betty, I try to live right, but for what? Look at me. The doctor is trying to say that I have three to six months left. I don't know what else to do. My heart is heavy, Mrs. Betty; I'm tired.

Mrs. Betty: Sweetie, I know it's hard, but you can't give up. No matter what, GOD gets the glory in this. You just have to be strong and believe GOD, not the doctors.

Simone: I hear you, but I'm tired, Mrs. Betty! And look at me. I'm here all alone, dying. Where are my friends? No one came to see me at all, but you? Is this what my life has been reduced to? Just pain, fear and loneliness. Where are my friends?

Mrs. Betty: Oh, those girls at work aren't your friends, dear. You see, I have heard them talk about you on more than one occasion, but I do my best to keep to myself. The first time that you were diagnosed with cancer, baby, I was praying for you every day like you were my own daughter. I even went on a fast because I just did not want you to leave like that. I could hear them speaking death over you, but I was canceling their words and telling them to watch their words. But, I know they don't care much for me because I'm a child of GOD. When I heard that you were okay, I celebrated. And just know that I am praying for you even now.

Simone: Thank you Mrs. Betty. I love you dearly. I can't wait to get back to work so I can get them straight. How dare they talk about me…

Mrs. Betty: No, no, no! Let GOD be GOD, baby girl. They talk about me, but it doesn't bother me. The last thing I heard was that my husband was leaving me. I just laughed. If they only knew.

Simone: He's not leaving you? Cause I heard that too.

Mrs. Betty: Oh, no way. I think that rumor came from a conversation I had with him some months ago. You see, we'd just heard that our daughter was in the hospital having her baby. My daughter lives in Wisconsin. He'd called home earlier, from work, and we discussed our initial plans were to travel down to Wisconsin to see her that coming weekend, but I knew that he was anxious to go ahead and go. I asked him clearly if he was going to fly out that day because I did not want to cook and waste all that food, and he assured me that he would wait until the weekend so that I could go with him. But, when I went on break, I heard a message from him talking about he's at the airport and that bothered me because if I knew he was leaving; I wouldn't have cooked all that food. Plus, I'd reminded him that I finished up on the spring cleaning and had been taking care of his mother, so I didn't feel like traveling on that day. I wanted to wait until the weekend.

Simone: But, what about that girl, I...I mean, that he was seen with in Wal-Mart.

Mrs. Betty: (Laughs) That's my daughter. Her and her daddy are very close. Her daddy took her on a shopping spree to get some things for her since she was pregnant and was flying out the next day. He knew he wouldn't get the chance to come to the baby shower, so he took her out that day. He just spoils her. I'm surprised people haven't seen them out for dinner, movies and where ever else they'd been. They are so very close. Every since she was little; they have been like best friends. Even her husband doesn't interfere when they make plans. I told him to just do like I do and jokingly give them a curfew. (laughs)

Horrified, Simone confesses to being the one who started the rumor, but to her amazement, Mrs. Betty didn't care. She just didn't want her to stress herself out any more about it.

Explanation:

Simone's action was to spread gossip. Not only did she gossip, but she put her mouth on a woman of GOD. Did GOD give Simone cancer? No. GOD said to not touch HIS anointed, but Simone kept on touching Mrs. Betty with her words. Not to mention, the countless other people who had fallen under the sword of Simone's words. You see, the Bible says that if we live by the sword, we'll die by the sword. That isn't just the bladed sword that most people think it is. The sword is words. The SWORD of GOD is the WORD of GOD. The Bible also says that life and death are in the power of the tongue and those that love it would eat the fruit thereof. So, what Simone did was she committed an action that caused a reaction. That reaction was the activation of the WORD. Simone gave herself over to gossip and envy since the two are very much linked, and as a result; she lived in the midst of demons. If you throw a woman in a prison full of sexual predators, do you think she'd be safe? Why is it that people believe that they can let sin imprison them in the realm of the demonic and they'd be safe as long as they went to church on Sunday? That's like throwing a cat into a room with a bunch of hungry dogs and locking the door. While Simone was speaking evil of others, evil was being born of her, and because she was its mother, it followed her around. GOD called Simone to operate in a particular realm and to live in that realm, but she went into the slums with demons to live there. Occasionally, she would talk right, but her heart was not in GOD. She loved gossip, but gossip did not love her.

Some people would argue that Simone's condition was a "chanced" result of some type of exposure, just as those same people would argue that seizures are the result of an imbalance in the brain. This is because they are bi-believers. They have two different belief systems. They believe, on one hand, that the Bible is correct; but on the other hand, they don't believe the entire Bible.

In the days of old, people understood the root of most ailments: ***"And as Jesus passed by, he saw a man who was blind from his birth. And his disciples asked him, saying, Teacher, who did sin, this man, or his parents, that he was born blind? Jesus answered, Neither has this man sinned, nor his parents: but that the works of God should be made manifest in him." (John 9:1-3)***

Here, you can see that the Disciples saw not just the blindness,

but understood that it had a root. But, JESUS explained that the root was not sin, in this case, but this was done so that GOD could be glorified. Now, let's see how sin ties into many of the illnesses that strike against the health and wellness that was declared for us in ***Isaiah 53:5:***
"And Azariah the priest went in after him, and with him fourscore priests of the LORD, that were valiant men: And they withstood Uzziah the king, and said unto him, It belongs not unto you, Uzziah, to burn incense unto the LORD, but to the priests the sons of Aaron, that are consecrated to burn incense: go out of the sanctuary; for you have trespassed; neither shall it be for your honor from the LORD God. Then Uzziah was angry, and had a censer in his hand to burn incense: and while he was angry with the priests, leprosy even broke out in his forehead before the priests in the house of the LORD, from beside the incense altar. And Azariah the chief priest, and all the priests, looked upon him, and, behold, he was leprous in his forehead, and they thrust him out from there; yea, he himself hastened also to go out, because the LORD had struck him." (2 Chronicles 26:17-20)
Further reading tells us that Uzziah died with leprosy.

Another entrance is through demonic infestation. Of course, demons enter through disobedience, generational curses and associations. ***"And it came to pass, that on the next day, when they were come down from the mountain, many people met him. And, behold, a man of the company cried out, saying, Teacher, I beseech you, look upon my son: for he is my only child. And, lo, a spirit takes him, and he suddenly cries out; and it convulses him so that he foams again, and bruising him seldom departs from him. And I besought your disciples to cast him out; and they could not. And Jesus answering said, O faithless and perverse generation, how long shall I be with you, and bear with you? Bring your son here. And as he was yet coming, the***

demon threw him down, and tore him. And Jesus rebuked the unclean spirit, and healed the child, and delivered him again to his father." (Luke 9:37-42)

Now, this doesn't explain the point of demonic entrance into this little boy, however, this does explain that the root of the seizures (epilepsy) was and still is a spirit (demon.)

Now, let's get back to Simone. Simone's disease was rooted in her sin. Simone did not understand that by gossiping and assuming Mrs. Betty's husband was leaving her, Simone was sending out a spirit against their marriage. Simone had drawn her sword against Mrs. Betty, but Mrs. Betty was praying for Simone and of course, we'd like to believe that Mrs. Betty knew to cancel words that were sent out against her since she knew people were talking.

Yes; we go through trials, but all too often, a chastening is mistaken for a trial. A chastening is basically a good old fashioned butt-whooping from the LORD. We are often times warned first. Someone comes along and tells us or we may hear the pastor speak on something and we know GOD is talking to us through him/her. Then, there are the times when we read something that we know is intended for us, or the times when we can hear the rebuke (conscious) come from within. Nevertheless, we refuse to yield and as a result; we have to go through, live with, or die because of that thing. Now, GOD can't be tempted with evil, which means, GOD does not bring evil upon us, but the chastening is that when we whore ourselves out to sin; sin gets a chance to pay us for our acts. The wages of sin is death.

Why use such harsh words like "whoring?" We have to get past the flesh and sometimes, we understand just what we are REALLY doing when someone calls it what it is. We are HIS children, we are NOT children of sin. So, when we lie down with sin, we get pregnant by sin and what is birthed is consequence. Sure, consequence is an ugly baby, but it is born to teach you that sin is an ugly thing.

Watch what you say as well and be mindful of what others are saying about you. The earth is created in a way that everything we say has to respond to us. ***"Death and life are in the power of the tongue: and they that love it shall eat the fruit thereof." (Proverbs 18:21)***

People are always cursing and calling other people names. Many are always gossiping and speaking the language of death, but when disaster, chaos, oppression, depression and all of Satan's seeds are released, people want to run and call on the LORD. Again, let's get graphic so you can understand it better. If you have intercourse with a man, he will release his seeds in the end, right? Did you know that the words you speak are doing something similar? Every time you speak a thing, it moves in the atmosphere and something is released as a result of it. Even when you release evil words against someone else, that evil impregnates your life as well. And if they are believers, canceling your words and living in obedience to GOD; what is sent out by you has a one-way ticket back to you. Words seduce curses and demons when they are evil. Words that are blessed birth blessed things in our lives. Speak life if you want to live!
"When GOD says no, your 'yes' is overridden."

WHEN SEXY DON'T WORK

"Sexy will only get you a [illegible], however wisdom draws in after its own kind."

It's only natural. We want to be somebody's wife. Many of us are anointed to be a wife and many are not. The sad part of it all is that many who are anointed to marry have been taught wrong, in most cases. Somebody told you several ways to "find a man," but they didn't tell you how to be found by your husband. They are not one in the same. A husband is anointed of GOD to carry on the role of a leader in his home, to love and procreate with his wife, provide for his family and to birth nations of believers. The terms 'husband' and 'wife' have been perverted by the world today so it's no wonder many women find themselves in the throngs of opinions, witchcraft and ideas as to how to get to the altar. They cook, they clean, they sew and they have babies. But, still, no man marries them.

Sandra is beautiful, single and ready to be married. She is a great cook, a great housekeeper and all of her friends come to her for advice. She is also a paralegal and has no children. So, by all accounts, Sandra is a catch, right?

It's Friday night and Sandra is adding the final touches to her makeup. She's showing off that curvaceous form, as usual. Her short and fitted gray skirt is shimmery and is more like a peep show where the curtains had just begun to come down. Her midriff matching top rests just above her belly button, showing off a thin waist line, and drops down at the top to reveal her much complimented cleavage. She finishes her look with a pair of stilettos and an up-do that shows off the beautiful bone structure in her face. Off she goes to the club where she is easily seen as the most beautiful woman there.

At the club, Sandra meets Jeff; a real estate investor who loves a good time, and they hit it off well. Jeff is mesmerized by Sandra's beauty and her form. He just can't get the first glimpse of her out of his mind.

Weeks go by and Sandra has invited Jeff over a few times, but this night is special. Sandra feels like it's time to take it to the next level. She has cooked for Jeff before and he has always complimented her cooking. He has taken her out once or twice and his friends have smiled at him, giving him the thumbs-up when they see them together. Jeff told Sandra how beautiful she was and how he just can't stop thinking about that first glimpse of her. They have shared more than one kiss and each time, the pressure to abstain is too great. So, after talking with a few friends, Sandra decides that tonight is the night that she shows Jeff another reason to consider her for holy matrimony. And she does just that.

The night was long and passionate and Sandra feels comforted in Jeff's arms. In the middle of the night, Jeff goes home; but not without giving her one last passionate kiss.

Sandra sleeps in the next day. She wakes up feeling perky and confident. She is so puffed up because she not only cooked food that Jeff had never eaten (and he loved it), but she got a few compliments in the bedroom as well. Her thoughts of the night engage her mind as she strolls to the kitchen to get her morning coffee. The day passes by, but Jeff doesn't call like he usually does. Sandra decides that he is just tired from the night before, so she dismisses it and continues about the day. The next day, it's the same thing. Sandra's phone doesn't ring. So, she checks the ringer. It's on. She checks to make sure the phone is not off the hook. It's not. Around nine p.m., she calls Jeff, but he doesn't answer. Feeling a boat load of anxiety, she plays the night back in her head again and again to see if there was anything she did that could have run him away. Nothing comes to mind.

Around 11 p.m., Jeff calls. He says his phone got stolen, and he had to get a new one. Sandra is relieved because she was beginning to feel used. Jeff asks if he could come over again tonight, and Sandra agrees. She, like most women, believes that this is the start of something amazing.

The night goes like the one before and by the middle of the night, Jeff gets up and leaves, saying that he has to work the next day.

For the next few weeks, the same scenario plays out. Jeff seems to answer his phone less and he calls less frequently. He answers sometimes during the day, but he always calls back during the night. And at night, he wants to see Sandra. Sandra excuses his behavior, citing to herself that he is a working man. So, she tries to be understanding, but she just can't shake the feeling that something is wrong.

One Friday morning, Sandra stays home from work because the streets near her job have been flooded and the company closed down for the day. The city was expecting floods to sweep through a lot of the neighborhoods, so some companies decided not to open their doors that day. As the rain continued to come down, Sandra thought of how romantic it would be if Jeff could come there and just spend the entire weekend with her. She plans to cater to him by serving him breakfast in bed, massaging his feet and completing the evening with a candlelit supper. She calls, but as usual, he doesn't answer. His phone never seems to ring long either. After two rings, she always gets the voicemail. Sandra decides to go to the store and get some supplies in preparation for the impending flood, and to get some thing to cook for Jeff over the weekend. “Tonight, when he calls, I'll ask him and I know he can't resist,” she thinks to herself. She throws on her shoes and her poncho and heads out the door.

At the store, Sandra is stocking up on canned goods when she sees a familiar face. It's Jeff. Her grin is cut short as she sees that his fingers are intertwined with another hand. He just passed the aisle, hand in hand with another girl. He didn't see Sandra; however, because he was pulling on this other woman who was laughing and almost stumbling trying to show him something. Sandra's heart races as she quickly abandons her shopping cart to go and catch up with Jeff. This has to be a misunderstanding. Maybe it's his cousin. As she rounds the corner, she catches up with Jeff and his friend. They had stopped to laugh at Jeff's three-year-old son, Zach, who was far behind pouting. Sandra didn't even know Jeff had a kid.

“What's this?” she asks Jeff. Petrified, Jeff says, “This is my fiancé, Deborah. Deborah, this is Sandra.... a friend of mine. Zach, come here so daddy can fix your shoes!” Sandra goes into a state of shock. She can't believe what she's hearing. Stunned, Sandra questions him. “Financé? Daddy? You have a fiancé? You have been at my house sleeping with me for the last few months and I don't recall you ever mentioning a fiancé or a son!” In defense, Jeff says, “Stop lying and get away from us! You and I have been over for a long time now!” He grabs his confused fiancé’s hand, picks up his son and storms out of the store. Sandra follows behind him yelling obscenities and crying.

She follows up her tirade by calling Jeff continuously as he backs out of the parking lot, but he doesn't answer. She calls him over and over again throughout the day, but still no answer. Later that day, his fiancé answers and screams, "Sandra, get over it! He told me everything. It was just sex, my dear! But, he's been with me a year and a half and one would think you would have gotten over him by now. He doesn't want you so get counseling! I wear the ring! You don't! You didn't even know he had a child, so what does that say to you about your importance level?! Let it go and stop embarrassing yourself!" At this, she hangs up the phone. "Gotten over him by now? What does she mean?" These questions haunt Sandra as she realizes that Jeff has lied to Deborah. It's obvious that he told her that he'd had a sexual affair with her before he met Deborah and Sandra has been stalking him every since. Sandra calls back again and again until Deborah answers. "Sandra, do you truly believe that your stalking is going to make him take you back?! Don't you understand that it was just sex?! Jeff and I are going to get married in a few days! Now, does this make the load heavy enough to break you into reality or do you still need a key?!"

The calls go on for a week until finally one day, without Deborah in his presence, Jeff answers his phone. A far cry from the low voiced in-love sounding individual that he once pretended to be, Jeff desperately pleads with Sandra to leave him alone. "Listen, Sandra, I'm sorry for how all of this went down. But, I never said I was your man. You assumed that I was your man. I enjoyed your company and all, but you're just not my type. It was just sex. So, I ask of you to get off your chest whatever you need to get off your chest and after this phone call, do not call my phone again or I'll be forced to file charges."

Explanation:

Now, we don't have to go any further with this story. Isn't this a common story? What happened? After all, beautiful Sandra was a great cook, a looker, a professional and she knew her way around the bedroom. You would think a man would consider her a perfect catch. After all, isn't this the image that Hollywood plays on our screens as the catch of a lifetime? The big fish that no man could throw back? Looks like even though Jeff caught her, he threw her back. That fish was too small.

What happened? Men don't marry sexy; they marry nurturing. Read that again. There are some women out there who just don't get it. There are certain qualities that a man looks for in a wife and he will immediately decide what he wants to pursue you as from the initial conversation, or at maximum, the first week of knowing you. Now, in many cases, a man may initially look at you as having wife-potential. But, after a conversation or two, he has moved you to the bedroom files. Why? Because she is too focused on being sexy and too focused on being married and it is not the nature of a man to be pursued. You see, a woman that spends too much time and money trying to be sexually appealing is chasing a man; even if she never approaches one. Men know this. We give them less credit than they deserve, ladies. Plus, Jeff met Sandra in a club. He wasn't looking for a wife in a club. Most men see clubs as brothels with music. Like most men that go to clubs, he was looking for a good time and just like the buzz from the alcohol wears off, his interest in a woman found on the prowl wears off when he has burned off some of his fuel.

Jeff came into the club looking, and there she was, already halfway undressed, like a piece of candy waiting to be unwrapped. Candice was irresistible because she looked easy and the bonus was...she was beautiful and shapely. He wanted to do the honors of unwrapping her. He knew all she needed was a few compliments, a little attention, a date or two, a phone call a day, and she'd be naked by the end of the month. He had a fiancé already. He was just a man with wandering eyes; not qualified to be anyone's husband, but even these type want decent women. He'd met his fiancé at the library and she has **never** slept with him. That's why she wears the ring. Funny thing is, Sandra is far more beautiful in the eyes of most, than his fiancé. But, what man cares?

This is what many women do not understand. On television, sexy counts. They like to say "sex sells." Sex doesn't sell; it rents. Imagine what a man does with a prostitute. He pays her, sleeps with her and drops her back off for the next man to rent. I know this sounds harsh, but the truth does not come in to bandage; it is a sword, so it comes to destroy any knowledge that exalts itself against the WORD of GOD. Every time a man gives you his time, money, attention; but does not commit himself as a husband to you before GOD, he is simply paying to lay with you and paying to be seen with you. Men can stay with a woman that they have no intentions of marrying for years!

Just like that man dropped off that prostitute; a man that finds a woman looking for a man and a man not anointed to be her husband is going to take that woman, pay that woman with time, compliments and a few dates and then bed that woman. After he's reached his point of destination, he drops her back off for the next man to do the same with. Ladies, please understand that if he's not anointed to be your husband, he will always try to be your lover. A husband will pursue your hand in marriage. He is interested more in what's in your heart and this intensifies the sexual experience after marriage because he is in love with the whole you. A lover pursues a sexual rendezvous with you. He is more interested in what's in your pants than what is in your head. He doesn't want to know your favorite colors or what your dreams are. He doesn't want to know how many kids you want. He doesn't plan to be around that long. He only wants to know what you like in a man, so he can pretend to be just that until he has had his fill of you.

But some may say, "Well, Sandra's case was obvious. She should have known better. I have been with my boyfriend for four years and we don't have those kind of issues." The man that came before the boyfriend was there three years and the guy before him was with her two years. But, no ring! The only thing that keeps happening is she is leasing herself out, if that term is preferred over renting. Because it does not take a man a long time to decide that you are his wife! If he needs years and years to think about it, chances are, he has already decided that you make a great girlfriend and a beautiful bed-buddy. That's it! Nothing more! Leave him and let him find a woman who will not accept being just a girlfriend; a woman who knows her worth and values herself, and she'll have a ring in as little as six months in many cases.

Sex is a bonus. Sexy is a bonus. But, it is not the deal maker. Ask yourself this: Would you go to a car lot and purchase a beautiful 2012 Mercedes Benz with a locked up engine for $35,000? Of course not! The car looks good, but what's under the hood is a mess, so it's not worth it! You may sit in the car, rub on the seats, open the glove compartment and stare at the gauges, but in the end, you'll get out and choose a car that runs; even if its not as pretty. Even if it's an older model, you'd pay more for something that gets you to where you want to be. Or would you go to the car lot and purchase a fully loaded 2012 BMW that's been obviously crashed and banged up a few times for $45,000? Why don't you believe that men were created to think that way as well? Why would he pay (supporting a home for the rest of his life) for a woman who looks good on the outside, but needs a new way of thinking? This is to get you to understand why you see so many women live their lives 'sexy' and spend their lives getting sexed, only to grow old still being called somebody's girlfriend.

Yes, learn to cook. Yes, be sure to keep your home neat and in order. Keep yourself looking beautiful. But, know this: Beauty will get you to the castle, but wisdom will bring you before the king. Sexy will make the king call you a concubine, have you 'committed' to a chamber to be used at his discretion whenever you happen to cross his mind. But, wisdom will make him call you wife, over all of the women in the kingdom!

When you get married, it is then that you can unleash the 'sexy' you in the comfort of your home.

Remember sexy will only get you sexed, but wisdom draws after its one kind.

The Prodigal Daughter

"When you go into sin, you come out with a sinner

It is very common to find a woman of GOD in a relationship with a man of the world. Some women have a tendency to get swept away in emotions and desires, never subjecting those feelings to the WORD of GOD to be tried by fire. What happens is, a lot of women enter sin looking for a husband and come out with a sinner.

Michelle wanted Richard. It was no secret. Sure, Richard was a bad boy. But, that's what Michelle likes. Even though Michelle is a believer, she has always been fascinated by boys of rebellion. She views their rebellious ways as their strength.

Michelle is like many women of GOD. She's not ready for a husband yet. Her mind hasn't been changed yet. She is still a baby, spiritually. She is attracted to rebellious men because she is rebellious, even though, in her, it isn't so obvious.

One day, while hanging out at the public pool, Michelle spots Richard diving into the deep part of the pool (10 feet). A great swimmer, Michelle dives in and swims in the direction that she sees him in. She is always flirting with him, but this time, she is determined to exchange numbers with him. She came to the pool for this very reason. She knows that Richard loves to come here, especially on Saturdays.

With the pool being so packed with people, Michelle feels anxious as she tries to swim around the kicking legs of other swimmers. She comes up for air and spots Richard just a few feet away. “Richard?!” Michelle screams his name. “Richard?!” She waves her arms to get his attention. Ah, desperation! Richard can smell it on her. He smiles and swims right on over. Nothing like a fish that throws itself on the deck.

“Hey you,” he says as he comes to the surface. “What are you up to?” Richard knows that Michelle likes him. He thinks she's a pretty girl, and probably would be more interested in her if she wasn't chasing him, but he decides that today is a good day to get to know her better. “I'm just here, cooling off,” replies Michelle. “You're looking good as usual.” She shyly awaits Richard's response, hoping that she hadn't scared him. Smiling, he says, “Let's get out of the pool so I can get your number.” Michelle agrees.

Months later, the relationship seems to be going well. Richard really likes Michelle and Michelle really likes Richard, and since Richard is not a church going-Bible reading man, Michelle has had to comply with his fleshly needs. A man of the world doesn't care anything about your beliefs because he has his own that are centered around himself and not GOD.

Anyhow, Michelle discovers that she is pregnant. She's been going to church less and less, and she has now changed her radio station from the gospel station that she once loved to listen to, and now she listens to jazz, r&b and hip hop. Jazz and r&b for romance, and hip hop because that's what Richard likes. She likes hip hop now as well because she was exposed to it a lot and now her way of thinking has changed. Even her clothing has changed. Her speech has changed and her hang outs have changed. She is a different woman. She has abandoned GOD to follow Richard and his devils.

A few years later, Michelle and Richard have two children together and are living together. They have spoke about marriage a couple of times, but this isn't something they are anxious to do. Sure, Michelle wants a wedding with all the trimmings, but she doesn't want to stress out Richard about it, so she just goes along with what he wants.

Richard has been going through his share of issues as well. Michelle isn't so pretty anymore. She's okay, in his eyes, but that's it. She just does not fascinate him anymore, and those hollering kids are getting on his nerves. Honestly, the sight of Michelle irritates him. Not to mention, they have cut Michelle's hours at work, so now, the funds coming in are even less, but Michelle is home more. What? Did you think Richard would work to take care of a family that he doesn't care much for? Men invest in women whom they want, but make women whom they don't want pay for them! Michelle's public aid has been helping to keep the refrigerator stocked. Richard does get out, every now and again, and get a few hundreds from the other women in his life. Even though Michelle pretty much knows that he is a philandering man, she excuses his ways, toying with the idea that the other women are foolish enough to help take care of their home. Because when Richard does get this money, he may go out and pay a bill, buy a few packs of meat or give it to Michelle. That's love, right? No. It's Richard's prideful attempt to feel like what he perceives as a "real man." It has nothing to do with Michelle or the kids.

The relationship gets so strained that Richard decides to move out and pursue Alyssa, a beautiful Filipino girl who he believes likes him, but just won't give him the time of day. He just cannot stop thinking about Alyssa, to the point where he's dreaming about her all the time. Every time he goes up to the bank where Alyssa works, she grins at him before shooting him down. But, her latest comment to him was, "You have a girlfriend. I am not a home wrecker." This prompted Richard to move out so that he could better his chances of getting her.

What about Michelle? Well, she's heartbroken and just cannot understand what happened. She'd planned their whole life together and thought that this string of problems that they were having was just Richard going through one of his down-times. After all, he's always putting her down. So, what's new?

It wasn't easy for Michelle when they were together. She'd been the bread-winner and she had to deal with other women calling her to say that they'd been with Richard. Her kids have come back to tell her that they saw daddy kissing this and that girl. He had no shame. Richard had been abusive to Michelle, as well. Anytime she went through one of her "nagging days," he'd silence her by punching her or choking her until he could feel that she was weak enough to stop talking and start gagging for air.
But, now, Michelle is going crazy, or so she thinks. She can't work because of the pain she's enduring. So, she quits. She's watching the house where Richard is now staying. He has moved back into his mom's house. Stalking is not an easy job. She notices that Richard is always going to the bank. She's confronted other women that she's found him with in the past, only to be met by fights, ugly words and a constant reminder by Richard that they were not together anymore.

Michelle enters the bank and looks to see where Richard is. He's in Alyssa's line and she's grinning from ear to ear. Instead of waiting to see what happens, Michelle approaches Alyssa in front of her customers. "Are you the home-wrecking tramp that stole my boyfriend?! Because if you are, just know that he is mine, always will be and we have not one, but two children together. Plus another one on the way!" Yep, Michelle has recently discovered that she is pregnant again, but this news does nothing to calm Richard's response. He leaps past the people in the line and begins choking Michelle. "Didn't I tell you that I don't want you anymore? Didn't I tell you? But, now I bet you'll get it this time when I cut your lights off..."

Security leaps into action and rescues a now consciously humiliated Michelle from the arms of her would be killer. The people standing around are stunned and frightened. Many duck, believing that this to be a distraction for an armed robbery, while others stand by recording the attack with their cell phones.
The police arrives and arrests both Michelle and Richard and questions Alyssa, who is in so much shock that she's trembling and crying.
Michelle's life is in shambles. With no money, no job, no man, two children and another one on the way, she doesn't know where to turn. She turned her back on her family years ago when they protested her relationship with Richard. And her pride won't let her go and ask for a place to stay. Broken and confused, she heads to the church that was once her sanctuary. It's Wednesday night, and Bible study is almost finished. She comes in and sits at the back of the church and hopes that no one sees her. She's rugged looking now, and her tattoos bear witness to the type of life she has been living. And the alcohol and drug use (marijuana) has taken its toll on her face. She looks older, and the stress has caused her to lose much of the weight that she'd gained. Her kids also look needy. Her son, Richard Jr., leans over her shoulder, a quiet two-year-old, not knowing what to make of everything. Her daughter, one-year-old Richelle is asleep in her arms, having been soothed by the sound of the choir singing.

Bible study is over and everyone leaves the church. Every one, excepts Michelle, her children and the pastor. He'd recognized Michelle and was happy to see her back in church after all these years, but he senses something is wrong. He makes his way to the back, calling his wife first and asking her to come up to the church to help him minister to the obviously broken Michelle and she does. Their house is not far from the church, so she's there in five minutes.

When the pastor's wife arrives, she could hear loud troubled talking from within the church. Panicked, she runs inside only to find Michelle is crying aloud and releasing years of pent up anguish and frustration. Her husband sits there quietly, understanding that Michelle needs to release before he can get a word in.

Michelle: I've been good to him, Pastor! I turned on my own momma! I turned on my own daddy! I gave this idiot kids! I loved him and I gave him all of me, but it wasn't enough! Now I've got a criminal record; I'm jobless, homeless, and he's out laying around with this and that woman and acting like he don't know me or his kids! I have cried out to GOD. Why did HE let this happen to me? I know I was wrong.... yes! But, I am not a killer. I haven't killed or raped anybody! I am just a woman who loved the wrong man! Now, I don't know where to go, what I'm going to eat, where my children are going to lay their heads, what my children are going to eat, and I just don't know! I just don't know!
Pastor John: Michelle, I understand that this is a hard time for you, and I'm not one to mix words. I believe the truth will set you free, so I'm not going to keep you bound by trying to find words to soothe your pain. I'm going to find words of love that are meant to destroy what's oppressing you and heal you. Daughter, you brought this on yourself. You took your life from GOD'S

hands to put it in the hands of a man who did not know GOD. You're like a lot of women. You believe that you can make a crooked man straight, but you can't, baby girl. No matter how many kids you gave him, no matter how faithful you was to him, no matter how much love you gave him, how much money you made; that man would have left because GOD never pairs HIS daughters with sons of the devil. And even though it hurts, you must understand that you were not wronged in this; you were delivered. You see, the season was up for your rebellion and now GOD is calling you back to servitude. HE allowed you to run out there so that you can understand that HIS no won't return to HIM void.

Michelle: I understand all that, Pastor. I really do. But, it just hurts so bad. It really-really hurts. I could feel GOD was calling me back, but Pastor, I was ashamed. Look how far I went away from HIM. Do you know what I've been doing these last few years? No matter how low it was, I have been doing whatever it takes to please that man! He had me to strip for his friends! What kind of man asks the mother of his children to strip for his friends?!

Pastor John: The kind of man that is the son of Satan. You have to understand that you know how you are supposed to be treated. That's why you hurt and that's why you fight with him. Because your FATHER showed you how precious you were and how you should be treated. But, the error was in you. You tried to put wings on a devil and call it an angel. That man did not wrong you. He did what he knew how to do. He did what was in his nature to do. However, you lied to you when you told yourself that you could love him enough to bring him to salvation, when he clearly didn't want it. You see, when a man of the world meets a woman of GOD, the two plan in their hearts to pull on one another. The woman of GOD believes that she can bring this man to GOD through her love and her teaching him. The man, in his darkness and conceit, believes that he can bring this woman into the world by his lies, sex, and by brainwashing her. A man of the world looks at the potential that you have to be worldly. So, you have two people in one relationship trying to pull it in two different directions, but the man is stronger. GOD created him that way. A house divided cannot and will not stand. And in the end, he will do you like he does a worldly woman. He'll use her up until his interest in her has passed. And when it does, he gets meaner and meaner. Because, to him, you are now the thing that's holding him back. To him, there is no more mystery left to you and now, you are his enemy because you won't sit back and allow him to pursue women and ideas that he is interested in.

Pastor's wife interrupts. To her, her husband is a little too hard on Michelle, so she tries to say what he is saying in a kind way. She signals for her husband to leave the room and he excuses himself to let the ladies speak.

Pastor Lydia: I know you're hurting. Michelle, you are beautiful. You are a great singer. I used to love to hear you sing. I have surely missed you. But, let me share my testimony with you. His name was Jerry Jordan. Jerry Jordan was a policeman, and he was very very very handsome. On the outside, that is. And I just had to have him. I lived across the street from him, and I would be at the window all the time trying to catch a glimpse of him. Here I was, a woman of GOD, but I was attracted to this man that I had heard curse, saw drinking and knew was a bad boy. But, what made him more appealing was the fact that he was a bad boy with a badge. I just had to have him. I had my own apartment, and I was young in the faith, still single and just hard headed. My dad would come by and he saw that my eyes would twinkle every time I saw Jerry Jordan. My dad looked me in the eyes and said, "Lydia, you can pour bleach on a zebra, but you can't remove its stripes. Lydia, you can paint a zebra, and it will still be a zebra. Lydia, that man you eyeballing ain't for you! You have a choice.

Wait on GOD for your husband or wound up getting with this man, and if you come out alive, you'll come out with a testimony of what GOD had to bring you through. Lydia, some testimonies you just don't have to have! Don't you go after this character! He ain't your husband!" But, you know, Michelle, I wouldn't listen. I figured my dad was just an old fogie and did not understand the times. So, one day, I put on the shortest skirt, and the tallest heels, and I marched on outside and stayed there until he came out. I just leaned on my car, and I eyed him until he came over. That was the beginning of the end of my ignorance. I got a testimony and some wisdom in that fight! Jerry believed in Wicca. Girl, I was so crazy about Jerry that he had me lighting candles and playing with witchcraft! Talk about turning your life around; I did a complete one-eighty! That man turned out to be the devil himself. We'd moved in together, had a daughter and he used to beat me up and down the road. The neighbors got so used to seeing me getting beat up and running for my life that whenever we had an episode, they would just call their kids in the house and wouldn't even bother to call the police. After all, Jerry was the police.

Anyhow, three years in, I had decided that I had enough. I had enough of the beatings. I had enough of the belittling. I didn't like who I'd become. I was no longer this church-going pastor's daughter. I was a woman who lived her life as a victim. That man would beat me for no reason. If I sneezed, he'd hit me. If I looked at him the wrong way, he'd hit me. But, when I saw him slap my daughter; that's when I decided that I had to get out, if not for me, for her. I remembered those words my daddy said well. He said, "If you come out alive, you'll come out with a testimony." I'd been through a test that I was not required to take, but I went into that classroom and took it anyway.

One Friday morning, I decided that this was the day for me to get out. I waited for Jerry to go to work so that I could pack whatever I could, get my daughter, and get out. Jerry had always told me that he would never let me leave him alive, and I knew he'd fight me with everything in him. Anyhow, he got up, got dressed, and I think he sensed I wanted to leave him because he lurked around the house a little longer than he usually did. He had beaten me so bad that I was unrecognizable, but I was used to it. I pretended to be getting ready for work, and to be getting our daughter ready for school. Finally, Jerry left and I put my plan in action. I was so scared! I ran through that house, throwing our clothes in garbage bags. I didn't care about my computer, my cell phone.... nothing. All I wanted was to get some of my clothes and my daughter's clothes, my important documents and get out. But, something was telling me to stop and just turn that television set on, so I did. I put those garbage bags in the hall closet and sat down as the door opened. Jerry came home pretending he'd forgotten something. He knew it was my habit to sit down and watch a little television before I headed out, so at first, everything to him, appeared normal. Then, he noticed I didn't have my morning coffee. He asked me about it and I lied like we were out of sugar. He checked and I nervously acted surprised when he found the sugar. He asked me if I was leaving him and I-was-trembling! I said, "No, baby. Why would I do that?"

Michelle, this man pulled a knife and told me that he was going to kill me and my daughter. Imagine that. His own daughter! He went to the hall closet as if he already knew. He found the bags and that's when the nightmare began. He grabbed his gun and....well, sometimes, those of us that come out alive, come out with a testimony.
(*Lydia pulls back her hair to reveal a scar on her left temple. It looked round, and the skin was dark in that area.*)
One bullet to the head almost destroyed my testimony.
Sometimes, those of us that come out alive, come out with a

testimony. They have to then warn the ones who want to stay in that we weren't called to give their lives to or for a man. We were called to live and declare the works of the LORD. I survived.

At this, Michelle is overwhelmed with shock and emotion. She covers her mouth in horror and yells out, "Pastor Lydia, what happened?!!!"

Pastor Lydia: When the devil couldn't have me anymore; he tried to kill me. What you and millions of women like you have to understand is that you weren't called to be a girlfriend; you weren't called to be a punching bag; you weren't called to be a sex worker; you weren't called to die for a man. You were called to live and declare the works of the LORD. I survived him, and this scar is a reminder to me of the price I almost paid for my rebellion. What you didn't know was that GOD said no, even when you were saying yes. And HIS WORD won't return to HIM void. You got out with your life. You got a second chance, just like me. Many women never get this second chance. You were blessed beyond recognition. Sure, it hurts. I went through years of counseling, depression, and suicidal thoughts. I could not understand how the man that said he loved me; how the man who gave me a beautiful daughter could turn around to be the man who would try to take my life. I believe that if I would have died; he would have killed my daughter, but GOD! That man tried to shoot me a second time and the gun jammed. After that, he fled and left me there to die. I praise GOD that Jerry left the door open. My daughter, who was only two-years-old at the time, was wandering around in the street, covered in blood. Someone saw her and called the police.

Men like that don't know love. GOD is love! We go looking for love in these men when GOD was and is love all by HIMSELF. And all HE wanted was that we would go so far in HIM that our husbands would have to go that much further and beyond to find us. This is when they have been released to be a husband.

I thank GOD for Pastor John. Girl, I tried to evade capture for years. I had gotten myself right with the LORD and here comes this man trying to get with me. I said no-way! All I wanted was to finish school, raise my daughter and to enjoy life without a man. I wrote them off. Forgave the last one, but just didn't want them kind of problems anymore. But, he wouldn't let up and at the urging of my daddy, I finally went out with him, and the rest is history. He has loved my daughter as if she were his own, and she adores herself some him. We have four children together, and sometimes I think she's closer to him than his own seed! But, he doesn't know the difference between her and his actual children. He treats them all the same, loves them all the same and disciplines them all the same.
What I'm saying is this. GOD said no. GOD said live. GOD said live for HIM! Get up and teach your children what your daddy taught you. In time, GOD will send a husband to you, if that is the desire of your heart. But, right now, HE has to heal you, clean you up, and direct you back in HIM. This isn't a time for tears. It's a time for celebrating. GOD delivered you because HE loves you. Satan kept shouting yes to the relationship because he wanted you to die in that sin. But, in all his shouting, all GOD had to do was whisper one “no” and HIS WORD would not and could not return to HIM void.

Explanation:

How many women have done this? How many of you have tried to understand how you could give all that you were to a man, only to be met by betrayal? So many women never come out of this alive. And there are others who come out bitter, untrusting and unforgiving; however, you were given another chance to stay in GOD and be focused on GOD and not a man. You survived you! Because you are your greatest enemy! But, don't let you tell you what to do. Let GOD be in control, always!

We all have wanted something, at one point, that GOD was saying no to. But, if you survived; you lived to testify to another woman who is lost in herself and her sin. You can share with her that there is no blessing in sin. You can't find a blessing in a cursed man. There are many women out there like Michelle and Lydia. Women who thought they could make a crooked man straight. Women who walked into the darkness looking for a man to light up the way. When GOD says no, your yes won't survive. Be thankful that you did.

ORDER OR DISORDERLY

"A wife that is hidden far in the LORD can only be found by a husband that has traveled that much further in HIM."

Everything that we come into, we come into as babies. When we came into our bodies, we started off as infants. When we came into CHRIST, we started off as babes in CHRIST. When we were young, our parents fed us, guarded us, taught us, corrected us and did what was needed to be done to raise us to be successful, healthy women. They'd hoped that we would get married to a successful, loving man one day, and for those of you whose parents were believers; they'd prayed that you would marry a man of GOD one day. But, when you were four years old, they would never consider releasing you to be any man's wife. Why? Because you were too young. You were still growing. You weren't mature yet. You were still a baby.

When we come into CHRIST, again, we are babes in CHRIST. Just like our natural dad, our heavenly FATHER won't release us to marry until we have grown up and matured. And when HE does give our hand in marriage, the man that HE gives it to will have to be in HIM and be able to take care of HIS daughter. But, all too often, as babies, we rebel and want to get out and be somebody's wife before we have even begun to take spiritual meat. This opens the door for catastrophe.

"Let go of my hair! Let go of my hair!" These were the rantings from the desperate Darcy who was entangled up in a fight with a woman named Catherine. Catherine was getting the best of Darcy, who by now, was bent over holding her head as Catherine pulled her hair with one hand and kept pounding her head with the other hand. This fight had to happen. And many were there to see it.

It started off with a runaway dog. Darcy was living with her husband, Jason and their dog had gotten loose one day. In heat, the dog ran into a neighbor's yard and was caught by the attractive Catherine. Seeing Jason running up the street, Catherine caught Snow and headed towards Jason with the trembling fur ball in her hands. (Snow was the dog's name, of course.) She was a white Pomeranian pooch who'd had enough of being locked away in the confines of a house. Nope. Nature was calling and Snow wanted to answer.

Jason: Thank you so much for catching this little rascal. She's in heat and has been going crazy trying to get out the house to mate.
Catherine: Well, she and I understand each other well. I guess that's why she didn't bite me. Good luck!

At this, Catherine winks at Jason and turns around and walks back to her house, but not before turning and giving Jason a smile. This was the beginning of the end of Jason and Darcy.

Two months into the affair, Jason was no longer going to church, but he insisted that Darcy go alone. This would give him a few hours to be with Catherine. He was smitten by the dark haired, gray eyed, long-legged bombshell who wasn't the tiniest bit shy. There was something about her that left him spent; mind, body and cash.

Let's rewind this story so you can get a more inept look at Jason and Darcy.

Darcy met Jason at church, of all places. He'd been going to the same church that she'd been a member of for years, but he was rarely there. He came mostly on holidays and sporadically throughout the year. Initially, Jason hadn't paid much attention to Darcy because she always sat at the front, and he could never really see her entirely. Jason was always late for church (whenever he did come), so he sat at the back and always left right before church ended.

But, one New Years Eve that all changed. Darcy was running late because she'd taken a nap earlier that day and slept later than she'd anticipated. Then, after waking up, she couldn't find the shoes she wanted to wear with her new dress. After 30 minutes of searching, she found the shoes still packed up in some boxes in the attic. She hadn't finished unpacking yet. After that, she had trouble finding her keys and to make matters worse, she was supposed to drive 45 minutes out of the way to pick up her mother for church. So, Darcy was more than 30 minutes late and arrived at the same time as Jason.

When Darcy and her mother arrived at church, service had already begun and Jason was pulling into the parking lot at the same time. When Darcy saw Jason, she grinned because she'd seen him a few times before and thought he was really cute. She assumed that he was single and available, since he always came alone. She was right. But, she didn't have time to entertain those thoughts; she needed to get into the building.

Jason rushed towards the door so that he could open the door for the beautiful red-headed woman he'd seen exiting her car. His eyes had never beheld such a beautiful woman. He wasn't usually attracted to red heads, but this woman who was in his sights was

breathtaking.
As he opened the door, Darcy's beautiful green eyes met his. “Thank you,” she said. “What a gentlemen.”

After service, Jason, for the first time in his life, was still there. It was a New Years Eve service, and it was late. They'd bought in the New Year in worship, but Jason bought in the New Year staring at the beautiful red head in the green dress. How did GOD pack all that beauty up and package it into one woman? Jason wanted to know, so with those very words, he surprised Darcy as she stood in the parking lot talking to some of the members. “Excuse me?” Darcy was surprised and flattered. Here was this gorgeous man standing there giving her compliments. The group that she was talking to smiled and bid her farewell as they left her with Jason. He repeated himself. “How could GOD gather up all that beauty and pack it into one woman without her exploding?" he asked. Before Darcy could answer, her mother, who was waiting in the car, leaned over and blew the horn. “I gotta go,” she said, looking back at her mother. “Wait. Can I have your number so you can help me understand this mystery?” Jason was corny, but charming. So, Darcy handed him her business card and left.

Weeks after meeting Jason, Darcy knew that he was nowhere close to where she was in CHRIST. He spoke mainly about his accomplishments and his dreams, but never about GOD or wanting a family. At first, Darcy wasn't going to let the relationship go any further than a few chats on the phone, but what turned the tide in Jason's favor came on one Wednesday afternoon. Darcy, who worked for a huge accounting firm, went to work prepared for a long day. She'd spent most of the night talking to Jason and trying to reason with herself about him. He seemed nice and boy was he cute! Not to mention, he did come to church sometimes and he did so on his own. Nobody was

pressuring him to come. So, he desired to do the right thing, right? He just needed a push. Then, on the other hand, her pastor's words echoed in her head shooting down those thoughts of reason. “A wife's height in GOD should never be greater than her husband's. If he isn't where you are or higher, forget about chances...he's not the one.”
Jason's words also played over and over again. “You are my wife and I know it. I know that I need to come to church more and do more for the LORD, but I believe HE sent you to help me to get there. Never turn away your blessings just because you don't understand them. Nobody can understand what GOD is doing between me and you. I respect you and I would never ever hurt you.”

A month after meeting, Jason and Darcy went on their first date and a year later; they were married. They moved into a new neighborhood, and Jason was feeling great. He'd married the most beautiful woman whom he'd ever laid his eyes on, purchased his first dream home, and now he was at peace. One of the neighbors had a pregnant Pomeranian dog, and he knew that Darcy loved dogs, so he decided to talk with the neighbor about getting one.

After the puppies were born, Jason took Darcy to the neighbor's house to pick up the pup he had asked the neighbor to hold for her. Darcy was ecstatic. What a great man! He'd picked out the beautiful white puppy who seemed to have trouble getting past the others to get to her mother, but she was unique in that she had a red patch of hair growing at the top of her head.

Six months later, Snow was in heat and she was going wild. Jason and Darcy were trying to keep her in the house. Jason wanted to eventually breed her, but Darcy wanted to spay her. So, at the moment, Snow was not spayed and couldn't see past getting out that front door. She finally got her chance when Jason opened the door to get the newspaper. Off went Snow, running from one neighbor's yard to the next with Jason behind her screaming her name.

Catherine, one of the neighbors saw handsome Jason running after the little white fur ball. Since they were headed in her direction, she took a piece of the hotdog that she was eating and coaxed Snow to come to her. Then she grabbed her and began to walk towards the handsome man that was now leaned over and wheezing for his breath.

Catherine was absolutely beautiful. She had the deepest gray eyes that he'd ever seen. And her hair; long and dark, flowed down her back. She looked even prettier than Darcy at that moment, and she wasn't shy at all. She liked Jason and he could see that. There was something about that girl that left Jason confused. How could he be attracted to another woman when he was married? Better yet, how could he be attracted to another woman so early in his marriage? Was Darcy really the one? After all, the only thing she wanted to do was go to church, go to work, talk about GOD and play wife. Everyday Jason went to the mailbox, looking up the road and hoping to get another glance of Catherine.

One day, he got more than what he bargained for. Darcy had just left to go to work and Jason decided to go and check the mail. It was too early. He knew that the mailman hadn't run yet, but he wanted to see Catherine. She came outside and began to walk in Jason's direction. She looked just like she'd looked in his dreams. She had just awakened and was wearing this pink robe. Smiling, she began a flirtatious play on words.

Catherine: Are you stalking me?

Jason: Maybe I am. What's my punishment?

Catherine: Well, I wrote you a ticket and you need to call the number on the ticket to find out.

Catherine handed Jason a piece of paper with her name and number written on it. She'd sprayed the paper with her favorite scent and had written her name inside of a hand-drawn heart. Jason wasted no time calling her, and this is how the affair began.

During the affair, Jason spoke very evil of his wife. He would complain about her going to church, going to work too much, and he'd even lied and said that he suspected Darcy was having an affair. Jason cast himself as the victim to relax Catherine even more about the affair, but his lies weren't necessary. Catherine was known to have affairs with married men. She couldn't care less who was the bad guy in that marriage. She'd laid eyes on Jason and liked what she saw.

Darcy suspected that Jason was having an affair. After a year of being married to him, she knew enough about him to notice when a change took place. He suddenly needs new under garments, new cologne and new clothes. Yep. He has suddenly taken a surprising new interest in his appearance, but he never seemed to care much about how he looked before. Plus, when he goes out somewhere with Darcy, he just throws on a t-shirt, some jeans and whatever shoes are by the door. But, now, when he heads out, he has to be extra showered, and the mouthwash has been taking a licking as well. He'd complained about holes being in his underwear, so he got new and fancier ones. He now gets his hair cut once a week, and he has new hobbies; playing pool and going to the mailbox. Even the mailman got tired of seeing him there everyday.

Suspicious, Darcy confirmed Jason's affair by hiding a live tape recorder in his car. She knew he would leave on Saturday night, like he'd been doing for the last six weeks. So, on Friday, she went out and bought a tape recorder and Saturday, while he was in the shower, she put it under the driver's seat of his car. She hoped that she was wrong, but to her surprise, the tape yielded much evidence; and it didn't take her long to recognize the voice of the all too friendly neighbor Catherine. Being from the South, Catherine's accent was undeniable. Catherine had been greeting Darcy every day to the point where Darcy was beginning to feel uneasy about her. Maybe she had some kind of mental illness or something. She'd stopped Darcy several times to strike up conversations with her about things as minor as an electric can opener malfunctioning. She claimed that her boyfriend had bought her a new one, but during a wild episode of sex, she'd accidentally kicked it off the kitchen counter. She even asked Darcy if she knew where she could buy some irresistible lingerie for her new boyfriend, and Darcy would always try to be polite and talk to her about the LORD. Now, it all came to light. Catherine had been toying with Darcy.

Darcy confronted Jason and after hours of denying the affair, he finally confessed, right before saying that he was leaving her because he was confused.
The next day, Jason was taking out his clothes and to Darcy's horror, he wasn't putting them in the car; he was carrying them down the street to Catherine's house. And Catherine, in true Catherine fashion, took the time out to wave at Darcy with the most evil smirk on her face. That was it. Darcy ran out of her front door after Jason screaming and crying, and Catherine ran out and met her with a few punches. Before she knew it, Darcy was on the ground trying to figure out how to save herself. She'd managed to get up, but Catherine still had her by the hair and was beating her head so hard that she could see the ground lighting up. Some neighbors sprung into action and separated the two. Still trying to catch up with her thoughts, Darcy broke loose and

stumbled towards her house, surprised that Jason was so cruel that he didn't even try to rescue her from the hands of his mistress.

Darcy decided to take the high road and file for divorce. She didn't want to be one of those women who found themselves fighting over a man. She got back in church and never came out of GOD again.

Explanation:

This story is short because, like the last story, the message is 'unfaithfulness.' We, as women, have to understand that when we are unfaithful to GOD; we meet unfaithful men. No mature, faithful man of GOD wants a woman who has not first dedicated herself to GOD. When Darcy met Jason, he was just a church-goer. He came to church some Sundays and attended a few programs, but he was still a baby in CHRIST. Jason had not grown up in HIM; nevertheless, they decided that they were mature enough to get married and ***try*** to spend their lives together. Darcy found herself trying to raise Jason and Jason's natural, manly instinct caused him to fall out of love with her because it is not the order of GOD for a man to be led by his wife. A man is supposed to lead his wife. Therefore, it was only natural that Jason went after a woman who he felt he could lead.

The message here is wait. Stay in CHRIST. Not every man in church is a man of GOD and not every man of GOD has grown up yet. Sure, he may be a grown man physically, but he may be a child spiritually and children do childish things. Jason, like many babes in CHRIST, was bound to come out of CHRIST and eventually find his way back in. Too bad, Darcy placed herself in harm's way when she decided to be a spiritual pedophile and marry a man who did not know what it was to commit yet. He hadn't committed to GOD, so how could he have committed himself to Darcy or anyone, for that matter?

In order for a man to be ripe enough to marry, he has to be planted in GOD and mature. This is the time when he is selfless, not selfish. This is the time when he is so focused on GOD that curves don't fascinate him. Sure, he's a man and finds many women attractive, but he's mature enough to know that only one woman has his other rib. He's not wasting his time chasing up behind the wife or concubine of anyone else.
The deeper that man goes in CHRIST, the further he walks away from the 'average' believing woman. A man who is so wrapped up in CHRIST can only unwrap a treasure of a wife. Go deep in GOD and your husband will have to go deeper to find you. Don't get the man who's knocking on HIS door. Wait for the husband who lives in HIM to knock at yours.

Get Better, Not Bitter

"Any fruit picked out of season will be bitter."

You want what you want when you want it. But, everything underneath the sun has a season. A plum, when it is not ripe, is green in color and is very bitter. And bitter fruit often causes stomach distress. Whatever it is that you are waiting on GOD for, be patient and continue to wait in HIM. Sure, the tree may not drop its fruit when your taste buds are screaming for it, but if it did, you wouldn't like the after-bite.

Sharlene is a shapely girl with a big attitude. She has beautiful, golden-brown skin, and her long hair always seems to drape her face perfectly. Short, arrogant and a little bit feisty, she has never had trouble getting a man, and some pretty good-lookers at that. But, she does seem to have a problem keeping a man. She's a no-nonsense kind of girl. Cheat on her? You're out! Raise your hand at her? You're out! Call her names? Bye-bye. Many of the younger girls in the neighborhood really admire Sharlene. They have watched her send away some of the most desired men around, and they all seem to keep pursuing her. In addition, Sharlene goes to church every Sunday. It looks like Sharlene has it made.

Sharlene wants to live right, but like many, she has her fair share of strongholds. To her credit, she has made some changes in her life. She is going to the club less and less, and she has disassociated herself from most of her evil friends.

Nevertheless, Sharlene is not ready yet. She is just a seed, but before she can grow, GOD wants to uproot the seeds that life and disobedience have planted in her. But, she never seems to understand the full concept of living right.

What most people do not know about Sharlene is that she is bitter. Tired of being dumped, cheated on and humiliated, she decided that she was going to take control of her life. She is nice looking, and she knows it. She knows how to dress, and she knows that men love to chase women who are running from them. Her feisty attitude has gotten the attention of some of the most prominent men around, as well, and she is one of the best dancers around. She loves to show off her moves at any party, club or event. What leaves most men captivated by Sharlene is the fact that she comes in half dressed, looking as if she is hunting a man, nevertheless, she always leaves without one because she has shot everyone down.

Terrence is a Pediatrician who has often seen Sharlene around. Unlike other girls, she has never chased him or hit on him; she's quite the opposite. She always ignores him, even when he speaks to her. There is something about that beautiful woman that he wants to get to know. There is a mystery about her that he has to uncover. It's a challenge. Game on!

Terrence sends flowers to Sharlene's job, but she sends them back. Terrence then sends 50 different vases of white roses to her job. Sharlene is impressed, yet she does not show it. Terrence decides to take it a step further. After all, this could be the future Mrs. He goes to the mall one day and orders a beautiful, flowing white

gown. He conducted on his private investigation and found out a lot about Sharlene. He knows that she likes red wine, and white is her favorite color. She does not like restaurants below three stars. It was said that a man once tried to take her to a two-star restaurant and when she'd realized where she was, she'd called a taxi and went back home. So, Terrence made reservations at four-star Riondi's. He had the dress delivered to her house with a note attached.
"Wear this dress and be outside by seven p.m. tomorrow.
~Terrence"

Sharlene is very impressed. She loves to be dined and treated like a woman of great importance. She'd decided long ago that she would not give her hand or her number to any man who was like the ones that took her heart and stomped on it. But, Terrence is different. He has gone above and beyond, plus he's not just any man; he's a doctor. And doctors don't ordinarily pursue 'club' women.

The next day, Sharlene stops in to see her beautician. "I have an emergency," she says. "Can you fit me in? I'll tip you real good." The beautician does just that and sweeps Sharlene's long dark hair up into an elegant French roll. She pulls some of the hair loose around her face, and Sharlene is off to the cosmetician to have her makeup professionally done.

Seven o'clock comes, and Sharlene is ready. She is beginning to feel anxiety, believing that every man should be early for a date, and she is the one who is supposed to hold them up. The doorbell rings at seven o'clock, on the dot. Sharlene answers and is amazed to see that the man at the door isn't Terrence. The man at the door wore a black suit, almost uniform like, and he says to Sharlene, "Your car awaits." He escorts her to the limo and opens the back door. Seated, she sees the handsome Terrence obviously captivated by what he sees. Smiling, she sits down and begins to buckle her seat belt. “Hello,” she says, noticing the near speechless Terrence still staring at her, trying to find the words to say. “Hi. Wow. I have never been nervous around a woman before,” says Terrence as he observes the petite princess like figure that had just entered the car.

The restaurant was nice, the food was great, and the date went well. Terrence is amazed to learn that Sharlene is studying to be a RN and has no children. She answers all of his questions, never speaking too much, or too little.
As time goes by, Terrence finds himself falling in love with Sharlene. Ordinarily, she wouldn't be his type, but there is just something about her and how she carries herself. There was a mystery to her, and this was captivating to him. One day, he takes her to meet his mother. He believes that Sharlene is the one, but mother obviously does not agree. The minute Sharlene stepped from the car; he could see his mother's disapproval. She was nice to Sharlene and made her feel very comfortable, but Terrence knows his mother, and he knows that when mother doesn't approve, it's because she sees something. Something that curves has blinded him from seeing.

After introducing Sharlene to his mother, Terrence starts paying closer attention to Sharlene. He'd thought about 'popping the question,' of course. That's why he wanted her to meet his mother, but now, there was something for him to think about. His mother wasn't the type of woman to downright say, “She's no good! Leave this woman alone!” Instead, she would always voice her disapproval by saying, “I'm praying for you, son. Your season is not here yet.” Plus, Sharlene's attitude has been not so great lately. That cute old feisty attitude has been made ugly by the now obvious venom that dresses it up. At one point, he thought her lack of tact was raw confidence, but now, he was beginning to view it for what it was; hurt, bitterness, fear, and unforgiveness. What a deadly, venomous combo.

It's the Memorial Day weekend, and Terrence is off work. The clinic where he works is closed, so he decides to spend the day with Sharlene. Their relationship has grown so much to the point where he now has a key to Sharlene's house, and she has one to his. He decides to shower first, stop by the store to pick up some roses and head right over to Sharlene's place. He gets into the shower, and as he is enjoying the water, he thinks he hears a sound. But, he dismisses it and continues. Maybe the neighbor's cats were fighting again.

After the shower, he gets out, gets dressed and heads out for the store. As he is leaving, he notices that his mail looks disturbed, and he can smell the familiar scent of Sharlene. Again, he brushes this off and heads out.

After going by the market, he heads up the walkway to Sharlene's house, happy and whistling. Sharlene opens the door, before he could unlock it, and she looks angry. "Hey baby. Beautiful flowers for a beautiful woman." Terrence hands Sharlene the flowers, and she shoves them back to him. "What's wrong?" Terrence is surprised. But, instead of answering him, Sharlene turns and heads back into the house, followed by her confused beau. Unable to contain herself, Sharlene snaps.

"Who is Marilyn?! Who is Marilyn, Terrence?! Did you think I wouldn't find out?!"

Before he could answer, Sharlene begins to scream for him to leave. She takes the roses from his hands and throws them in his face. She even goes so far as to slam the door so close behind him that it almost caused him to fall.

Terrence heads to his car confused and heartbroken, but somewhat relieved. He had begun to see a lot of venom in

Sharlene, but he didn't know that she could be so vicious. Before he could leave, Sharlene bolts from the door and she wants to fight. Terrence tries to calm her down to stop a humiliating public scene from unraveling; after all, he's a well known physician, but she's livid.

Sharlene: So, Marilyn loves you?! Right?! Right?! And you love her?! What was this between you and me?! Huh, Terrence? She's sending you Christmas cards professing her love for you? And you're sending her Christmas cards professing your love for her?! And you're talking about taking her to Hawaii?! Are you serious?! Did you think I wouldn't find out?! You obviously don't know me! You obviously didn't hear about me, but, let me give you something to remember Sharlene by!
(She picks up rocks and begins to throw them at the doctor as he attempts to enter his car. One rock struck and shattered his passenger side window. The good doctor exits the car and begins to head toward Sharlene.)
Terrence: Let me tell you the truth about Marilyn; if you will listen. So, I don't have to wind up losing my religion over here.
Sharlene: Tell me, Terrence! Tell me! I'm all ears!
Terrence: Marilyn is my mother! You psycho....she's my mother!
Sharlene: Whatever! Whatever! Your mother's name is Mary!
Sharlene then pauses and a light bulb comes on. Uh-oh.
Terrence: We call her Mary, but her name is Marilyn. Now I know who has been disturbing my mail. Have a good life, Sharlene.

At this, Terrence tries to go back to his car, but a now humiliated and humbled Sharlene grabs at his arm. With tears and a heavy heart, she was begging for him to stay.

Sharlene: Baby, I'm sorry. Baby, please forgive me. Please don't go. I'm so sorry.

Terrence doesn't answer. He gets into his car with a now desperate Sharlene standing in front the car crying and pleading with him to get out and talk to her. She stands in front of the car, preparing to throw her body on top of it, but Terrence puts the car in reverse and drives in reverse until he reaches the cross streets. There he turns, puts his car in drive and drives away hurriedly.

Sharlene's calls go unanswered. Her visits to the house and Terrence's clinic have now been blocked by a restraining order, but this doesn't sway her. She's been arrested three times already, yet, she just doesn't get it. Her email has been blocked. The tons of pictures she sent of the two of them together have been deleted. But, her worst deed had yet come. One day, while pruning her flowers, Marilyn (Terrence's mom) notices an unfamiliar car pull up in her drive way. Before the car is fully in park, out jumps Sharlene. Marilyn is aware of the story and tries to get into the house to call the police, but Sharlene is quickly standing in front of her door blocking her.

Sharlene: Momma, just talk to me. I'm sorry, Momma!
Marilyn: I'm not your momma, girl! Move out of my way or I'm calling the police.
Sharlene: Please! I need someone to talk to. I can't live without your son. I am literally going crazy.
Marilyn: You were already crazy, Sharlene. Now move!
Sharlene: I just need someone to talk to. I can't eat, I can't sleep and I can't function. He was my man, Momma. He was mine and I messed it up! I was just scared! You can understand me; I know.
Marilyn: How many men have you done this to, Sharlene? How many men have you stalked like this? I know that Terrence isn't the first and at this rate, he won't be the last. You were broken before Terrence even knew you. I saw that. That makes you

dangerous because women like you believe that men are to blame for your issues when you are to blame. You run out here dressing like a floozy and giving your body away, and then you're surprised when it doesn't work. My son was not in love with you.

Sharlene: Yes, he was Momma. He said it. We talked about marriage. Please talk to him for me. I know you can understand my pain. I know I may not be the daughter in law type, but I'm a good woman. I'm just hurting. Can't you see that?

Marilyn: Dear Sharlene, he wasn't in love with you. Terrence is a man. Terrence fell in love with the mystery of you, and you fell in love with his degree. You were evading him and men like the thrill of the chase. He's designed to hunt. He thought you were better than other women because you were letting down men all over the place, but he found out that you weren't better; you were bitter. Understand how a man works. Once he finds you out and discovers that great mystery about you, there is nothing left for him to search out in you, but in CHRIST; your husband will search you out and rejoice every time he discovers something new. Just when he thinks he knows you, GOD will put more in you for him to discover. But, a man will search out a woman and there isn't much to a woman, but an orgasm. Don't you get it? Terrence didn't hurt you. You responded to the hurt that was already in you. It was only a matter of time before you hurt him. Women like you wound up hurting their boyfriends, their husbands and even their own children because, instead of letting GOD take the wheel in your life, you decided to steer yourself into the arms of this man and that man. Now, my son is your latest victim, and you want me to push him into an early grave by telling him to get with a woman whose demons I can see? Darling, I'm not trying to be hard on you, but I have to tell you the truth, whether it sounds good to you or not. If you continue to pursue Terrence like this, it won't end well. He does not want you. I raised Terrence to know the difference between a woman and a wife. You are a woman in the world, but if you would only come to CHRIST and let HIM heal you of that hurt and unforgiveness; let HIM remove the souls of all of those men whom you have lain with, then you might find yourself listed as a wife. You can't keep throwing yourself around like this! It's up to you if you want to do something with your life. Go and clean yourself up. Get into your WORD and refuse to come out! Your husband might not be a doctor or a lawyer, but darling; a man after GOD'S own heart will take care of you far better than a man of the world with a degree on his wall!

Sharlene: I just can't let him go. I can't. I'm sorry for bothering you, but I can't let him go.

Months later, Sharlene is back at it. She has slowed up with calling and going by the doctor's office. She's back to looking sharp and wowing crowds. Her beauty still draws men to her, but is never enough to keep them with her.

Explanation:

What was Sharlene's problem? Sharlene was a seed that was growing, but there was still a lot of growing that she had to do before she would be ripe enough to be called a wife. Like most men, Terrence was mesmerized by the thrill of the hunt. He wanted to know the mystery of Sharlene and he found out that Sharlene's heart was buried under bitterness. Nowadays, Terrence does not mistake a feisty attitude for strength or confidence. He prefers a humble woman, like his mom. Sharlene did leave him alone, but not before trying to destroy his name. Sharlene lived her life giving herself to successful men and failing to ever be taken down the aisle towards a happily forever after. Instead, she was brought in and tossed out so much that bitterness began to show through her once beautiful face.

You have to know that a bitter woman cannot be changed by a nor can a bitter man.

man. GOD has created us so that we can only be repaired by HIM. A fruit that has ripened is always sweet, and it is healthy for you. Every tree planted in GOD is watered by HIM. It's your choice, though: You can let the LORD plant you in HIM, to grow up in HIM and be hand-picked by the husband in HIM, or you can cast yourself to the ground bitter where parasites will finish you off. GOD wants you to wait for a reason. In doing so, you will learn to understand the seasons.

The seasons don't just tie-in with relationships either. There is a season for sowing and a season for reaping. How do you tell the difference? Look at the farmer. When he's planting corn, he isn't gathering corn because there is no corn to be gathered. Instead, he has seeds and a field to plant them in. Life is like that. When the season to sow is upon you, you may not bring in much. It is during this time that you are to take the seeds that you do have and plant as many of them as you can. If a farmer stored up his seeds and consumed them, the only harvest he could expect would come from his bowels. Even though there are times when he feels the impact of being a farmer, he knows that the season to reap will come and plenty will be his reward.

As an entrepreneur, I have met many women of GOD who are entrepreneurs, desired to be entrepreneurs or were once entrepreneurs. I can always spot a successful woman before success manifests itself, but the shocking fact is, most women don't stay planted in one thing long enough to bud. Women tend to lack patience when it comes to establishing a career or a relationship. A woman will stay with a bad man for 10 years, but will give up on a good business idea in less than a year. What happens is many of you keep looking at the next woman's success, and because you can't see success in what you're doing, you uproot yourself and try to plant yourself in the soil that GOD has planted her in. However, the LORD will water her only because she is in the right place, but you are not. When you see that this didn't work, you go off and plant yourself in another woman's anointed place, then another and another. Her gift will make room for her; not you! Failing at everything, you go out and work at secular jobs, making a buck here and there, but you can never shake that feeling that success is yours.

So, you go back and plant yourself in your gift, but your patience wears thin. Another woman comes along, and she shares with you how much money she is making creating jewelry, for example. Now, you want to create jewelry. You put yours on every website that you can think of, but no sells. However, every time you see her; she's bragging about how much money she's making. Now, you can't stand her. She brags too much. If you had something to brag about, you'd love her right back.

Your season of success will fall upon you if you have gone through the process. Are you planted in GOD? Stay there. Did you remember to stay rooted in the WORD so the winds of doctrine could not blow you away? Have you asked the LORD to build a fence around you so that the animals won't come along and dig you up? Did you know that you will **NEVER** find your place of success in another woman's (or man's) gifting? Nevertheless, many women live in this earth and leave this earth poor because they see one woman's shoes and they decide that they want to try them on for size. This is error and this is envy and it causes them to fall every time.

My testimony is known by most that know me. I started in 2007 with designing. By 2010, I had grown so much in my gifting that I went from being a graphic designer to a successful graphic designer. There is a difference. There are many things that I have done, but GOD is glorified. I went through MUCH learning, much warfare and through it all, I held on to GOD'S unchanging hand. GOD began to elevate me and the rest is history.

But, I often meet women who think that they can skip over GOD'S plan and go right to success. So, they try to link up with successful people, not understanding that linking up to a successful person does not automatically equal success. It only avails them access to some of the knowledge and understanding of how to get to success. You could get a book for that! You still have to do the work and go through the seasons! And this is where I have found that most women fall off. They thought someone was going to hand success over to them and when they saw otherwise, they got angry at that woman and sometimes at GOD. They develop tactics (wiles) and schemes trying to go through the window to success rather than letting the LORD open the door for them in their own anointed places. They refuse to let the seasons play out so that they could grow in their gifts. No. Instead, when the season of bloom finds them, they are holding up another woman's blood-soaked gifts and wondering why they can't prosper. It's normal for the human mind to look for different ways to get to where we want to be, nevertheless, GOD designed us to fail outside of HIM. Even if you praise the LORD while trying to put your feet in another woman's shoes, you will not go far. Her shoes will either be too big for you, causing you to fall; or they will be too small for you and make your journey a painful one. Imagine walking 10 miles in some really painful heels, only to find that you went in the wrong direction. And, please know this. When you desire her testimonies, you just might get her tests!

"To every thing there is a season, and a time to every purpose under the heaven: A time to be born, and a time to die; a time to plant, and a time to pluck up that which is planted; a time to kill, and a time to heal; a time to break down, and a time to build up; a time to weep, and a time to laugh; a time to mourn,

and a time to dance; a time to cast away stones, and a time to gather stones together; a time to embrace, and a time to refrain from embracing; a time to get, and a time to lose; a time to keep, and a time to cast away; a time to rend, and a time to sew; a time to keep silence, and a time to speak; a time to love, and a time to hate; a time of war, and a time of peace. What profit hath he that worketh in that wherein he laboureth? I have seen the travail, which God hath given to the sons of men to be exercised in it. He hath made every thing beautiful in his time. also he hath set the world in their heart, so that no man can find out the work that God maketh from the beginning to the end." (Ecclesiastes 3:1-11)

A bad seed produces a bad tree and any tree that is not yielding fruit is reserved for destruction. Recall the story of JESUS and the fig tree.

"And on the next day, when they had come from Bethany, HE was hungry: And seeing a fig tree afar off having leaves, he came, if perhaps he might find anything thereon: and when he came to it, he found nothing but leaves; for the time of figs was not yet. And Jesus answered and said unto it, No man eat fruit of you hereafter forever. And his disciples heard it." (Mark 11:12-14)

Why did JESUS curse the fig tree? The Bible verse tells us that the tree had leaves. This means that it was in season to produce fruits, but it did not produce anything. It gave off the appearance of a fruit bearing tree, nevertheless; JESUS found it bare.

Many women, who are believers, give off the appearance of being fruit bearing women of GOD, but when the season comes for them to show their harvest, they are found bare. This is because they kept uprooting themselves and planting themselves in all manners of evils. You have to stay where GOD has planted you if you expect to be blessed. Through the storms and the rain, you have to be there. Through the dry seasons, you have to be there. Otherwise, CHRIST may come and find you bare. And you don't want that!

Kidnapping Daughters (A Case of Sin-Taken Identity)

"If you can't distinguish between your daughter and your sister, you are obviously blind."

Being a leader isn't an easy task because your life has to stay in line with the WORD of GOD, not just for the sake of your soul, but for the sake of the souls that are learning from hearing or watching you. There is one common issue that is plaguing a lot of female leaders and I like to call it mistaken identity or sin-taken identity. Let me explain.

In my walk alone, I have come in contact with many women who did not know who they were to me or who I was to them; so they assumed that they were my "spiritual mothers." This happened especially with women who had been ordained. Many of them know that they weren't called to 'head' you up, but in an attempt to grow their followers, they'll sign you up before you realize that they've got a pen in their hands; especially if you have an obvious gifting or anointing. *Many of you know what I'm talking about.* If you're gifted, and someone realizes how your gift can benefit "their" ministry, they will become a-d-a-m-a-n-t about having you join. Some even going as far as to say the LORD called you to their ministry. Many will even offer to ordain you. This is an illegal act going on in the church, as many women and men alike were not called to lead you, some were called to sharpen you or be sharpened by you. But, because of conceit and the desire to have a large ministry, many have forsaken GOD to chase after that in which they believe will help them achieve this greatness that they so desire.

Even when I was a baby in knowledge, I didn't fall for this. I almost did. But, there was something in me...SOMEONE...(*You know who HE is*) that would not allow me to link up with them the way they were trying to link up with me. For me, how it would happen was; I would talk to someone, and they'd hear the WORD that came from GOD'S mouth through me. Then they'd ask me my 'title' and finding that I was not ordained by any man; they'd offer to ordain me. Some would even claim that the LORD is leading them to ordain me. But, how can you ordain someone if you don't know who they are in GOD and who they are to you? As I grew up in the LORD, I found that this very act is being carried out in a lot of the churches. Not just by women, of course, but men do it too. I could list many many stories to demonstrate just what type of spirits there are standing in pulpits. But, then again, you have to understand that there are many who are GOD'S daughters and sons who ordain people or bring people under their wings out of lack of knowledge. So, it's not that they are evil; it's just that they don't know any better, but GOD always corrects those whom HE loves.

My Testimony: One particular situation came on the heels of me turning my life over to the LORD some years ago. I was designing websites, and a woman came along and ordered one from me. Once the order was completed, she wouldn't just go away. She began to try to attach to me. At that time, I didn't have any rules in place, so I was like a kite. Whichever way the day blew me, that way I was flying. I didn't command my day; I went with it. Well, this woman said that the LORD told her I was an Evangelist, and she wanted to ordain me. Problem was; she lived in another state, so she offered to do it via mail. What struck me was the fact that she kept referring to me as "her" Evangelist as in her own personal Evangelist. Not GOD'S. Again, I was a baby, but the LORD was warning me from within, and I could feel the tug of war. She even sent me an ordination certificate in the mail with my name on it along with Evangelist written in bold. I opened the envelope, but the LORD wouldn't let me do anything with it, so I put it on top to the TV and left it there. I didn't know why at the time.

About a month or so into our communications, she was calling me several times a day; every day. (*Sigh*) Plus, she was very very controlling and she knew it (unrepentant.) But, I saw her title and didn't want to disrespect the title. I felt deep down in the depths of my soul that something was not right. At that time, I didn't understand the depth of Matthew 7:21-23. ***"Not every one that says unto me, Lord, Lord, shall enter into the kingdom of heaven; but he that does the will of my Father who is in heaven. Many will say to me in that day, Lord, Lord, have we not prophesied in your name? And in your name have cast out demons? And in your name done many wonderful works? And then will I profess unto them, I never knew you: depart from me, you that work iniquity."***

There were many incidents that vexed my spirit in this relationship, but what finally caused me to start pulling away were a couple of situations related to my marriage. My husband was living in Germany (He's not American). He wanted me to move to Germany, and I wanted him to move to America. Finally, we decided that America was best for a while since I had a job, and he had a degree; plus I didn't speak Deustch (German). So, while waiting on him to get his work visa to come and work here, we'd discussed me just coming there. Since he was not filing for a permanent visa, and he was married to me, immigration laws made it hard for him to move here. To come here, he would need to file for a permanent visa, and he didn't want that. They'd denied him once so I'd pretty much reserved myself to the fact that I would more than likely be moving to Germany; and she knew about this. So, one day she asked me if all was well with him coming here, and I told her that I wasn't sure; but if not, I was moving to Germany. (I was actually beginning to get excited about the thought of living in Germany, so I didn't care either way.) She told me that she'd be praying that he could come and if not, she would pay for my divorce, because "we had work to do for the LORD." I paused, trying not to say anything that I would regret. I was still a baby, but I knew this wasn't right. No way. So, I just got off the phone.

I had a spiritual brother who the LORD was using to mentor me at that time, and I called him and was telling him about what was going on. "She's a pastor!" I would tell him. But, some things just weren't right about her. When I told him about all of the controlling and what she'd said, he immediately said, "Sis, sounds like you're dealing with a Jezebel spirit. Go and read up on that spirit as soon as you can. You're going to have to get away from her. She senses that anointing on you and she's trying to control you." I agreed, but I didn't do anything immediately because I was hoping the situation would just fade to black.

I also talked to a sister in CHRIST and told her what was going on because it was all too confusing to me. Ministers weren't supposed to act like that. This friend said to me, "Oh, girl, that's a Jezebel! You're going to have to get away from her. As a matter of fact, go online and read some articles about that spirit and its characteristics." When she said that, I was floored. This was the second time I was hearing about a Jezebel spirit, so I went online and read some articles and then found a video on YouTube that made the hair on the back of my neck stand up. This man, on the video, described this woman to the core of her being! It was like he knew her. A few days later, this woman tells me that she just got some kind of partnership (or something) and I would be traveling the world with her. I declined stating that my husband and I were newlyweds, and we wanted to have children, so I wouldn't be going. At this, she was very offended and said to me, "Children?! Children?! Well, I will pray for you to have **one** child! You hear me?! ONE! Because we've got too much work to do." She went on to tell me how foreign men always want to keep their wives barefoot and pregnant and how one of her friends was married to an African, and he wanted to keep her knocked up. She said that her friend had to divorce him. I responded by saying that her friend was stupid. I knew this was it for me. I couldn't lie to myself anymore, and I couldn't bite my tongue any further, so I decided to pull out.

Trying to disassociate from her was no joke. Seriously. If you have every come in contact with that spirit, it is one of witchcraft and will stalk its prey like a lion stalks a wounded deer.
I decided the best way to get rid of her was to just stop answering her calls. (Wrong!) And boy, did she call over and over again. She started leaving me threatening voice mails (because I wasn't answering her calls), even threatening to come to my city/state and come to my church and talk to my pastor about me. (Again, my crime was that I wasn't answering my phone. Nothing else.) The last call she made to me, her voice message was, "You'd better watch your back!!!!!!!" This was after she'd called me like 20 times in a five minute span and I kept clicking the hang up button on my phone. Finally, the LORD delivered me with a new knowledge of the Jezebel.

Explanation:

I asked the LORD why HE'D allowed this situation to happen. HE reminded me of a prayer that I'd prayed not long before I met her. In the prayer, I'd asked HIM to teach me about the different kinds of spirits and how to get rid of them. I laughed. "LORD, I thought you were just going to drop the information in my spirit." I love HIM for that situation because not only did I learn what a Jezebel is, I learned the characteristics of it. I can identify someone with that spirit by just hearing their voice now. This situation eventually helped and continues to help me educate a lot of young women who are babes in CHRIST. Many of them are trying to figure out why some woman (or man) is trying to control them, and I'm able to share my testimony with them. And, in the majority of cases, GOD confirms what HE shares through me by using someone else not in association with me to tell them the very same thing. So, every situation that we go through isn't about us. It's about the members of the body of CHRIST.

What I have since witnessed is a lot of leaders Jezebellin.' That's my term for it. Jezebellin' is to take on a role that was not created for you. Jezebel was never supposed to be Ahab's wife or the Queen of Israel. But, because of Ahab's disobedience, this evil and accursed woman was given the fame, the wealth, and the power to contaminate the people of GOD with her gods; to destroy the Prophets of the LORD, and to destroy the temples of the LORD.

Don't get confused. Men do this as well. I remember one man (ordained as an Apostle) that first tried to get me to join his ministry. I told him I would pray on it. He'd told me the LORD said I'd outgrown the ministry I was going to. Of course, I asked the LORD and the LORD responded by fire. What I mean is, the LORD will send a consuming fire that will burn away our blindness and expose the demon in them. This man began flirting with me; asking me if I was attracted to him, even though I am married....and so was he! I told him to never contact me again, but he wasn't the first man who did this and probably won't be the last.

The whole point here is you have to understand that there will be many people who will attempt to kidnap your anointing because you were not called to be their daughters. That's why there is so much chaos in the church. You hear all the time about members being hurt by their leaders. Sometimes the member is wrong and sometimes the leader is wrong. It happens when someone is out of place. Nevertheless, when you belong to CHRIST, HE will not leave you under a head that was not made for your body.

When a woman assumes that she is your spiritual mother, she will always try to feed you, but can never eat from your table or be sharpened by you. If the LORD gives you a mature seed that has not grown up for her yet, and she doesn't understand the message that HE is birthing through you; she'll try to downplay or cast down that message as untrue. Why? Because in her understanding, you are too young to deliver to her something that GOD has said. Therefore, she will attempt to correct you in her conceit, but not understanding that she is steering you in the wrong direction. You may know HIS voice and hear HIM clearly. You teach the message, and this woman will come along and tell you that what you're teaching is not true. This doesn't mean she's not of GOD; she may be young in HIM and has not yet been fed with this because it's too rich for her belly right now. But, if she thinks that she's your mother; she's going to try to force feed you with what's in her. When you don't latch on, or you regurgitate what's being fed to you, a woman who doesn't know who she is to you will react in offense. That's because you weren't supposed to be led by her and many times, women try to give milk to women who are hungry for meat.

You could have come into the knowledge of GOD three years ago and be older than someone who has been in HIM for 37 years! I have seen it! Why? Because many women and men get to a certain age in HIM and refuse to grow up any further. They keep eating the same things, and refuse to eat anything else. Many don't realize that GOD may seat you under a ministry for a season. That is until you get what you need to get, but then after you've been fed all that's being fed there, HE may seat you elsewhere. HE is birthing not just a child for HIMSELF, but HE is looking to create leaders. That's why you'll see, in some churches, people that have an anointing will be seated at all times, never to be ordained there or lead there. Everyone with an anointing was not called to be in a particular building. Some were called to do as the Apostles and go about teaching the WORD of GOD without walls.

Many have gotten their rightful titles, and some were not called to the titles that they use. Nevertheless, to them, their title bears witness to who should be over them and who should be under them. Meaning, they are leaning to their own understanding! Which is sin in itself! That's why you are called to knowledge (meaning to know) so that you can know the difference between who is HIS and who is not HIS. You are also to come into the understanding of seasons and how they work. If you truly understand seasons, you will know the weather of every season and know when it is your season to sow, and it is your season to reap. You need to also understand where to sow and where to reap.

GOD taught me a lesson that keeps me humble to this day. HE told me that a Jezebel spirit (and other demonic spirits) can only attach to a person that goes outside of the GOD ordained authority; uncovering their heads. What does this mean? A woman who tries, for example, to be equal to her husband or lord herself over her husband will have a Jezebel spirit. Point blank. Because her husband is her covering. If she tries to be his head, she is no longer under the covering authority of the CHRIST! Because CHRIST is the head of man, and man is the head of the wife. A woman cannot head her husband. If she tries to cover another woman who she was never called to lead, she will pick up a Jezebel spirit because she is stepping from under the lineup as set up in CHRIST. Jezebel made herself equal to or greater than Ahab. Even the least Israelite was greater than a Phoenician woman. Read the stories of Jezebel and Ahab and the story of King Xerxes and Queen Esther. There is a difference. Queen Esther understood that she was not her husband's head, equal, or covering! Look at Abraham and Sarah. Sarah, like most women, wasn't perfect, but she stayed covered by her husband. She told Abraham to put Hagar out; he refused, and she didn't say another word about the matter. She didn't complain or nag him. Because she laid the seed and let GOD yield the increase. She said what she wanted, and GOD commanded that Abraham listen.

As for me, I still meet women who assume that I have some kind of servant's anointing in their ministry, or they assume that they are here to mother me. In such cases, wisdom tells me to love them, pray for them, but back away from them. Not just for my protection, but for theirs because if a person oversteps who they are in CHRIST and hinders their sister or brother; the LORD will humble them. And the word 'humble' sounds nice and friendly, but when one is being humbled, there is nothing pretty about it. I have met a lot of women; even online that, if you eat one piece of bread (knowledge) from them; their conceit leads them to assume that they were called to feed you. They get offended when you reject something they are teaching, because again, in their own conceit, they are there to teach you. Not knowing that GOD can use the least to sharpen the greatest because HE is GOD alone. And again, I have found a lot of babies that have a great anointing on their lives. But, because they are babies, they look for people to lead them without praying about it first. What happens is, some woman or man operating in witchcraft will bring them under the subjection of their titles and start to spiritually oppress them. Believe it or not, this is very very common! Too many people are out trying to grow their 'fan' base. They couldn't care less about the soul that they are hindering; they care about numbers. Listen up. GOD can take two women who are the same height in HIM, but one may have more knowledge in one area while the other may be more knowledgeable in another area. HE will use these women to sharpen one another! As you grow in HIM, you will know when someone is sent to lead or mentor you, or if they've come to sharpen or be sharpened by you.

As a leader, you may have those times when lust tries to take a seat in your heart. It has to be cast out, if it wasn't cast down when it introduced itself to you as a thought. After having met that woman with the Jezebel spirit on her; I can truly say that I have met that spirit a lot of times after her. The common denominator in all of those women was the fact that they got out of line somewhere. Somehow, they got into themselves and decided that they would grow their ministry or direct their households because, to them, it wasn't the LORD'S ministry, and their husbands belonged to them only. They believe that their husbands are supposed to follow their lead, because, many times, they feel like their husbands don't know as much as they do about the Bible or about the LORD. They don't understand that CHRIST is the head of man! The head directs the body! They want a mega church or to be the next celebrity televangelist. Then, there are the ones that were hurt by men and never delivered from this hurt. In these cases, she was doomed to pick up that Jezebel spirit because she, in her hurt place, does not trust men or anyone in authority and will always try to oppress them.

When you take on a young lady and call her your spiritual daughter, what you are saying to GOD is that you are sent to feed and grow her up. A mother raises her daughters to be women after her. But, if she wasn't called to be there, you are out of the will of GOD and so is she. Therefore, you'll find much contention in your ministry because devils thrive in ignorance; devils flourish in disobedience, and devils dwell in disorder. Disaster always loves to add the finishing touch. Remember, even Lot and Abraham parted ways.

Understand that many times these women are not called to be your daughters or your mothers, but they are your sisters in CHRIST. The LORD may use one woman to mentor another woman FOR A SEASON. That's it. Even a spiritual daughter has to grow up eventually. Don't let conceit deceive you. There are many of you that were called of GOD and operate in GOD that have strayed because you see women and call them "daughter", and you attempt to operate as their "mothers." Many of you don't mean any harm by it and for me, I have met so many beautiful and anointed women of GOD that will lovingly call me daughter (because it's habit for them), but never try to take on the role itself.
If you are young in CHRIST and you know it, please do this. Pray and ask the LORD to keep you away from the people that HE did not call into your life and to position everyone in your life where they should be; even if that means HE has to move them from your life. Ask the LORD to protect you from the spirit of witchcraft. You will offend many women in your walk when you know who you are and who they are not. Many go out with witchcraft on their breath; seeking to adopt daughters who they don't spiritually know or recognize, and they will feed off of their anointing. Read your Bible e-v-e-r-y-d-a-y and talk to the LORD

every day; several times a day. In knowing HIM, you will find out who you are and who people are to you so you won't assume that this woman or that man is called to head you up when they were not and vice versa. We have to know our function in the BODY in order to operate in the way in which we were designed. A hand trying to operate as an eye cannot see because it wasn't designed to see.

If some woman just starts feeding you with information about 'her' ministry and then she goes on to call you 'daughter,' get away from her, cover yourself with the armor of GOD and be led by GOD as to how to deal with her. Get the knowledge that you need so that you won't become subject to someone's devils or conceit.

Remember, in this walk, sometimes you have to offend the wrong to defend what's right. I have met many many women of GOD who are babies in HIM that find themselves being pulled on by this and that woman to be <u>under</u> their ministry. There are women calling them daughters; giving them assignments and even ordaining some of them. But, because they were not called to lead these women, when the woman (student) begins to rise up in knowledge or understanding; the other woman (kidnapper) is offended. In many cases, the kidnapped daughter tried to rescue herself and was met by what we like to refer to as "church hurt." She was called wicked, prophelied to and made to feel as if she has offended GOD by trying to free herself of this woman's leadership. Many of them were told that a curse would come upon them. And this is plain ole witchcraft at its dirtiest!

We are not to get offended, but pray for the people that are in CHRIST and those that profess to be in HIM, but are not. One prayer that I send up to Heaven when I meet a woman of GOD is for the LORD to open her eyes so that she can see who everyone is all around her (including me), and for the LORD to open my eyes so that I can see who she is. This kicks out assumption and helps us develop sisterly relationships where expectation doesn't come in as a burden. Because expectation always acts as a yoke when someone does not know the truth about you or vice versa. The truth comes to deliver; not condemn. And the truth is never a burden, but assumption and expectation are evil twins that will wear a woman down to the bones of her faith.

None of us, that love and fear the LORD, want to get caught up in this religious craze that is sweeping the churches. Most of us just want to serve HIM in a manner that HE is well pleased with and we have to be very careful. There are many churches that are sprouting up, being run by men and women who only want to promote their agendas, and they need numbers. They need many people to fulfill the lust that is in them. You have to know when to say, "You are not my mother!" Day by day, as you learn more about HIM, you will get the answers to many of the questions that are plaguing you. Chapter by chapter of your life, revelation will open itself up to you and reveal the purpose of even your darkest hour! That's because you are loved of the LORD.

Speak it...I am the redeemed of the LORD! Believe it...GOD will never suffer the righteous to be moved! Live it...I will not die, but live and declare the works of the LORD! If your heart is set on serving HIM, realize that there are many things sent out and set up by Satan to hinder your walk. Many leaders are mature enough to know when to release you. GOD will speak to HIS own. You were called to be in one place at a particular season, but if you are somewhere else, the season will not yield the fruit of increase for you because you are in disobedience. And in disobedience, you can only expect thorns and barren ground.

There is a lot of witchcraft out there. Don't let your life get twisted up in it, but instead, come against it at all times. Again, many people do it out of ignorance, whereas there are many who kidnap daughters out of rebellion. The ones that are HIS will more than likely hear from HIM and be rebuked by HIM, but those that are not HIS don't care what HE says. They only want to be the next big mega-star out, and you are just a footstool for them to stand on.

Trading One Problem For Another

"If you were being attacked by a lion at the water's edge and a shark rescued you from that lion, it wasn't love that made him do it. He was hungry, too."

Relationships come and relationships fail. Sometimes, in the midst of a relationship, we just know that it's not going to work. Maybe things have heated up and so much damage has been done that the two of you are spent. But, there is a fad sweeping the nation with women. A lot of women are falling for one of Satan's schemes. Women of GOD in adultery and they think that it's justifiable.

The argument has heated up again. Hanna and her husband (Mark) are fighting over his secretary. Hanna wants Rebecca, the secretary, fired. It's no secret. Mark and Rebecca are having an affair. Everyone at the law firm knows and the news has gotten back to Hanna, and truthfully; she didn't need to hear it. She came to Mark's office once before and noticed a chemistry between Mark and his secretary. Now, people are talking and Hanna is humiliated, hurt and angered by it all.

"Fire her!" Hanna is unrelenting. But, Mark fires back. "No! I won't fire her just because you are insecure! I don't care what

everyone else thinks! You want to leave, the door is wide open! But, I won't fire her!"
Hanna is very hurt at this. He would rather lose his wife and two sons than to fire Rebecca. What woman wouldn't be hurt?

But, Hanna's not ready for it to end. After all, it came all of a sudden. This was not expected. They have a vacation coming up in a couple of weeks where they were going to travel to Greece, and the new school term is almost here. Hanna doesn't know what to do. So, she endures, trying to keep quiet and absorbing shock after shock as Mark's brazen behavior gets bolder and bolder. He starts staying out until the next day, coming in smelling like perfume and worst of all, Hanna notices that thousands of dollars are coming out of the account often with no explanation. But, she keeps quiet because she's not ready to leave yet. She's trying to build up her gut to leave; however, Mark is feeling like he's gotten his way of having both women.

It's Sunday and Hanna's just arrived home from church with the boys. She notices that her husband's car isn't home. She knows where he is. He's at Rebecca's house. Not wanting the children to see her pain, she asks seven year old Jayden and five year old Cameron to go to their play room while she prepares dinner.

In the kitchen, Hanna's emotions get the best of her. All of that anger and hurt that she's been trying to hold back is now having its way with her. She tries to cry silently, but her sobs could be heard in the playroom. Jayden asks Cameron to stay in the playroom while he goes to ask mommy something. He knows that his mother is hurting, but he doesn't know why. He knows that daddy is the one hurting mommy, but he doesn't know how. So, he has developed an anger towards his dad and at seven, he has already taken on the protective nature of a big brother, shielding his brother from the pain.

Jayden: Mommy, don't cry anymore. When I grow up, I'll marry you and you can divorce daddy.
Hanna laughs and tries to wipe away the tears.
Hanna: Come here, baby. (*Jayden goes into his mother's arms.*) I'm not crying. I was cutting an onion and it was hurting my eyes. I love you and Cameron with all of my heart. And no, you can't marry Mommy. You will meet a beautiful woman one day and she will make you the happiest man in the world. Just tell me that you will never hurt her.
Jayden: I won't.
Hanna: Okay, baby. Go back and play with Cameron, okay?

Jayden agrees and goes back into the playroom. For a moment, Hanna is comforted, but the thought of her children being fatherless brings her back to tears. She is so emotional that she doesn't notice her husband's Mercedes pull into the garage. Mark comes in and finds his wife in the kitchen, cutting up vegetables and sobbing. He looks at her, and his disgust is obvious. He turns around and walks into the playroom with the kids, not acknowledging his wife's pain.

Hanna: Mark? Can you come here for a minute?
Mark: (*Sighs and comes into the kitchen.*) What, Hanna?
Hanna: Mark, where were you?
Mark: I went by the office to look over some case files. Happy now?
Hanna: On a Sunday? Was Rebecca there?
Mark: Maybe she was. What's it to you?
Hanna: Mark, baby? What are we doing? I'm your wife, but I feel like your rug!!! What have I done to you to make you hate me like this?
Mark: You woke up.

Mark walks away, heading to the playroom. Hanna's belly is filled with shock, rage and hurt. Mark has become colder and his affair has become more obvious over the passing months. Mark doesn't want to divorce Hanna because the divorce would be too costly and embarrassing. So, he has elected to break Hanna into being a woman that does not question or complain about his affairs. In truth, he wants to stay with Hanna because she is a good woman, whereas, Rebecca is more of his bedroom buddy. Mark often dreamed about having both women under the same roof getting along and catering to his lusts.

The next day, Hanna goes to the gym to do her daily workout. The conversation from the night before still playing in her mind, she doesn't notice that the fitness instructor has turned off the music and is now staring at her.
Instructor Keith: Hanna, are you okay?
Hanna: Huh? Oh. You stopped the music? *Laughs.* Is everything okay?
Keith: I need to ask you the same question. Are you okay?

Keith is not just an instructor. Keith owns the gym and is a licensed counselor. So, he's not only strong and good looking, but he has some textbook sense.
Hanna breaks down and tells him everything Mark has been doing. What he hears upsets him. Hanna is a beautiful GOD fearing woman. She actually reminds him of his mother. And he can't understand how any man could be so cruel and heartless to his wife and the mother of his children. While Hanna is pouring her heart out, Keith pulls up the Internet on his cell phone and goes to his favorite florist website to order flowers. He has them sent to the gym while Hanna is still standing there crying her eyes out. She didn't notice what Keith had done because she kept pacing back and forth as she told him about her marital problems.

The flowers arrive and Keith goes to unlock the door. "Hold on a minute," he says to Hanna. He heads to the door and tips the deliverer as he retrieves the dozen red roses from his hand. Hanna is now standing around the corner feeling ashamed of herself. She can't see Keith with the flowers, but after unloading so much hurt, she's now conscious that she just told her problems to her instructor. How can he work with her after that?

Keith rounds the corner with a bouquet of roses and hands them to Hanna. On it is a note that reads, "He may have chipped your wings, but you're still an angel." Flattered, humiliated and shocked, Hanna doesn't know what to say.

Hanna: Wow. Thanks Keith. I'm sorry for unloading you on like that. It has just been so hard and...
Keith: Hey, don't worry about it. I'm glad you talked about it. You don't deserve to be treated like that, Hanna. You're smart, you're beautiful, and you're a good wife and mother. Any man that doesn't recognize that is brain dead.
Hanna: Thanks, Keith. I'd better go so I can pick the kids up from daycare and get supper started before Mark comes home.

At this, she leaves and Keith can't stop thinking about her. He wants to rescue her from Mark. He wants to beat Mark into a pulp. He wants to take Hanna away from all of her pain.

Arriving home, Hanna notices that Mark's car is already there. She gets an uneasy feeling as she pulls into the driveway. The anxiety is so thick that it makes Hanna feel sick. As she enters the house, she can see boxes and suitcases sitting out. She decides to take the children to the neighbor's house, fearing what they might witness.
When she comes into the house, she finds Mark removing his clothes from their dresser and placing them in a suitcase.

Hanna: Mark, what are you doing?
Mark: You can have the house and I'm willing to give you a generous amount for spousal support. All I want is custody of my boys and to be free from you.

Feeling light headed, Hanna sits on the bed.
Hanna: Mark, please tell me what's going on.
Mark: Today, I looked in the mirror and realized I wasn't in love with you and the more I stay here, the worse I feel about you. I don't want my kids to see this. So, I think it is best if we got a divorce, and if you would just sign over custody of the boys.
Hanna: Mark, I'm feeling really sick right now. Please tell me it's a joke. Please, this room is spinning. Please tell me it's a joke Mark. A really really cruel joke.
Mark: Unfortunately, it's not. Now answer my question. Are you going to sign over custody of the boys without a problem or do I have to fight you in court?
Hanna: I would never give you and your whore my children. Please hurry up and leave my house. I won't fight the divorce, Mark. I won't fight. *Sobs.* I just want my peace back. Lord, I want my peace.
Mark: Have it your way, then.
(*Mark storms out the house, but as he passes Hanna's car, he notices the roses. He unlocks the door and reads the card, but it doesn't say who it's from. He storms back into the house and attacks Hanna.*)
Mark: So, you're cheating on me! You out here worrying about who I'm lying with and you're cheating on me!
He releases the now afraid Hanna and she's shocked. Mark has never touched her violently before.
Hanna: If you're talking about roses, they are from an admirer, not a boyfriend.
Mark: Yeah, well, I'm not leaving this house. If you want out,

you leave! And my Jayden and Cameron are not coming with you!
(*Mark has had a sudden change of heart. He realizes that someone else is trying to get his wife's attention and this sparks an interest in him to stay with his wife and win the tug of war. It's all bout pride, not about Hanna.*)
He questions Hanna about the sender, but she claims to not know.

One evening, Hanna goes to the gym and Keith is already there, but he's not wearing work out clothes.
Keith: Don't panic. Just let me show you a good time. No worries, no doubts...just two friends hanging out.

Hanna does not shoot down the idea. It actually feels good to be admired. Keith takes her into the gym where he has a table set up with a beautiful cloth that draped the table, and candles fill the room with its soft lighting. He leads Hanna to the table, hand in hand, and pulls out the seat for her. "I'm going to serve you, so relax and just let me show you a good time. You deserve it." Keith's strong arms stretch out, and he relaxes his hand on Hanna's chin. He doesn't know it, but Hanna has already given in. There is no more need for romance. Being starved of affection and attention, Hanna is enjoying every moment of Keith's pursuits, and the night is perfect in her eyes. He starts the night off by bringing out the appetizers and then the main dish, followed by dessert and wine. They talk about Hanna's marriage, Keith's dreams and what they both want. They find that they both want many of the same things. Soft music echoes from the speakers as Keith stands up and asks Hanna for a dance. In his arms, she feels safe. In his arms, she feels loved. In his arms, she feels wanted. They dance and dance until finally their lips meet, and Hanna finds herself losing track of the time.

At 12 a.m., Hanna comes home. She'd already called her mother and asked her to keep Jayden and Cameron. As she unlocks the door to her home, she prepares herself for Mark's counterattack. Sitting in a dark living room, Mark is anxious and angry.

Mark: Where have you been?
Hanna: Today, I looked in the mirror and realized I wasn't in love with you. And the more I stay here, the worse I feel about you. I don't want my kids to see this. So, I sent them to mother's house. I think it is best if we got a divorce and if you would just not try to fight me about the kids, because not only will I fight you, but I will expose all of your dirty little secrets.

Mark jumps up from his seat, enraged with his hands extended.
Hanna: What are you going to do, kill me? You already did that to this marriage. Now, go to your new home with your whore and leave mine before I show you a side of me that you never knew about.
Mark: Yeah! I slept with Rebecca! And you know what? She's so much better than you are! I can tell you that. She cooks better than you, smells better than you...she's just better...period! You disgust me! I wonder what I ever saw in you!
Hanna: (*Laughs*) You're right. For you; she's better. She's a whore; you're a whore and together you make a great pair. Just like me and him make a good match. I didn't know that sex outside of you could be so good. Heck, I even forgot sex is supposed to last longer than two minutes!

Mark launches and puts his hands around Hanna's throat.
Mark: So, you ARE cheating on me?
Hanna, well versed in martial arts, quickly grabs and twists Mark's arms behind his back.
Hanna: You didn't know that I took martial arts classes, did you? Oh, that's right. You were so busy trying to pay Rebecca's bills that you knew nothing about me, your own wife!

(*Mark screams from the pain as he tries to pull his arm loose. He is now on the floor with Hanna's knee in his back.*)
Hanna: Dear Mark, let me introduce you to the new Hanna. How can I cheat on you? Remember, it's over between you and me. So, my act tonight was a single woman making love to a single man.
Mark tries to get up to get the best of Hanna, but she twists his arm tighter and steps on his back.
Hanna: Let me share something with you. The next time you get married, pay attention to your wife before you put your hands on her. She just may be a third degree black belt in karate, a karate instructor or Yondan as they call it.
(*Hanna dislocates Mark's arm before she leaves him on the floor.*)
Hanna: Oh yeah, call the police. I'll see that you never practice law again.

Hanna leaves to go and sleep at her mother's house. Mark manages to get himself up and calls for an ambulance. The paramedic is able to snap his arm back into its socket before taking him to the hospital for further observation, but Mark claims that he'd fallen downstairs causing his arm to be dislocated.

The next day, Mark is back at home. For some reason, Hanna's new attitude and love interest has sparked an interest in him. He now wants to patch things up with his wife, but she's now the one being evasive. Day in and day out, Hanna comes and leaves, sometimes not coming home until the next day. Mark has tried everything. He has purchased flowers and sent them to her job, brought her lunch to work, and he has even tried apologizing, but Hanna won't have it. She wants a divorce, and she doesn't stop until she gets it.

Two months after the divorce is finalized, Keith and Hanna are living together. Hanna is head over heels in love, but now, Keith seems distant. Just like his predecessor Mark, he avoids talking to Hanna by focusing on her sons.
A few months later, he asks Hanna to move out, even though she's now pregnant with his son. He doesn't understand why he lost interest in Hanna and Hanna can't figure out what happened.

Explanation:

Men are hunters by nature. Men are territorial and competitive. What Hanna didn't realize was that Keith's mother had been through the same thing with his father. He'd cheated on her, beat her up, and eventually killed her. When Keith heard Hanna's story, all of those emotions came flooding back. He began to see Hanna in a similar view as his mother. He wanted to protect Hanna because, in reality, he was shielding his mother, in his view. Plus, he wanted to win. The natural need to compete and win took over. It's what drove him, and once he'd accomplished that; there was nothing else behind the wheel of his love. I ask you again; whose mouth do you feel safer in? A lion or a shark's? Relationships not birthed in GOD are consuming and many many women find themselves jumping from one man to the next. It's hero-syndrome. It's easy to fall in love with a man you like who's treating you right when the one you love is treating you wrong.

But, GOD designed us to learn from our mistakes and to not repeat them. Unfortunately, a lot of Christian women find themselves believing that one man is the cure to get over another man. When in truth, any man you find outside the will of GOD will take you into the will of Satan. You cannot expect a blessing from a sin. It just does not happen, despite what your heart is saying. That's like believing a cat could give birth to an elephant. It's not natural. GOD created the things in life to birth after its own kind. One blessing births another. A curse births a curse. A fruit tree will yield only the fruit of its own kind. ***"A good tree cannot bring forth evil fruit, neither can a corrupt tree bring forth good fruit." (Matthew 7:18)***

How can one sow the seeds of fornication and adultery and expect to reap GOD'S blessings? We only think that way when we are bi-believers. Sometimes, we believe GOD, but we also believe whatever report matches what we want or what we fear. So, if we want to believe that an illegal relationship will give us residency in the blessings that GOD has reserved for the obedient, we all the same have to believe that we can convince GOD that our sin is justifiable and unlike others, we deserve to be pardoned. GOD is no respecter of persons. You either live right or die wrong. If your relationship is birthed from the womb of sin, what's going to be born is chaos and a failed relationship. We either believe the report of GOD or the other report. We cannot loan our thoughts to reprobate thinking and expect the desires of our evil hearts to manifest and glorify GOD. GOD designed us to praise and glorify HIS Name, not just through speech, but through our lives. HIS Name is glorified either by our obedience, which consequentially attracts HIS blessings, or through disobedience, which attracts HIS wrath. Either way, HE is glorified. The fall of an evil man or woman bears witness that GOD does not tolerate sin. The rise of a righteous man or woman bears witness that GOD will lift up the righteous and bless them well.

You have to stay in the will of GOD to inherit the blessings of GOD. There is no shortcut and there is no window to get to the season you want without first being processed in the seasons you need. No woman can give birth without having first been pregnant. Everything has to grow and mature before the birthing. Don't be anxious. Wait on GOD. And never try to solve a problem with a problem. If you want to see how that works, enroll in school and when you go to math class, answer all of the equations with another equation. When you get that failing grade back, ask the teacher why he or she gave it to you. Their answer will undoubtedly be, "The problems that were given to you required solving. You can't answer a problem with another problem. You only create more problems, and nothing is solved."

Obedience Is Better Than Sacrifice

"If the Devil ain't mad at you, he must be proud of you."

In today's society, people tend to seek acceptance. We want to be loved, recognized and be a part of something great. We don't like standing out because that draws too much attention. So, we try to merge who we are called to be with who we want to be and that doesn't work. And when people voice or display their disdain for our beliefs, we're hurt. Why? Because we have built a relationship with what and how we want people to perceive us and when they do not, we suffer the effects of breakups from our fantasies, and we mourn the sight of our realities.

Kate is a woman of GOD. She's an ordained pastor and a woman after GOD'S own heart. But, Kate is in the heat of the battle with the members of her church. Sure, we know it's all spiritual and so does Kate, and she knows that she was called to lead this church back to GOD. Nevertheless, she is being met with much resistance. The building had once been led by Pastor Luane Stellars. Pastor Luane has recently passed on, and the church's board voted that Kate would take her place, against Pastor Luane's written request to put Jamie Johnston in her place. Pastor Luane, spiritually, wasn't right. She was hateful and bitter, but boy could she preach, and you didn't go to her for advice unless you wanted to be hit hard with the truth....or beat down with Pastor Luane's opinion. Many wrote off her angry demeanor and her harsh words as her being a woman of strength who didn't take hostages. But, in truth, Mrs. Stellars had a very obvious Jezebel spirit. Her husband, Deacon Joe Stellars was meek and tried to stay away from her wrath. He did as he was told and when he didn't, he was met with some of the harshest words when he arrived home. And her angry outbursts could go on all night.

But, now that Mrs. Stellars has passed away; her husband has left the church altogether and Kate now faces a crowd of people who have been controlled for so long that they are demanding that she operate as Mrs. Stellars did.

Kate wants to move to a newer building that is only $100 more a month and is in a better neighborhood, but the church board won't sign off on the deal.
Kate wants to get rid of those old choir robes and get the choir new robes and the church board doesn't want to hear it.
Kate wants to get a website and a logo for the church to better represents its image, and the church calls her a waster of money.
Everything that Kate wanted to do, they shot it down. They wanted Kate to come to church, preach those high lighted messages from Pastor Luane's old notebook and then release them to go home. That's it. But, here she is trying to change the church for the better, which puts her in bad lighting.

Kate is tired. It's normal that she wants to walk away from this church and be planted somewhere that believers believe! She is in constant prayer and fasting and finally; she gets the answer. Kate is the leader and she has to lead, no matter who likes it or not. Initially, Kate was so worried about losing the 60 members that she would comply with their demands, but she was always convicted by her choice. Kate is led to preach and teach as GOD has instructed her, and to go forward with the renting of the new building, purchase a website and a logo and to have the choir robes custom created by a woman that she knows. She pays for these things with her own money. She doesn't know what GOD is doing, but she just trusts HIM.

The following Sunday, Kate gives the sermon and many of the members sit in their usual places looking stoic. They hate the fact that Kate taught from the book of Revelations, whereas Pastor Stellars never went there. After the sermon, Kate makes an announcement that shocks this congregation to the core.
Kate: Many of you know the ordeal that I have been going through since I took on the responsibility to lead this church. But, until right now, I didn't know why GOD had me to go ahead and lease the building on Main Street. As you know, I have been trying to redirect the use of church funds to go from paying a bunch of people to come here and preach to using those funds to build up this church and bring the people in. But, something I read just now woke me up. ***2 Corinthians 5:17*** states, ***"Therefore if any man be in Christ, he is a new creation: old things are passed away; behold, all things are become new."*** This is a new day. Many of us are in CHRIST, but many of you are not. Just like the old man has to pass away so that he can become a new creation in CHRIST, old ways of thinking have to die so that we have to become new creations in CHRIST. You are to be changed by the renewing of your minds, but this church has not moved a lick in 12 years because it's run by evil, religious worshipers who do not care for the things of GOD. Yes, I said it and ain't nobody mad, but the Devil, himself! Therefore, this is what I'm being led to do. This building and the dirt in it is cursed. New Strength Christian Ministries will remain at this place and whatever Jezebel they appoint over it will serve the members and not the LORD. But, if you want to be taught of the LORD without fear, starting next Sunday, come to 1201 Main Street, across from Big Lots to the new and approved Renewed Strength Christian Ministries Worldwide. There will be a side for the Women's ministry which will be headed up by me and there will

be a side for the Men's ministry, which will be headed up by Brother Carlos Prather. I don't expect all of you to come. Only those of you who want the unchangeable and true WORD of GOD. We will have a website! We will have a logo that looks worth having! And we will NOT be controlled by a church board! We will be headed by CHRIST!

The congregation is stunned. A clap rings out in the back. Sister Leulah is excited to see someone finally stand up against the evil that had been New Strength Christian Ministries. Following Ms. Leulah's clap, another clap rings out and then another. One by one, some of the members got up and begin to leave, some excited about the new building and others furious that she wouldn't just comply with their standards.

The next Sunday comes and Kate is in the new building, bright and early. The building has the capacity to seat one thousand people and Kate is beginning to question if she'd made the right move. After all, the old building only had 60 members, 20 of them, which rarely came to church. Not to mention, more than a third of the members wanted to keep things the way that they were and were more than likely not going to come.

With no choir, no podium, and few decorations; Kate knows that this is a for sure faith walk. At 9:27 a.m., Ms. Leulah is the first to enter; followed by the Marshall family and a few others. When service starts, there are only 10 people seated and ready to receive the WORD of GOD. Refusing to be swayed, Kate teaches like she has never taught before.

Back over at New Strength Christian Ministries, only 20 people came to service. People are still talking about what transpired and Mrs. Bertha stands up to announce that the board has already appointed Sister Traneka Peters to be the new pastor. Pastor

Traneka wastes no time to stand up and preach her sermon. One by one, the member's eyes are opened. Traneka is preaching just like the old and now dead Luane Stellars and the 'front seaters' are now shaking their heads in agreement. She does not dare upset them. As a matter of fact, if it isn't highlighted in Pastor Luane's old notebook; Traneka won't touch it. The first to get up and head out the door was Deacon Horsham and his family. Quickly behind him, trying to catch the door was young musician Larry Mullers. One by one, 10 newly awakened souls headed out. "Who knows the way to Kate's church?" The voice comes from a car nearby. "I do," replied Larry. "Y'all can just follow me." And they do.

Kate is in the new building, comforted and knowing that GOD has a plan. What HE uses her to teach is ministering to her as well. Suddenly, the door opens and in comes the blessed 10. They want to be changed. They want to see the real hand of GOD move in their lives. They come in and take their seats, the men being led into the other side where Pastor Carlos is teaching. Kate not only manages to do everything that she set out to do, but one of the members offers to help her televise from within the church.

Membership grows and by the end of the first three months, one third of the seats are full. Kate recognizes that she is going to have to expand the building soon, as she witnesses the crowd grow larger and larger.

And she doesn't keep the members in the four walls. Kate brings the congregation to the streets of Detroit where they walk into the roughest areas singing and praising GOD and evangelizing the WORD of GOD to anyone who wanted to hear. Souls are saved, people are healed, and GOD is glorified.

One day, a man named Sylvester comes to her. He is now the pastor of a new church, but the old members were opposing him with everything in them. Sylvester is angry and wants to find out what he could do to turn his church around. He even speaks of leaving the church. Kate responds:

"The spirit of that kind of thinking is not of GOD. You have been called to teach the WORD, reach the world and breach the devil's security. Don't be distracted by their flesh. You aren't fighting with people. This war is spiritual; it always has been. Stay focused and brother, don't be offended when people come up against you. If people are applauding you everywhere, something is wrong. Remember if you're not fighting against spiritual darkness, you must be fighting with it. I get notes all the time calling me every bad thing underneath the sun, but you know what? I don't get mad; I dance and celebrate how GOD has used me. Brother, I am counted worthy to suffer shame for HIS Name's sake! Do you know the value in that?! And it's not even about me! That's the problem with most leaders. They start taking things personal when the battle isn't about them. No. You offend me when you strike at my GOD. If people are mad because you are doing what GOD tells you to do, then you need to celebrate! That means you are opposing d-evil or shall I say the Devil in them. Keep this with you at all times: if the devil isn't mad at you; he must be proud of you."

Explanation:

The Israelites had been delivered from Egypt by GOD. But, they were so used to being in captivity that they murmured and complained. This is still common amongst believers today. Many are so used to being in captivity that when GOD sends deliverance their way, they complain and wish they'd never left their bondage. Imagine this: You go out and act as the lawyer for a woman who has been falsely accused of a crime. She's freed

because of your hard work, and you even let her stay in your home to help her get on her feet. While there, she complains about your cooking. She says that the prison food was better and she wished that she could go back to those days. Even though prison is not a desired place, she'd gotten comfortable there. You'd probably want to strangle this woman.
Well, this is the case with many newly rescued slaves. They get comfortable in their bondage and they are offended by anyone that threatens to release them. People are afraid of change because they don't know what's on the other side of it. But, they do know what to expect in their bondage.

In many churches today, people control their leaders. (Well, we know that it's the darkness in people that tries to control the light in their leaders. This war is spiritual.) And sadly enough, there are many leaders who follow their congregation's lead. These are people that don't want change; they want familiarity. And anytime we live in familiarity, we are living in shackles.

THE PRICE OF ELEVATION

"No one ever reaches the top of the staircase without having first been at the bottom."

It's easy to look up and see people at the top waving down at you. But, they didn't jump to the top step. They had to take it one step at a time in CHRIST. Every step in sin is a step down. Many are distracted by where they want to be so much that they don't pay attention to where they are and in which direction they are heading.

Portia is married with three children. She has a humongous house, drives a BMW, and has a successful career as a Dentist. Portia's husband, Victor is a Pilot for a popular airline. He brings in a six-figure salary from his job, invests in property, and brings in seven figures from his investments. Not to mention that he is the pastor of a well-known church.
The two are not just successful financially, they are blessed all around. They have perfect health, a sound mind and mountains of wisdom to share. And their children are blessed.

Portia is a very humble and meek wife. She lets her husband take the lead as he is called to do. And Victor wisely listens to his wife as well, so in their united front; they have seen the arrival of many blessings.

It wasn't always like this, though. Portia was raised in Texas to a single mother. Portia's mother was a drug addict who was rarely home, so Portia was left home alone to care for her three brothers and four sisters. Some days, they wouldn't eat at all. School, to them, was important because it gave them the opportunity to eat twice a day. When she was 12, Portia was raped by one of her mother's boyfriends. When she told her mother, she was called a liar and forbidden to tell the story to anyone. She wound up giving birth to his baby; a daughter named Zia. When asked about the little girl's paternity, Portia would tell the lie that her mother coached her to say. She would say that she didn't know where the dad was, but he was some guy that she had met only once and she didn't remember his last name. At the age of 16, Portia dropped out of high school to work full-time at a local market to take care of her siblings and her child, since every dime the government gave her mother went towards her mother's habit. When she was 18, Portia's mother died and Portia found herself having to raise her seven siblings and Zia all alone. She struggled, but she managed to raise them well. Sacrificing her own education, Portia pushed every last one of them to go to college and graduate. Portia wouldn't have it any other way. At the age of 30, Portia decided to go back to school and get her High School diploma, and then she went on to college to become a Dentist.

Not long after graduating, Portia had met and fell in love with Scott, a local drug dealer. Many wondered how could a Dentist be interested in a drug dealer, but the fact was, Portia never had time to make those crucial mistakes that most of us did as young women. After a two-year courtship, Portia gave birth to Scott's son, Scott Kinston, Jr. During this time in her life, Portia suffered mental and physical abuse at the hands of her boyfriend. Portia had started growing closer to GOD and wanted her family to follow in her footsteps, but Scott wanted Portia to stay away from

the church. Almost losing Zia came as a wake-up call. One night, while Portia and Scott were fighting, Zia stormed out of the house. She was tired of their fighting, and she decided that she was going to go out and get high to calm herself down. While driving, however, Zia was struck by a drunk driver. She was in a coma for almost two weeks, and her full recovery took almost two years. The day of the accident was the day that Portia decided to change her life. Her prayer life grew stronger, and it was at that time that she fully dedicated her life to CHRIST and she left Scott for good.
Back in 2004, Portia got a call that her youngest brother had been killed. He'd gotten involved with drugs and owed some local drug dealer. They found his body behind a trash compactor. Heartbroken, Portia managed to pull her family together as she always did. She encouraged them to give their lives to GOD and every one of them respected her so much that they began going to church and learning the WORD of GOD.

In 2006, Portia had to fly to a convention in nearby San Diego, and this is where she met her husband, Victor Nesbit. She was sitting in the airport waiting to board when this tall and handsome man walked by her. When he spotted Portia, his heart leaped. It was like he knew her already.

Victor also came from a broken background. His dad had been abusive to his mother and she died by his hands. At the age of 11, Victor was sent to live with his grandfather and grandmother, but they seemed to be bitter towards him because he was his father's child. So, there wasn't much love in that household.

At 13, Victor ran away from home and was arrested for shoplifting. His grandfather's sudden death, back when he was 14, drew him and his grandmother closer together, and they remained that way until her death when he was 17. After her death, he was sent to live with his Uncle Rollins. Uncle Rollins was a decent man, by all accounts, but he had one problem. He kept borrowing money from loan sharks, so he would have to uproot Victor again and again; moving from city to city to avoid being killed. Nevertheless, Victor continued to go to school, wherever he was. And they never seemed to have a house. Uncle Rollins always seemed to know somebody that knew somebody that would let him stay with them. They lived like this until Victor graduated high school and went to college, where he stayed on campus.

At 24, Victor had married his first wife, but three years in; he found out that she had been having an affair with one of his friends. She even attempted to end Victor's life, which is how the affair was revealed. She'd given him a soda with arsenic in it, and Victor was hospitalized for a week. While in the hospital, doctors found the arsenic in his blood, called the police and an investigation ensued. As a result of the investigation, his wife was arrested and eventually convicted of attempted murder. She was given 20 years in prison with the possibility of parole after 15 years. Victor divorced her and tried to pick up the pieces of his life. He began to pray more and seek the LORD more and more. With two children now in his custody; he moved to Oceanside, California where he went to Pilot School and joined a local church, later to be ordained a pastor.

Victor and Portia's meeting was inevitable. Portia was always flying out for conventions, not to mention, unbeknownst to them, they went to the same church. Months of conversing and finally going out together led to one of the most publicized and anticipated marriages in California.

Nice story, but it doesn't end there.
Portia is content as she is and so is Victor. With Zia now in

college and Scott, Jr. enrolled in elementary school; Portia's hands are full. Throughout her struggles, her family was never there, save her brothers and sisters. She had aunts and uncles, cousins and so on, but as she was raising her siblings and dealing with the struggles of life, she found herself doing it all alone. Of course, GOD was there.

Now that Portia is successful, she has had to change her phone number seven times. Sure, she forgave her family years ago, but wisdom tells her to steer clear of them.

Victor and Portia's marriage has had its fair share of struggles in the beginning, but now, it's smooth sailing. They are in love and it can be seen every time they look at one another. It's almost child like.

In addition, there are many women attempting to attach to Portia. This began when she started going to school to become a Dentist, but has escalated since she has gotten married to a successful man of GOD and moved into one of the biggest homes in Oceanside.

Arielle goes to Restored to Rise Ministries. She is a member and a volunteer for the helps ministry. Arielle, like many that have met the Nesbits, admires their lifestyle and has offered to take the First Lady out to lunch on more than one occasion, but her invitations are always met with a friendly decline. Portia would always try to explain why she couldn't hang out with Arielle.

"Arielle, I love you, but I don't fraternize with the ministry team or anyone, for that matter. When we go out as a group for the ministry, that is okay. I hope you're not offended. You have to understand that if you got familiar with me, you wouldn't be able to receive from me. A prophet is not without honor, except in his own country. Please understand."

You see, Arielle believes that by connecting with the First Lady that her dreams of being successful will come to fruition.

Arielle was in school at one point, but she dropped out to move closer to her boyfriend. When that relationship failed, she moved back to her hometown and got a job at a local coffee shop. Now, Arielle has been even more ambitious. In the last few years, she has tried her hand at several work at home jobs, started selling plate dishes from within her home, and finally found her niche in creating jewelry to sell online. The jewelry store does okay; averaging around $100 a week. Of course, that's not enough, but it's a start. However, Arielle sees the First Lady as a great opportunity to help her promote her jewelry store. So, she's always trying to link up with Portia, but is always gently let back down.

Explanation:

Arielle is like many women. She sees the final product that is Victor and Portia's success. Rather than doing as the Nesbit's did and relying on GOD, Arielle has decided that she would find her way up by connecting with Portia. In Arielle's eyes, it's a friendship that could serve as a huge business connection and opportunity; but Portia understands what Arielle is doing. She is trying to step over the LORD'S way and fly to the top of the stairs without having to climb them.

Women like Arielle try to connect with any woman or man that has reached their successful place.
Many women will look and admire, even envy the success of other women. They see where they are, but they don't see where they came from. Every one of us has a dream and a story, but no one can reach the top of the staircase without first starting at the bottom. Plus the way to Portia's success is not going to be the way to Arielle's success. Many never arrive at success because they spend their lives trying to overstep the LORD and get to success on alternate routes, when there is no other way! In the

next chapter, we will discuss what success is and what success is not.

And please know this. What is considered the top of the staircase for someone else, may be your bottom step. This includes those of you who were brought up in financial wealth and inherited this wealth from your parents. Their wealthy place is your place of poverty. That means, you have to start where you are and seek the LORD to get where HE has called you to be.

Chasing Success (Why It Keeps Evading Capture)

"Anyone that follows success is lost. Anyone driven towards success will run out of fuel. Anyone driven towards GOD will be accompanied by success."

You have to know what success is and what success is not before you will understand it. Success is one's heart arriving in faith. Success does not mean to have plenty. Nowadays, there are many women chasing behind wealth because they believe that wealth will buy them all of the things that they need to make them happy. They believe that wealth is the answer to all of their problems, when, in reality, wealth without wisdom is the start of a whole new set of problems that they are not equipped to handle. So, to many, success is the absence of need coupled with the ability to get anything one wants without worry.

Ashley has a drive and so does her twin sister, Asia. Both are women of the faith, and even though they are identical in appearance, they are driven by two different forces. Both women are landscapers and have their own landscaping companies, but Ashley's company seems to be doing better than Asia's. Asia isn't swayed by this because she loves her sister and is happy for her. Originally, they had one company that they both were co-owners of, but Ashley's drive for success drove Asia out.

WISE HER STILL

Ashley is always working on something. If she isn't advertising online; she's somewhere shooting a commercial. Her business is always in her forethought. Asia, on the other hand, believes in hard work, dedication, and planning; but, she refuses to overwork herself to get there. Asia likes to focus much of her attention on the LORD.

Asia is always talking to Ashley, trying to get her to slow down and let the seasons have their way. However, Ashley believes that Asia's interference is driven by competitiveness and envy. So, she doesn't listen. Instead, she continues to amp up her advertising even more, and she began to create negative ad campaigns about companies that didn't offer what she offered. She was indirectly targeting her sister's company.

Most people are drawn to Ashley because Ashley seems to have already arrived at the peak of success, where Asia can be seen working hard and long, but never overdoing it. Don't get me wrong. Asia is driven, just not by the thoughts of success. Asia sees her vision as a whole. She wants to live for the LORD, get married one day, have children, have a successful landscaping company and live joyfully ever after.
Ashley wants the same things, but she's more driven towards financial success and afterward; she plans to focus on each dream individually. Besides, Ashley has had a boyfriend for the last two years, and marriage isn't at the top of her priorities right now.

One day, Asia meets the man of her dreams. He's perfect! He's a landscaper as well, and best of all, he's a man of GOD! As time passes, Asia and Michael, her new beau, grow closer and closer until one day, nine months after they met, Michael proposed and Asia accepts.

No one is more shocked about this than her twin sister, Ashley.

She believes that it is too soon and that Asia's focusing on the wrong things right now. Why doesn't she just focus on her business and worry about marriage later? After all, Ashley has a boyfriend, but both of them are extremely driven towards success, so neither one of them is considering marriage as of yet. In true Ashley form, she delivers her disapproving words to Asia, but they fall on deaf ears.

A year after the marriage, Michael and Asia are doing well. They have merged their landscaping businesses and success is written all over it. Michael brought ideas to Asia and Asia brought ideas to Michael. Together, they created a landscaping business like no other. You see, Michael's family bought properties, when he was a teen. They would buy them, fix them up and sell them. Michael is a regular old handyman. He can fix just about anything, so he would always help his dad with repairing the houses and whatever they couldn't do, they would hire someone to do.

And now, Asia's pregnant with their first child. Unable to do much of the work herself, Asia takes to studying as much as she can about foreign plants and ponds. She took an interest in ponds when she saw one in one of her customer's yards. Michael and Asia joined together and came up with an idea that would launch their business to unimaginable heights.
They would go and buy foreclosed properties and properties from people who could no longer afford their mortgages. They would paint the homes, put ponds and fountains in the yards, and give them the best landscaping designs in town. And it worked! Not only did the houses sell for way more than they'd expected, but neighbors of these homes would feel so embarrassed that their yards didn't look as good as the yard that Michael and Asia had landscaped, that they'd call them to hire them to do their landscaping.

Business took off so fast that before Asia had the baby, Michael had to hire more landscapers to keep up with the demand. He would teach them something he knew, but he would never teach one agent everything he knew. Michael's idea was to teach one man about ponds, for example, and teach another about foreign plants and another one about another area. This way, no man could run away with all of that knowledge, and they had to learn to work together to get it done the way Michael and Asia would do it. He would also encourage each one to bring something new to the business. They had six months to do so.
And their business was a huge success. But, despite it all, Michael and Asia never lost sight of GOD. They were more committed to serving HIM than serving that business.

Ashley can feel the competitive pressure. Her business does okay, but it's not where she wants it to be. She seems to have peaked, and her profits have been about the same for the last few years. Her business does well, but now, Ashley is trying to find new avenues to invest in because her landscaping business isn't buying her the houses and the cars that she felt entitled to. Plus, she cannot believe the success of Asia. “It's short-lived,” she would always say to others. “I love my twin, but it's all happening too fast.”

Years later, Michael and Asia's landscaping business continued to flourish as they kept implementing new ideas. Guess where those ideas were coming from? GOD, of course.
They have three children and because they have a large landscaping company that pretty much runs itself, they are able to travel and live the life that a workaholic doesn't have time for.

Explanation:

Success is not financial freedom. Success is arriving at your appointed place in GOD and reaping the benefits. Success does not require you to give up one blessing to get to the next. For example, there are millions of people who have financial success, but they don't have success with being healthy, success with being at peace, success with being happy, or success with serving the LORD without fail. So, they sacrifice all of these things for what they worship... money. You sacrifice to what you worship. This is why you find that many celebrities die from drug overdoses because they replaced GOD with monetary success. That's not success, since success comes as a whole and cannot be portioned out. That is the sacrificial offering that doomed the person. If you can learn to successfully seek the LORD and find HIM every day, you have arrived at success, and the material things will come along shortly. You don't have to sacrifice your health and your peace of mind, as Ashley did. Everything has a season, but in order for the seasons to work, you have to stay planted in obedience and rooted in the WORD of GOD.

"Therefore I say unto you, Take no thought for your life, what ye shall eat, or what ye shall drink; nor yet for your body, what ye shall put on. Is not the life more than meat, and the body than raiment? Behold the fowls of the air: for they sow not, neither do they reap, nor gather into barns; yet your heavenly Father feedeth them. Are ye not much better than they? Which of you by taking thought can add one cubit unto his stature? And why take ye thought for raiment? Consider the lilies of the field, how they grow; they toil not, neither do they spin: And yet I say unto you, That even Solomon in all his glory was not arrayed like one of these. Wherefore, if God so clothe the grass of the field, which to day is, and to morrow is cast into the oven, shall he not much more clothe you, O ye of little faith? Therefore take no thought, saying, What shall we eat? or, What

shall we drink? or, Wherewithal shall we be clothed? (For after all these things do the Gentiles seek:) for your heavenly Father knoweth that ye have need of all these things. But seek ye first the kingdom of God, and his righteousness; and all these things shall be added unto you.
Take therefore no thought for the morrow: for the morrow shall take thought for the things of itself. Sufficient unto the day is the evil thereof." (Matthew 6:25-34)

Check your heart's GPS. What is it set for? If it's not set in arriving in a place where your life is pleasing to GOD, you need to reset it. Many children go to college, graduate, and live a life of lack. That's because they went out looking for something that did not exist. They looked for financial freedom when this is not an address; it is a state of mind that is only found in GOD. Sure, many people who do not serve the LORD arrive at financial wealth, but this is not the state of financial wealth that's in GOD. It is perverted and they often pay handsomely to get there and an even greater to stay there. And they still don't have joy on the inside, health on the outside and peace all around.

The blessings of the LORD are peace (sound mind), health (sound body) and the absence of lack. Sure, some things can make people happy, but here's the thing about 'happiness.' Happiness is brought on by external situations, but joy comes from within. So, in my successful peaceful place, I'd rather have joy than happiness any day! Joy is when you can be at home, alone and just enjoy yourself more than you could in the presence of people. Joy is when you can laugh while seated in a restaurant all by your lonesome self because your mind is playing back something you or someone else said or something you are planning to say. Joy is when you don't care about what anyone else thinks, they can think you're crazy over there in your vehicle, praising the LORD at the red light!

Look at your GPS and ask yourself, “What am I going after? What have I been chasing?” If it's not the LORD, ask HIM to change your destination.

The Anatomy of a Man Versus the Anatomy of a Man of GOD

"Every man is not anointed to be a husband and every husband is not anointed to be 'your' husband."

The majority of single women alive believe that if it's a man, it can be a husband. They are both built the same way; they have deep voices, strong arms and are anatomically correct. But, there is a difference. A mere man is not in GOD and is found in his flesh, led of his flesh and dies by his flesh. A man of GOD is released and anointed to be a husband and is only found in GOD, led by GOD and lives in GOD. Even when he leaves his natural body, his legacy lives on, and he leaves an inheritance for his children and his children's children.

MAN

IS TREAD ON BY SERPENTS. SECONDARY BRAIN.

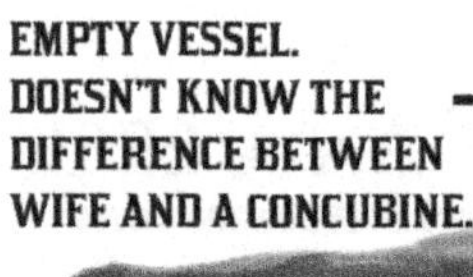

DECIDES TO LET OTHERS DECIDE HOW HE SHOULD LIVE. (FOLLOWER)

USED TO SPEAK DEATH AND WHATEVER EVIL IS ON HIS HEART. USED TO TEAR DOWN WOMEN AND THE CHILDREN THEY BARE.

USED TO FIGHT, STEAL KILL AND RESIST.

USED TO DO THE WORKS OF HIS FATHER (SATAN)

USED TO CREATE SOUL TIES WITH WOMEN. SPREAD DISEASE. MAIN BRAIN.

FOLLOWS THE DIRECTION THE MAIN BRAIN AND MONEY GIVES IT.

SUPPORTS THE RIGHT LEG THE WRONG WAY

MAN OF GOD/HUSBAND

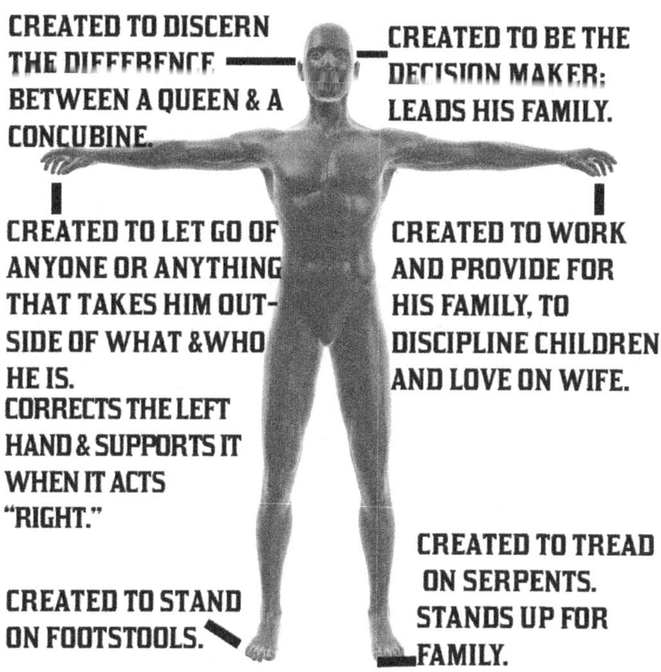

Knowing the difference between a man and a man of GOD is imperative to your destiny.

GOD is coming back for a church without spot or wrinkle. That is, this church has to fully align with the WORD of GOD and cannot be found with a blemish. This means that the church has to get it right before it can be accepted by GOD.

Let's talk about a man versus a man of GOD. A man is a creature that has rented himself to sin, but a man of GOD is more than just a man. He has sacrificed the dead man to walk in faith. He has overcome the flesh and the desires of the world by living in the WORD and refusing to come out. Just like the BODY of CHRIST has limbs and each limb has a purpose, a man and a man of GOD has limbs that all have a function.

When a man is just a man, his mind is perverted, perverting the use of his limbs and his walk. A woman can get mad at a man for acting like a man, but this only shows how immature she is because a man cannot go outside of what he is or who he is. He can only be elevated in CHRIST when he reaches up and wants to do better with his life, but talking to him and yelling at him won't change him. It'll only infuriate him because he has reached his flesh's limits and cannot legally be what his wife wants him to be without first being elevated by GOD.

A man walks after his flesh. Satan uses the flesh to expose the man and destroy the man because the desires of the flesh are strong. No....they are STRONG, and they render us weak. That's why we have to have the WORD in us so that we can fight the flesh. We have to have a relationship with GOD so that we can ask HIM to kill the flesh and quicken the spirit.
A man cannot tell the difference between a wife and a woman. Many men can marry a wife and leave her for a woman. It's not a reflection of <u>who</u> you are; it's a reflection of <u>what</u> he is, but you were in error when you stepped down to court and marry him.

A man will follow after opinions, ideas and fads. For example, if hip-hop is popular, he will morph into a pimpin'-limpin' reincarnation of the rapper that he idolizes. If ballet is the in-thing, he'll dance circles around you. Whatever and whomever defines to him what a man is supposed to look, act, talk and dress like, is what and whom he will listen to because there is no wisdom in him. He needs to be told how to live, where to live and who to live with. He even needs to be told how to dress, how to speak and how to walk. If his favorite rapper, pop star or actor walks like someone shot him in the foot, he will walk like someone shot him in the foot as well.

A man's mouth is his undoing. His heart is evil, so his mouth speaks evil things. Whatever woman gives herself to him will find herself subjected to all types of verbal abuse. He doesn't bless the name of the LORD; why would he treat you any better?!

A man's hands are used for war. He'll fight whomever he thinks he can beat up. For example, if he doesn't think that he can overpower that guy that is his height, his weight and just as mouthy as him; but he thinks he can beat you, prepare to taste the floor. That's what makes him feel like a man. He's trying to discover who he is and you will serve as a punching bag until he does. He will steal or do whatever his evil heart pushes him to do.

A man's feet are slaves to his heart. Wherever his heart tells him to go, he will go.
A man's loins were supposed to be used to create life that his hands would toil to take care of, but because he is a man and not a man of GOD, his children are just proof that his parts are working. He may even stay around and take care of his children (slightly) for a while, but break up with him, and he will break up with his children, in many cases. And the ones that do stay in their lives, often don't have much to teach them except the ignorance that they have come to find bliss in.

A man of GOD walks after the WORD of GOD and refuses to go

any other way. His desire is in pleasing the LORD at all times.
A man of GOD knows the difference between a wife and a woman. Wisdom has taught him a lot!
A man of GOD follows after the WORD and will offend others by disregarding their opinions and ideas. He doesn't care about pleasing others. He wants to please GOD and his wife. Anyone else doesn't matter.
A man of GOD will bless the Name of the LORD at all times. He blesses his wife with kindness and blesses his children. He knows what to say and when to say it. He knows to keep his mouth from evil because his heart far from evil.
A man of GOD will use his hands to praise GOD, pray, work, discipline his children, love on his wife and hold the family together. If he needs to war, he will war in the spirit.
A man of GOD'S feet will follow after GOD and lead his wife.
A man of GOD'S loins are for the sole purpose of mating with his wife and pleasing his wife. Every child he creates, he takes care of, teaches and disciplines. He teaches his boys how to be men and he teaches his daughters how to differentiate between mere men and men of GOD.
A man of GOD is selfless, but a mere man is selfish.

Problem is, many women don't know the difference because many women are mere women. They are not women of GOD. Being a woman of GOD is not dependent on how many times you go to church, how many times you say "hallelujah," whether you are baptized or not or how much of the Bible you know. Being a woman of GOD is serving the LORD with all of your heart, mind and soul. Being found by the man of GOD appointed for you is all about being in the right place at the right time. But, to do this, you have to do the right things the right way. Because a season will come upon you where your husband is scheduled to arrive, but if you're not there, GOD will not curse him by sending him you when you're off in sin somewhere.

Women say they want a man of GOD, yet they continue to fornicate with the men that they wish were their husbands. Years and years later, they scream, "I'm so tired of waiting for my husband! When is he coming? I have been waiting 33 years and still no husband! My biological clock's batteries are wearing down by the minute!" It's not GOD'S fault; it's her own. Because to be found by a man of GOD, you have to first be a woman of GOD. If you still wrestle with offense, fornication, backbiting, gossip, slander, laziness, and so on; you are not ready yet. GOD'S son has prayed to HIM for his wife and stayed in obedience to find her. Why would the LORD send this man of GOD to a woman who is still wrestling with some issues? The LORD doesn't want to hear, "LORD, why hast thou forsaken me?!" HE wants that man to bless HIS Name and tell others how he found such a beautiful and wonderful treasure.

What's sad is there are so many women out there waiting for a husband. I mean, seriously waiting. But, they want the man before they want GOD. This is out of order. Many women still dance with sin, but they lay down with a Bible in their hands. They can't even be faithful to GOD, but they want HIM to send them a man after HIS heart? The moment that man steps on their toes, they'd be out there with another man who is like themselves...a man of and in the world. You need to know that when you are not in GOD or haven't arrived at a particular place in HIM, you will find men of the world attractive and they will be drawn to you as well. But, once GOD has cleaned you up; sagging pants, profane speech, perversity and the ability to fight won't entertain you. They'll disgust you. There is nothing like a man who is strong enough to follow the LORD, and a leader that does not care what anyone thinks!

If you're reading this because you want to be found by your man of GOD, then first ask GOD to make you that woman of GOD that will compliment him. Being a woman does not entitle you to a man of GOD, but it does make you available for mere men and believe me....you don't want that.

I am a women of God: So that entitles me for my husband to be a Man of God not just a mere man.

What Real Forgiveness Looks Like

"Refusing to forgive is the same as refusing to live."

If you're like most of us, you do not want to know the day that you are scheduled to pass away out of your body. You just want to live in peace each and every day. But, did you know that when you refuse to forgive someone for what they've done to you, you are refusing to live past that day? So, the day that you died was the day that unforgiveness tagged you. But, thankfully, through CHRIST, you too can be resurrected.

Janice blow dries her beautiful blonde hair and prepares to go to the prison. She's going there to visit her mother's killer, her dad. It's been 24 years since Janice has seen her dad. Twelve years old at the time of her mother's death, Janice spent much of her childhood grieving the loss of her mother and hating her dad for taking her away from her.

An only child, Janice was raised by her mother's twin sister Patricia. Patricia did her best to help Janice through the ordeal, but she too had trouble forgiving Janice's dad, Rocco. It wasn't easy for Janice to grow up with a woman who had the face of her mother. When Janice was little, there were times when Patricia would enter her room to tuck her in, and she would wake up thinking that her mother was visiting her. Patricia would always explain to her that her mother is asleep now, and her spirit would not and could not travel in the earth realm without an earth suit, but the notion that her mother was watching over her was far more comforting to Janice.

The loud sounds of the doors opening at the prison spooked Janice. She sat down at the table waiting for her dad to emerge. He had been writing her for the last 23 years, and she'd never answered him or read his letters. She would always return them to the sender and pray that he got the message, but he didn't. A call from him in late October of that year sparked some old emotions, and she decided to go to the prison to ask the questions that she wanted to ask.

The door opens and Janice looks for her dad's face, but instead sees a guard coming in pushing something. She looks down to see the fragile remainder of her dad being wheeled into the room. He is in a wheelchair and far skinnier than Janice had remembered. His skin was no longer the smooth skin she'd remembered, but was now replaced by wrinkles and liver spots. Most of his teeth were gone and his eyes had a glaze on them that wasn't there before.

Janice and Rocco sat there for one minute before Rocco began to break down and cry. His daughter had grown up to be a beautiful woman. Her face was so very similar to her mother's face to the point where Rocco, for a second, thought he was seeing a ghost. But, she had her daddy's unmistakable chin.

Sitting across from his daughter, Rocco attempts to hold her hand, but isn't surprised when Janice snatches them off of the table. His tears pour out even more as he thought about the precious gift that he'd taken away from his daughter. He had dreamed of this moment for 20-plus years and now that it was here; he didn't know what to do with it, so he just began to speak.

Rocco: Thank you for coming to visit me. I have prayed for years that I would be able to see your face again at least one more time before I leave this earth. You are beautiful just like your..... *(Rocco pauses) Janice tears up and opens her mouth and a familiar voice comes out.*

Janice: My mother?

Janice's voice has matured. She was sounding just like her mother.

Rocco: Yes. Baby, I wrote you for years. I don't expect you to want a relationship with me. But, I wanted to tell you face to face that I am sorry. I was so stupid back then. I would give anything to rewind the hands of time to undo what I did. When I found out that I may not be on this earth much longer; I decided to try harder to contact you. I gave my life to CHRIST years ago, and I have asked HIM over and over again for HIS forgiveness. Baby, I love you more than the beat of my heart, and I am begging you to forgive me.

Janice: It took me a long time to even consider forgiving you. I had to wake up everyday and look at a woman who reminded me so much of my mother. Sometimes, to escape the pain, I would convince myself that she was her. I would watch Aunt Patricia with her kids, and it reminded me of how my mother was with me. Aunt Patricia loved me and she was a great parent, but the love between a mother and her own children is unmistakable. She did her best with me. I went to visit my mother's grave every Saturday. I would tell her what happened all week long at school, my first date, my first kiss and just ask her all kinds of questions about life. But, she wouldn't answer me. She couldn't answer me. My momma was gone, and she wasn't coming back. Ever. So, I decided that the best place for me to be was to go with her. One day, I played sick, so I wouldn't have to go to school. I was planning to take a butcher knife and slice my wrists as soon as

Aunt Patricia and Uncle Jesse went to work. When they left, I went to the kitchen and picked up the sharpest knife they had. I went into my room, and just as I was trying to get up my nerves to do it, I heard glass breaking in the living room. I ran to see what had happened, and one of momma's pictures had fallen off the wall. I broke down right there and while I was laying there beside her picture, Aunt Pat came back through the door. She didn't ask any questions; she just knelt down beside me and began holding me and we cried together. We stayed there for more than an hour just holding one another; not saying a word, just crying. I wanted to know why GOD let you take my momma away from me. I was mad at HIM for a while about it. But, I was comforted on that particular day because I felt like HE had let my momma come and visit me. HE let her come and stop me from taking my life. After that day, Uncle Jesse started to speak to me more and more about GOD. At first, I didn't want to hear it. But, something he said comforted me. He said that murderers would not enter heaven. I realized then why HE didn't let me go through with that suicide. My momma is in heaven, and if I'd murdered myself, I would be separated from her for eternity. When he told me that the Angels rejoice every time one soul is saved, I decided to get saved because I believe my momma is an Angel, and I have always wanted to make her proud. I thought I wanted to ask you a lot of questions, but now that I'm here, daddy; I have my peace. I came here to say that I love you despite what you did, and I want to offer one of my kidneys to you so that you will live.

At this, Rocco is inconsolable. He'd prayed for this day to come and his prayers had been answered. Janice reached over the table to wipe her daddy's tears away. This act made him cry all the more. Through the tears, he manages to speak.
Rocco: My baby. My daughter. My love, I could not imagine taking your kidney. But, I am overwhelmed by your offer to give me another chance at life after what I've done.

Janice: Daddy, I forgive you, but you have to forgive yourself. I know that my mom is in good hands now.
Rocco: One of my kidneys is functioning well. The other one is not doing so well, but the doctor says I can survive on one. It's just that my health has been deteriorating, and I know it's old age. If you want to help me, daughter, do me this one favor. I will be released within the next few months, and I need somewhere to stay. If you will, call around to some nursing homes to see if I can get a bed in one. Social Security will take care of the bill. But, what I really want is to see your face there at my bedside as much as you can visit.
Janice: When will you be released, Daddy?
Rocco: In January.

They continue to talk until his time limit is up. Janice has a plan, but she doesn't want her dad to know. She kisses him before she leaves the prison; watching the guard push her frail daddy away.

January comes, and Janice goes to the prison to pick up her dad. She has purchased a new van with a wheelchair lift, but Rocco doesn't know that the van is new. He wonders who the van is for, thinking that maybe Janice had borrowed someone's vehicle. After hugging, they make their way on the two-hour journey back to Flemingsburg, Kentucky.

Rocco: I love you, daughter.
Janice: I love you too, Dad. We're almost there.
Rocco: I've been meaning to ask. What's the name of this nursing home and how far is it from your house?
Janice: Well, it's called Family Love Nursing and we're here now.
Rocco looks up to see a beautiful brick home. It doesn't look like a nursing home.
Janice: Wait one second. I'll be right back. I have to get some help unloading you.

Afraid to ask any questions, Rocco sits there and nods his head. A few minutes later, a tall gentleman walks out of the front door. He goes around the back of the van and gets Rocco's wheelchair and opens it. Then he opens Rocco's door to introduce himself as another man comes out of the front door putting on his coat.
James: Hello, Granddad. I'm James, your grandson; James.

Rocco begins to tremble as he lets the tears break forward. A handshake won't do. He struggles to his feet to hug his grandson. Janice's husband comes to help put him in the chair and introduces himself as well. In the house, Rocco is met by two little girls; one named Samantha and the other named Paula, after her deceased grandmother.

There, he finds out that he will be staying with his daughter and her family. He lives with them for five years before he passed away. He was able to make peace with all the family; even Aunt Patricia.

Explanation:

Now, most people in this situation would say that they could never forgive Rocco. Because some acts are cruel; while others are crueler. But, Janice and her family decided to take the high road and forgive. And in doing so, she was refusing to be stuck in the past. At the same time, she was freeing herself from the wretched life that Satan wanted her to live and from the pits of hell that awaits the unforgiving. When we refuse to forgive, we refuse to live past the day of our hurt. In unforgiveness, the day that the crime occurred against us was the day that we passed away to purpose. By forgiving, Janice was not only ripping her soul out of the hands of Satan, but she was helping others to do the same.

Many cannot have success in jobs, relationships, or success in anything because they are plugged in; but the only three buttons working on them is pause, rewind and fast forward.
Pause: They can't seem to get past what was done to them. They can't move forward with their lives because their tape will play only up until the point of the incident.
Rewind: When they aren't pausing; they are rewinding the memories.
Fast Forward: People who do not forgive tend to look forward to someone getting what they believe is due to them.
Push Play Please: There is only one button that we should press and leave it alone and that button is 'play.' We have to take life scene by scene, day by day, minute by minute and sometimes, one breath at a time. Don't worry about tomorrow, for tomorrow will worry about itself. Yesterday is intended to be a lesson for today, but never to be carried with you.

Sure, people have come your way and hurt you. They have betrayed you. They have talked about you. They have done a lot to you. But, the worst thing you can do to someone who has wronged you is to forgive them, move forward and better your life. Give the gift of forgiveness; not to them, but to yourself! You'll thank yourself that you did.

Elevate or Imitate

"If discovering the whole heart of GOD was your job, you would never be unemployed."

GOD'S heart is unsearchable. His depths, heights and widths are without measure. HE is lifted up, yet who can discover HIS height? HE is wide, but there is nothing or no one that could measure HIS width. HE is deep, yet no one can uproot HIM or reach the depths of HIM. Getting lost in GOD is in the same as finding one's self. This is true. Who we are is found in GOD, nevertheless, most people live and die never knowing much about themselves; only their names, their likes and dislikes and their family's names. They trace their lineage back to the grave, since the people that birthed the seed that enabled them to come through that family are dead and gone. But, rarely do people trace their lineage back to CHRIST, as they should. This is why so many people spend years and thousands of dollars trying to discover details about their ancestors on earth. So, again, they trace their lineage to the grave. Discovering who you are is wrapped up in discovering who GOD is. Sure, you know HIS name, and you know that HE created the Heavens and the earth and HE created you. But, your parents came together and all they knew was that you were found in your mother's womb one day. They did not watch you form, and they don't know you inside out. GOD not only created you, but HE built you, piece by piece, limb by limb and hair by hair. So, it is no wonder that HE knows you from the inside out. But, in your natural walk, you have gone away to follow after the natural things in life, when the everlasting you is called to the spiritual things of eternal life. The flesh shall die, but the spirit remains forever. When we don't follow the LORD and when we don't search HIM out continuously, we lose touch with who we are and we begin to emulate others. It's because one of our key parts, called the brain, requires answers. Our original makeup or build was designed so that those answers would come from the LORD to complete us or upgrade us season by season. But, as people pull more away from GOD to follow the things of the flesh, it is of no wonder that this world is turning to drugs, promiscuity and every evil underneath the sun. Do you know who you are? Or are you still studying earthly books and watching television to discover who you want to be?

Chasity Bridgewater is a college student studying medicine. She has always wanted to be a doctor, and here she was in her junior year, studying to do what she always dreamed of doing.

In her spare time, Chasity likes to party and hang out with friends. Last Friday, she partied so hard that she couldn't remember much after one o'clock in the morning.

Her friends adored her. They felt that she was one of the funniest and brightest women they have ever known. She's humble and she's extremely honest. Tears or no tears, she would tell you the truth; no matter what it did to you and her friends loved her for that.

One day, while walking to the store, Chasity was interrupted by a homeless man who tapped her on the shoulder to ask for a few bucks. Disgusted, Chasity sharply rebuked him for touching her and continued on her walk to the store. Later that day, she told her friends about the encounter, and they all laughed. They imagined that Chasity had probably said some pretty funny or rude things, and they all wished they could have been there to witness Chasity unleash Chazz; what they referred to as her alter-ego.

A few days later, Chasity was studying for a big exam in front of her apartment window. She could see the homeless man outside apparently begging another woman. But, the woman's reaction was different from Chasity. She excused herself for a brief few minutes and reappeared holding a big bag full of groceries. She also handed him a few sandwiches in some freezer bags. He thanked her as he attempted to walk away, but she asked him to wait again. Obviously, she'd forgotten something. Moments later, one of her roommates came out of the apartment to hand the homeless man a Bible. They stopped to pray with him and let him continue on his way. “Yuck. How could they feed him? Don't they know he'd be like a dog and keep coming back?” Chasity thinks to herself. “He just wants money to buy alcohol or drugs. Or maybe he's a gambler. Who cares? He won't be robbing me.”

Around six p.m. that day, Chasity remembered she needed to head to the store and get a loaf of bread. She'd been putting it off all day and wanted to get there before it got dark. While walking, she could see the homeless man leaning up against the side of the store. She braces herself for his bothersome antics and tries to think of something funny to say to him, should he approach her. But, nothing. As she passes him by, he does not stop her. Instead, he sits quietly, eating one of the sandwiches that the all-too-friendly neighbor had given him. When she left the store, she didn't see him.

Almost to her apartment, Chasity came upon an abandoned building. It was a sore sight in such a decent neighborhood. It used to be a church, but the doors had closed a few years back, and it was said that the landlord was so evil and wanted so much money for it that the local newspapers even refused to list it. And the pastor that had once rented it out had somehow went crazy.

As she was passing by this church, she suddenly felt a blow to her head, and she found herself falling backwards. She couldn't scream because someone had muzzled her mouth with their hands. It was all happening so fast. The assailant dragged Chasity into a small alley beside the church and began to punch and strangle her. She fought for her life, but could feel herself slipping in and out of consciousness as his grip around her neck grew stronger with every passing breath. Just when she was ready to give up, out of nowhere, she made out another figure who'd come behind her attacker. He began to fight with her assailant as she wheezed for breath and tried to focus on regaining her sight. She stumbled and held on to the building as the blur began to clear up. She looked back and could see the homeless man wrestling with the guy who'd attacked her. By now, the homeless man had gotten the best of the assailant and was now sitting on him and screaming at Chasity to call 911. She does.

When the officers arrived, they found the attacker on the ground begging for help. After cuffing him, they searched him and found a hunting knife in a holster on his side. They also found rope and a set of car keys. After locating his vehicle, the police believed and later proved that he was a man responsible for a string of murders in the nearby city of Miami. He was later discovered to be Robert Spangling; a serial killer who loved to choke out his victims before dragging their unconscious bodies to his van. There, he would sexually assault them and then take them to a wooded area where he would strangle and stab them to death before dumping their bodies. His victims were usually dead one to two hours after his initial attack.

At the hospital, Chasity is kept overnight and is still a little shaken up. She struggles to make sense of the day and is comforted when her family arrives at the hospital. "She's going to be okay." She could hear the doctor reassuring her obviously distraught family. "She's just a little banged up and scared; quite understandably, but she's okay." This event had done something to Chasity. She felt bad that she'd been so cruel to the homeless man and had refused to help him, and yet he still risked his life to save hers. This situation made her think about how far she'd walked away from GOD. She'd seen her life flash before her eyes, and she cried uncontrollably as she thought of how the day could have went.

The hospital only allowed four people in her room at a time, so when her friends arrived; her mother and siblings agreed to go in the waiting room to let them visit with her. When they came into the room, they found Chasity sitting up on her bed. They were expecting her to look worse than she did, but she was fine; minus the redness and swelling around her neck and a little bruising around her eyes. Chasity felt uncomfortable with her friends being there and she didn't understand why. It didn't take her long to find out either. Right after they'd hugged her and she'd told them what happened, one of the girls, Emily, started laughing. When asked to share what had her so tickled, she said, "I was thinking how that could have been this big romantic scene if the homeless guy wasn't some old, funky man. How beautiful would that have been if your rescuer was, for example, Leonardo DiCaprio or the Rock." *Chasity's disgust turns to downright anger when the rest of her friends join in to laugh and talk about her rescuer.* Chasity interrupted, "This man saved my life and all you can talk about is what he has and what he doesn't have? He's a human being that deserves respect too. Especially for what he's done."

Emily: Yeah, yeah, I know. But, I'm just saying. Did you get a whiff of his armpits when he reached up to put the guy in the headlock? I'm imagining that's what took the guy down.

The room erupts with laughter as Chasity has a moment of realization. Here, she'd lost touch with who she was trying to amuse a pack of jackals. She'd walked away from the church and gotten so caught up in the idea of being this big shot doctor that she'd befriended people that, in her humble state, she would have never befriended. True to her nature, Chasity opens her mouth, but not before pushing the buzzer on her bed. When the desk asks Chasity what she needs, she responds.
Chasity: Can you send security up please?
Operator: What's wrong?
Chasity: Please, just send them up.

Chasity's friends are stunned now. Why does she need security? Olivia interrupts...
Olivia: Wait. I know you're not getting upset that we are talking about some nasty old homeless guy? Especially since you used to be the ring leader in talking about him. Maybe the choking cut off some vital oxygen to your brain or something. Call the nurse again so we can ask her to run some scans.

Security enters the room. Instead of sending in one guard; the nurse sent two. Chasity's doctor also rushes into the room to see what all the commotion is about.
Chasity: Hey. Please escort these vultures from my room.

At this, the now angered pack has begun gathering their purses to leave.

The next day, Chasity is released to go home. Throughout the night, she'd thought about the bravery of the homeless guy. She'd forgotten to get his name. The police had taken a report from her the previous day, but she'd forgotten to ask for his name.

Leaving the hospital, she turned her cell phone on and was infuriated by the text messages she'd gotten from her so-called friends. She'd never really paid attention to how ignorant they were. Her mother wanted her to come and stay at her house for a couple of weeks, but Chasity wanted to get back to her apartment so that she could study for the upcoming exam.

When she arrived home, the lady from across the street came over. She'd heard about the attack on Chasity and wanted to offer her support. Chasity smiled as she came over, knowing that this was her ticket to getting the homeless man's name.

The woman introduced herself as Tara. She began to minister to Chasity and spoke of the goodness of the LORD. She smiled as she rejoiced over the fact that Chasity had been spared and Chasity could not seem to get past this glow about the woman. She seemed almost radiant. After Tara finished talking, Chasity asked her about the homeless man.

Chasity: Thank you so much for your kind words. I can only cry when I think about how great GOD has been to me when I haven't deserved even a second of HIS mercies. I can truly say that I know GOD is with and in you. Before this incident, I'd become this monster. I was driven to be a doctor, and my identity was wrapped up in my soon to be title and my associations. I got around the wrong people, did the wrong things and now everything is so clear to me. The guy who saved me, I am ashamed to say how bad I'd treated him in the past. And he came, like an Angel in disguise, and saved my life. I want to say thank you to him, but I don't know his name.
(*Tara smiles.*)

Tara: His name is Pastor Fred Ponderosa.
Chasity: Pastor?
Tara: Yeah, well, I still call him pastor. He used to have church services at that abandoned building where your attack occurred. The landlord saw how the church had grown and kept demanding more and more money. Pastor Fred had put up all of his life savings trying to keep that church, but he wound up losing everything seven years ago. We tried to urge him to rent another building, but he always said that this was the building he was called to; so he refused to let go of the idea of renting another one. He lost his home and his family as a result. His wife wanted him to work at a factory nearby and he did at first. But, after paying the bills around the house, he kept storing up the rest of his check, pawning away for that building. She got tired of him, put him out, divorced him and then sold the house. She moved back to Alaska with their daughter, but he stayed behind; living wherever he could live. He does odd jobs for just about everyone around town. But, he's still storing up money to get that building. I just admire his drive. And he is a powerful man of GOD. I ask him to come this way often so I can feed him and be fed wisdom by him.
Chasity: I didn't know. Wow. I didn't know.
Tara: Don't cry for him now. Seems that him helping you has generated him a lot of public support. One guy that worked for a local news station came out to talk to him about the incident yesterday.
Tara laughs.
Tara: At first, he was shooing the guy away, but he decided to talk to him, so he could see how you were doing. The interview was aired early today and some guy who saw it decided to start a fund for him and the last time I checked, they have generated more than $200,000 for him! You see, what happened to you was set in motion by the Devil to kill you, but GOD had another plan. HE allowed this to happen so that you could come back to HIM,

and HE set the good pastor up for a blessing as well.

After they finished the discussion, Chasity retreated to her apartment to cry and just talk with the LORD. She repented and asked the LORD to bless Pastor Fred, wherever he was. She also decided to call her estranged dad, whom she hadn't talked to in more than three years. They'd had a disagreement about a boy Chasity was dating and her dad had let it slip that he didn't want Chasity to end up making the same mistake he'd made. Anger turned into hurt as Chasity came to the realization that she was the mistake that her father was referring to.
For years, her dad, Joseph Bridgewater, tried to get in touch with her, but to no avail. She now wanted to make amends and forgive him.

Joseph Bridgewater is the founder of Bridgewater Construction; a multi-million dollar construction company located in New York, New York. Chasity had tried to disassociate herself from her dad so that she could prove that she could live without him and his money.
She called her mother and got his number. Her mother was so happy that she'd asked for it. She'd wanted her to reconcile with her dad for years now.
She called the number, but there was no answer. She left a message and decided to clean up her house and take a nap.

Later that day, there was a knock at the door. Who could this be? Hopefully not one of the old friends that she was trying to rid her life of. Chasity's friends never knew that her dad was "Big Joe" Bridgewater. This was one secret that she'd decided to keep so that she could develop her own independent identity. Plus, she didn't want anyone getting any ideas and telling him where she was.

Groggy, she walked to the door, murmuring, “Who is it?” But, she got no answer. She looked out of the peephole and there were three characters standing there. One had his whole body turned around, and the other two were looking at the door. The only one she recognized was Tara from across the street. She opened the door and the man who'd been facing the street turned around. It was her dad. She hugged him and let out a flood of tears. She hadn't realized that she'd missed him so much. He cried as he held his firstborn daughter in his arms yet again; apologizing again and again for running her out of his life. For five minutes, Chasity stood there crying and holding her dad before she consciously realized that two other people were standing there. Tara and some guy who looked strangely familiar smiled and cried as the scene unfolded. The other guy looked familiar. His white hair and well maintained beard made her think that he was some tycoon from New York that had traveled with her dad. But, he looked too familiar. Tara introduced him as Pastor Fred, the man that had rescued her from the hands of a serial killer. Chasity asked no questions, but hugged him as hard as she'd hugged her dad. She felt, in a sense, like he was a long-lost Uncle, and it felt good to wrap her arms around him. She cried and thanked him again and again until he finally belched out, “I can't breathe.” They laughed and went into Chasity's apartment to talk.

During the discussion, Chasity learned that her dad had found her when her mother called him to tell him about the attack on Chasity. Her mother wanted to tell her dad where she was all along, but feared Chasity would disassociate from her if she did. So she would always encourage Chasity's dad to let her calm down and reach out to him. When he found out about the attack, he'd searched the Internet and found a story that had been put up a couple of hours after the attack. He decided to get a plane ticket and come down to see his daughter and to bless the man who saved her life. When he landed, the first thing he did was to locate the man who owned the abandoned church. It turns out, he'd been arrested for embezzling money from a company that he'd worked for and was in dire need of cash for a decent attorney. So, he'd taken the price of the church under market value to get up this money. At this point, he didn't want to rent the building anymore; he wanted to sell it and Mr. Bridgewater purchased it from him. He'd also found Mr. Ponderosa trying to hide from the swarm of paparazzi that was looking for him. He was hiding in the store near Chasity's house. The storekeeper had loaned him some clothes and was letting him sit at the back of the store, out of the window's view. Mr. Bridgewater, by chance, had went into that same store to ask the direction to Chasity Bridgewater's house. When the homeless man heard him asking about Chasity; he came out the back wanting to know why he wanted her address. Mr. Bridgewater immediately recognized him from the Internet story and told him who he was. It took a while for Mr. Ponderosa to believe him, but a call from the store owner to Chasity's mom cleared up the issue.

Mr. Bridgewater thanked Fred for saving his daughter's life and handed him the deed to the church, along with a check for five million dollars. At first, a teary-eyed Fred would not accept it. He was a man of GOD, but he was stubborn. But, Mr. Bridgewater took him out to eat and explained to him why he HAD to take the money.

Mr. Bridgewater: I heard about your story. I know that you want to earn every dollar to buy that building, but often times, our blessings don't come from the direction that we thought they'd come from. This is to glorify the LORD. Mr. Ponderosa, I haven't seen my daughter in three years. She got mad at me some years ago because of something foolish I'd said. I have waited and waited to see her again, hold her again and that opportunity was almost ripped from me. I bless GOD that you did what you did. Now I can hold her again and I am so thankful to GOD that you did what you did. And if you do not take this deed and this check, I will not go back to New York; but I will stay on the streets with you until you take it. I'll erect my cardboard box right next to yours and sing lullabies in the wee hours of the night. *(Mr. Bridgewater was a business man and he knew how to sell someone. He was as stubborn as stubborn gets.)*

After lunch, Mr. Bridgewater took Mr. Ponderosa on a shopping spree, took him to get a haircut and took him by his hotel room so that he could clean himself up. "I want you there with me when I go to see my daughter," he'd told Mr. Ponderosa.

Explanation:

The lesson here is this. Sometimes we get lost in who we want to be, and we never arrive at who we are to be. Fred Ponderosa never lost sight of the LORD, and all that fell away from him during his transition was not to come with him to the next level. He was being prepared for greater and to the world, he looked like he was at his worst. However, Chasity lost sight of GOD and began to focus on vain things. It took an almost fatal event to wake her up.

Sometimes, who we really are will cost us all that we have. Not because the LORD wants to break us down, but because the LORD will remove everything and everyone who supports the person we'd become. Why? Because those things and those people cannot embrace who we are. Be yourself with your friends. Talk about the LORD and try to serve HIM wholly and you will see the amount of friends that you have around you will quickly begin to disintegrate because people love the character that you present, but who we are in GOD is rarely welcomed. Many events come together looking like tragedy, but wound up being a set up for greatness.

You can't get far enough in GOD. But, you should try to go as far as you can in HIM, in this lifetime. The further you go, the more you will discover about HIM and the more HE will reveal to you about your true identity. After all, HE built you, so HE knows what parts of you are being fed and what parts are being starved. HE knows what fuel would power you and what fuel would destroy you. HE knows what you need to operate at your maximum potential, and HE knows what takes you to your lowest place. HE is your Creator, and you are HIS creation. But, when you walk away from HIM, you walk away not knowing who you are and what you need. So, you emulate others. You fuel up on whatever is fueling them. You try to become anything or anyone who fascinates your 'right now' way of thinking because the brain is designed to ask questions and require immediate answers. When we do not get the answers that we need, we accept anything that makes sense to us so that we can pacify the mind and move on. Problem is, we start to get filled up with lies and misconceptions, and we get further away from who we are and this is when peace eludes us. You are and you were created to worship HIM. You were created to serve HIM. But, Satan will take you on a strange path that leads away from GOD, but promises to answer your questions as you get further away from HIM. GOD created you, and it is only HIM that could power you up on the fuel that is HIS WORD. Without HIM, you wound up trying to power up on drugs, alcohol, sex and whatever comes in and introduces itself as your god.

The sad part is, many go into HIM and find a resting place, refusing to go further into the knowledge of GOD to learn more about HIM. There is so much to you that you do not know, but it is found in HIM. There is so much to HIM that you do not know or understand, but the answers are found in HIM. The more you discover, the more joy you will find in you because peace is not found in this world. Peace is being in alignment with the WORD of GOD. Peace is resting in HIM and knowing who you are. Chaos is living anywhere else.

Accepted Rejection (The Change That Changed Everything)

"It is better for you if man rejects the GOD in you than to be accepted by man with the Devil in you."

When you're wrong, you're accepted. When you're right, you're rejected. Most of us have experienced this truth firsthand, and it can be a hard pill to swallow in the beginning. In the world, we came to accept that everyone would not like us. We came to understand that envy is ruler over many. And many of us changed who we were to fit into the group that we felt we belonged to. They accepted the character you portrayed yourself to be when you rejected who you really were. And then, there was a change in you. The LORD'S hand was upon you, and you could no longer deny who you were. So, you came into the 'Christian' fold and were immediately accepted, for a minute or so. But, you were trying to be 'too' holy for most. In a world where holiness is unacceptable to many, those that try to live a life of holiness often find themselves rejected and alone. People love to quote scriptures and play church, but when they come face to face with someone who radiates holiness, they get offended and convicted. So, maybe...just maybe, you put on another mask, one like theirs. The one you'd go to church wearing, where you'd cut up in the building and then invite the crew over for a barbeque later that day. Everyone would show up and you'd all sit in the backyard, drinking beer and talking about Sister Beulah's wig falling off and how Deacon Macabre carefully kneels down before prayer as not to hurt his 'bad' knee. You'd blast your secular music as your children would get up and show off their seductive dance moves. For many, it is all fun and games playing fake church until they got some real issues.

Lukewarm Christians are of the religious Sadducee and Pharisee spirit. They rejected CHRIST, yet they came to church (building.) They rejected the ONE who sent CHRIST, yet they held religious feasts in HIS Name. And here you are sitting amongst them, still trying to be accepted; not understanding that acceptance by man is rejection by GOD. They wanted to kill the CHRIST because HE is holy, and now they want to destroy anyone who comes nears them walking a holy walk.

There are many who have this story. Many who live a life where they say they love the LORD, come to the building and religiously worship HIM, but their hearts are far from HIM. They love their worldliness and when someone comes and rebukes their ways, whether it's directly (through speaking with them) or indirectly (through living right), they become offended. Unbeknownst to them, their offense is not at you; it's at HE who is in you!

But, if you are of the small percentage who have truly sacrificed the things of the world to embrace the things of GOD, please know that you are not alone, but more importantly GOD is with you.

“Girl, did you see how Elder Banks cut up on Sunday? He fell out and then peeked with one of his eyes! It was a mess!”

Laughter erupted as Tina spoke with her friends late one Sunday

evening. This was a common gathering. They would always come together to eat pizza, fry fish or barbeque and gossip about the church members and leaders. They were all on the ministry helps team, some of them singing in the choir, some of them ushering and some of them ordained ministers.
Tina and her crew are very common church-goers. They know every hip hop song, every rock/roll song, every R&B song and every pop song out. They know how to shake their derrieres all over the front lawn and in the clubs and then, they could do their foot-loose dance all around the church when the piano player would get "happy." They even knew a few scriptures. Get in their car and you'll find the gospel CDs mixed with the secular CDs. Because they are mixed up. They haven't quite decided who they want to serve.

Traci, on the other hand is a young woman of GOD who has been going to that same church for a little over a year. And they just don't like her. Period. Originally, they'd tried to bring Traci into the 'crew,' but one by one, they discovered that not only did Traci not listen to secular music; but Traci didn't like gossip, she didn't backbite, and she loved and feared the LORD with everything in her. So, Traci was no longer invited to the barbeques, fish fries and cookouts. But, that was good because she had a mission there and she was determined to carry it out before leaving.

Traci watched as the 'well-off' members would sit at the front of the church every Sunday in the same place, even though there was no assigned seating. She observed that the leader seemed to take more of an interest in the members who tithed the most and ignore the members who she felt were nobodies. But, she had a mission and in this season, she was called to observe and be quiet.

Traci was perceived as a 'nobody.' Because she was poor and with that being a small town and a small church, it was no secret.

So, every Sunday, she would come in and slip under the radar, rarely being noticed unless someone from the gossip crew chose her to be that day's gossip buffet. Her Pastor, Rita knew of the things going on, but she said nothing because she wrestled with gossip. She loved to hear the latest news from the 'crew' and would use them to do her errands. It was like they did nothing wrong. And she didn't care much for Traci, either. But, she came to the church, so what could she do?

One day, Pastor Rita's son was arrested for shoplifting and the news spread like wildfire. The 'crew' had it, and it was one of the juiciest stories of the season. They loved the taste of fresh blood. Especially the blood of the son of their dear pastor! And he was caught stealing lip gloss?! They couldn't wait until Sunday for their meeting. They arranged the meeting on Friday night; each one bringing a dish and preparing themselves for the gossip fest. Tina came in ready, stating that she didn't wear too much makeup because she knew that she'd cry it off while laughing. They turned on the news to see more of the story, since there were details that were not revealed yet. While watching, they discovered that he'd attacked a male security officer after the officer tried to apprehend him and that his mother, Pastor Rita happened to be there with him. According to the news, Rita Longhorne had tried to help her son fight off the guard. Both were subdued and arrested by two off duty police officers who happened to be in the mall at that time. Their photos flashed on the screen, with more of the focus being put on the fact that Rita was a pastor.

This was THE story of the year. They laughed and talked about what had happened and what probably led to his arrest. They even joked about what they believed their dear ole pastor said as she was being arrested.

Back at the church, some of the ministry helps team came together to clean out the building. While all of this was happening, they found out that Pastor Rita had not been paying the church building's rent. So, they had less than a week to evacuate the building. But, who was going to teach on Sunday? They discussed this, but no one could come up with an answer. They decided to call around to some local pastors to see if anyone would fill in, but no one would. This was going to be their last service, and they didn't want to just not show up. After all, many of them were paid, not much, but a little cash for their help.

Sunday came and everyone was early coming to church. Including the people who were on the 'sick and shut in' list and the people who rarely showed up came for this big event. They'd seen the news and wanted to have their front row seats to Pastor Rita's speech. But, of course, Pastor Rita didn't show up. Even though her boyfriend had bailed her out on Friday, she decided that it was too embarrassing to show up. After all, she'd feasted on the news about everyone else, so she knew the church would be swarming with hungry gossipers looking to be fed the latest in Christian entertainment. This was the last Sunday that church would be open anyway, so she sat it out at home and watched television.

Back at the building, the choir proceeded to sing, as they usually did. Deacon Macabre got up and prayed as he always did and Mrs. Swinson got up and read the announcements as usual. She didn't have to read the 'sick and shut in' list since everyone was there, except one member who was in a coma. She jokingly thought to herself how surprised she was that this member did not wake up from the coma to come to this show. Someone obviously hadn't told her what happened.

After the announcements were read, the church went quiet.

Everyone looked around to see who would be preaching on today. They thought maybe Pastor Rita would send someone in her place, but five minutes of silence, and then the doors opened and in comes Traci and three men and two women whom they'd never seen before. Traci's not wearing the usual attire, but she was wearing the robe of a leader. With a key in her hand, she locked the door. Everyone's eyes followed her as she went to every single window and closed the windows. They wondered what she was doing as she went and turned the air conditioner's temperature so low that the air felt like ice as it blew from the vents.
Finally, she went up to the podium and began to bless the Name of the LORD. Everyone was confused, astonished and could not understand what was going on.

Traci: You're probably wondering why I locked the doors, right? Why did I locked the doors? Why did I turn down the air conditioner? Because it's about to get really hot up in here. The Fire of GOD is about to come through this place and no devil will escape!

Traci began to give a sermon, and the people were astonished at the wisdom that was in her. She'd been so quiet all this time, who knew? Who knew that she was an ordained pastor who'd been sent there to rescue the ones who wanted rescue and to warn the others? Who knew a sharp sword was in her mouth?

As she began to teach, a scream was heard roaring out from the back of the church. Everyone's eyes turned to watch as one of the crew-members fell down and began to convulse. As Traci approached her, she kept screaming in fear. And when Traci laid lands on her, she convulsed and screamed loudly before passing out. This continued throughout the church. Devils were put to flight and people were set free. Tina, the ring leader (one of the principal demon hosts or principality hosts) tried to run to the door. There was something different about her. She looked like she was growling. Her friends did not recognize her anymore. But, Traci went after her asking her if she wanted to be set free. One moment she would shake her head as if to say "no," but she whenever she could muscle out a word, she would say "yes." Tina was set free this day and everyone was warned. When a demon goes out, it always tries to come back and if it were permitted, it would bring seven demons more evil than itself.

Explanation:

Again, it is better for you if people reject the GOD in you than if they accept the devil in you. Holiness is required for you to enter Heaven. It is more dangerous to be a hypocrite and pretend to be GOD'S servant, all the while being a slave to sin than it is to be a sinner who isn't ashamed of what they are. We won't always be accepted, but that's okay. Being rejected is a blessed place! A lot of people don't realize the significance of rejection. You and I are never rejected. It is the GOD in us that people want no part of. Yes, even religious people. Because living religiously and living holy are two different lifestyles! The Pharisees and Sadducees lived religiously, but GOD says ***"Be ye holy, for I am holy." (1 Peter 1:16)***

When we walk in holiness, we are rarely accepted. If you ever want to see who your real friends are, live holy. In this, you will see people begin to disassociate themselves from you. Many of them will think that you are trying too hard to be holy, while others may think that you've got the devil in you because you are different than what they are accustomed to seeing. People don't understand that holiness is peculiarity (a state of being like GOD), not familiarity (a state of being common; unlike GOD.)

You will find that a lot of people (even in leadership) strive to know what the Bible says, but don't put much effort into doing what the Bible says. People often believe that they can sin freely, as long as they go to church, and as long as they pray. This simply means that they truly do not know the heart of GOD. They know HIS Name and they may even know scriptures, but that's it.

Traci was living a life of holiness, so she was shunned. Beware when the crowds accept you! Because, in holiness, you will find yourself in the less than popular crowd.

The choice is yours. Give up the world and get into GOD and be accepted by HIM or stay with the world and their justifications and deny GOD and be rejected on that Great and Awful Day of Judgment. Choose wisely; your eternity is depending on it.

Paired Up....Singled Out

"Two can't sit on a throne that GOD has built for one."

One of the syndromes that have been hitting young Christian women is what I like to refer to as BFF syndrome. Don't get me wrong; it's okay to have a friend, as long as they are in CHRIST and the relationship is called together by GOD.

Take a look at your fingers and pick up the mouse from your computer. Notice how your fingers work together, but they all grab the mouse in different places?
Well, that's how we are in the BODY of CHRIST. Every last member of the BODY has a function, and all of these functions work together for the good of the BODY. Now, take that same hand and try to pick up something heavy. Notice how the heavier the object is, the closer the fingers come together to grab it? We are to be the same. When our sisters and brothers are carrying something that is too heavy for them, we come together and lift it up to JESUS. We are not to be singled out and paired up to create a separate body, but we operate as one for a collective purpose.
Nevertheless, a lot of women are pairing up; focusing more on being a BFF than being in purpose, on purpose for CHRIST.

You have to understand how Satan works. He will single you out, pair you up and hinder you from walking the path that GOD

created for you to walk. That path is narrow, but the path to destruction is wide. That's because we have to answer individually for what we did or did not do. Like fingers, we work together to perform a function for the BODY. We ball up our faith as a big fist and give a two and three-fold cord blow to the enemy when we are challenged. We help one another when something feels too heavy for us to carry, and we just try to be a help and a blessing to one another.
But, the devil has singled many out to pair them up so that their focus is on being a 'friend' and not a 'daughter.'

Again, this isn't against friends and friendships when they have been called by the LORD. This is to tell you to be careful when someone is trying to pair up with you. Often times, the enemy has singled you out to pair you up and drain you of your purpose.

"We're about to go and make this money!" The voice came from a green Nissan parked in front of Tonia's house. The neighbors all knew this green car. It was always at Tonia's house and it belonged to her best friend, Beatrice. Tonia was getting into the passenger's door, dressed to impress, obviously heading out to their next big idea. They'd tried to start a daycare together and that didn't work out. They'd sold insurance at one time, but that didn't work. They'd even started selling plate lunches together in an attempt to start their own restaurant, but that went nowhere. Beatrice always seemed to be the more driven one. She was always pepped up about the newest idea that seemed to promise them a big future.

Widowed neighbor, Ms. Samantha looked out of her window and shook her head as she watched Tonia load into the car with

Beatrice yet again on another get rich quick scheme. She knew that Tonia was a work in progress. Tonia loved the LORD and wanted more of HIM, but Beatrice was self-centered and simply wanted to be rich, and she would use whomever she could to help her reach her goals. To Beatrice, it wasn't about the partnership. It was a strategy. Because Tonia was not only smart, but Tonia was gifted. She had so many talents! Beatrice had one talent, and that was making her face look grossly distorted. But, no one was going to pay for that. And she'd went to college for business management, so Tonia felt like she'd be able to handle the back-end of the company.

Beatrice always seemed to know someone. She was always calling around and doing much of the leg work, while Tonia just went along. In a way, it was like Beatrice was Tonia's agent; but in reality, she was trying to sell herself. Tonia was the idea girl. She'd come up with some amazing ideas and research what needed to be done to put her ideas into motion.

One Friday morning, one of Beatrice's friends (Raven) contacted her about joining this new business opportunity that she wanted to try. She was very excited about the idea and knew some people who swore by this company. They would be independent agents selling computers to large organizations. These computers were a new brand of computer, manufactured by a small company out of Korea. Raven invited Beatrice on a business call and from that initial call, Beatrice was sold! You could come in as an individual which would cost you $1,000 or you could come into the business with a partner and of course, it would cost you $500 each. So, Raven and Beatrice opted to come in as partners.
Beatrice's new business with Tonia, however, seemed to be going nowhere. They were now selling gift baskets and trying to get

them listed in some of the local and large stores.

When Beatrice didn't call her or come into their newly rented space, Tonia tried reaching her, but to no avail. A couple of days went by and no Beatrice. Finally, that Wednesday, Beatrice sent a text message to Tonia notifying her that she would no longer be a part of the company and that she'd got involved in another gig. Tonia called and called her, but she wouldn't answer her phone nor did she return Tonia's calls.

Sullen and angry, Tonia tried to figure out what to do with the company. They'd only had it one month and Beatrice had bailed on her already. Thankfully, the building was rented in Tonia's name and the business was registered to Tonia only; so she decided to change the company from being just a basket company and let it be a mini mall. The building had 80,000 square foot, more space than what she needed. She called the landlord and asked if she could rent out booths in the building and he happily agreed. And it was located in a busy part of town.

Tonia placed an ad in the newspaper seeking individuals who would want to rent out space and it wasn't long before she got her first call; then a second; then a third. Before the month was out, she'd rented out all of the booth space and was already projecting a profit from that. She'd made sure that everyone knew she was changing the place into a woman's mall/ sanctuary. So, the only people allowed to lease space had to have something that would benefit women.

The new space contained a spa, a gift basket center full of soaps and body washes, a gym, clothing and jewelry stores, restaurants, a bride center, cosmetic center and salons. Tonia's business thrived and when Beatrice saw the front page article about Tonia's success, she tried to call and patch things up; citing that she'd found the LORD. But, of course, this didn't work.

Without Beatrice, Tonia's business began to boom. You see, Beatrice was all about herself and her success. She'd attached to Tonia because she saw that Tonia was gifted, but when opportunity presented itself outside of Tonia; she took it and dismissed Tonia from her life.

Is this your life? When talking about your walk, you will find that many women will say 'we.' What the LORD taught me was any and everyone trying to arrive in righteousness will take his/her or her own way without complaining or worry. But, those with motives or alternate destinations tend to pair up to try to get there and they love the word "we." You can't get me in Heaven, and I can't get you in Heaven. You can want to have friends; that's normal. But, pray and ask the LORD to send wise people in your life who understand that your journey begins here, and theirs begins there. An immature Christian will always try to pair up because they have singled you out as their footstool.

This is very common amongst women and rarely rebuked behavior because we don't want to offend one another or turn away a woman who is obviously trying to befriend us. However, there comes a time in your walk that you will mature (if you're not already there) and understand that when GOD called your name and said, "Come here," HE did not ask you to bring a friend.

WISE HER STILL

One of my favorite stories in the Bible is the story of how Abraham separated from Lot. I love that Abraham was wise enough to separate (in body) from Lot, but still came to Lot's rescue when Lot was taken into captivity. Not to mention, Abraham interceded for Sodom because he knew his brother was there and GOD sent Angels to get Lot and his family out of Sodom before HE destroyed it.

What this teaches is that we are still brothers and sisters in the LORD when and if we separate. It doesn't mean that you want nothing more to do with her or she wants nothing more to do with you. It simply means that your time walking together has ended and when you stay around in something that GOD has left, you are choosing to be her friend instead of HIS daughter. In doing so, not only will she hinder you, but you will hinder her as well.

Someone that is not walking with you is not necessarily marching against you. Often times, separation is needed so that we can complete our individual tasks in the LORD.

After the death of Solomon, his son Rehoboam became king over Judah. The Israelites came to Rehoboam and said that they would serve him if he lightened the work load and the yoke that his father had put on them. Rehoboam asked them to come back in a few days and he would have an answer for them. Initially, he'd consulted the wise men who'd advised his father Solomon for many years, but he took the advice of some unwise men over their advice. He reported to Israel that he would make their burdens heavier. As a result, Israel separated from Judah and refused to serve Rehoboam. Rehoboam wanted to go to war against Israel to try to bring them back under subjection. ***"When Rehoboam***

arrived in Jerusalem, he mustered the house of Judah and Benjamin—a hundred and eighty thousand fighting men—to make war against Israel and to regain the kingdom for Rehoboam.

But this word of the Lord came to Shemaiah the man of God: "Say to Rehoboam son of Solomon king of Judah and to all the Israelites in Judah and Benjamin, 'This is what the Lord says: Do not go up to fight against your brothers. Go home, every one of you, for this is my doing.'" So they obeyed the words of the Lord and turned back from marching against Jeroboam." (2 Chronicles 1:1-2)

As you can see, GOD caused them to separate and as a result, Rehoboam wanted to attack Israel. GOD told him not to attack his 'brothers and sisters,' and GOD informed him that the separation was from GOD. (Glory to GOD that Rehoboam was wise enough to listen.) When the time comes to walk in different directions, a lot of women tap into their emotions and become belligerent towards one another. This is why GOD called for the separation in the first place! Because an unholy dependency and expectation had begun to form, and the women went from serving the LORD to serving the terms of the friendship. They had begun to place yokes on one another! GOD wants us to love one another and be closer than brothers and sisters, nevertheless, you should never trade your place in HIM for a chance to serve someone's definition of what a friend is and what a friend does. Our walks take us onto different paths; and if we are in the LORD, walking in obedience, these paths all lead to GOD. You will find yourself meeting up along the way, with no love lost. In truth, some of the closest and best friends one can have are friends that can go weeks, months and even years not communicating and still come together as if they'd seen you just yesterday! Remember....not all separations are from the devil, and not all separations are evidence of contention. Sometimes,

GOD has to separate you so that HE can get your friend back on her path, and you on yours. But, anyone who refuses to go their own way, where GOD has called them, is someone who has chosen to come outside of purpose and redefine their lives and their friend's lives. This is a very dangerous person to be around because their purpose now involves you, and the only way that you can fulfill their requirements is to be absent from your purpose as well.

Think about it this way. When two women are single and the best of friends, they often spend a lot of time together. This is because they are single! But, when one is found by her husband, she spends her time with him and does not have time to hang out nearly as much with her friend anymore. And what usually happens is, the friend who has not been found, becomes angry with her now married ex-best friend. She wants her to ration out her time between her new husband and her. But, the newlywed has to serve as a wife and prepare for her role as a mother. And yes...many times, the newly married woman wants to continue the friendship, but now the terms have to be redefined because she has a newer and more important role in life. In most of these cases, the friendship is lost forever because the unmarried friend feels betrayed. *(Please note that if the unmarried friend had been found first by her husband...chances are, she would have done the same thing! But, she won't tell you that.)* This painful contending would not have happened if they hadn't tried to redefine themselves and their roles toward one another. The best thing that you could do is to consider the most important roles that you intend to serve one day. If you intend to become a wife and a mother, then understand that hanging out with 'her' everyday isn't a good idea. Because, when the time comes for you to fill your new roles, chances are, she won't understand if she has never had these roles. But, if you go about everyday serving your most important role as a child of GOD, you will learn how to define the friendships in your life so that they won't become yokes around your neck or your friends' necks. And the women who walk around with yokes in their hands, looking for someone to wear them will always separate themselves from you quickly when they find that you aren't willing to wear them.

Driver....Let Me Out Here

"Everyone you meet has somewhere they are trying to get to. You're either their driver, their stolen vehicle, or their passenger."

Everyone....Yes, everyone that you meet has a destination plugged into their hearts. People who love the LORD are focused on HIM and arriving in the perfect knowledge of HIM. People who are focused on people are the most dangerous because their final destination is wrapped up in a piece of meat. But, most people are focused on arriving at a place of success; some want fame, and others want to just be comfortable. This is the perversion of the world. Because, in reality, if your destination isn't to arrive at the unveiling of the MOST HIGH GOD, you're going to find yourself jumping from this vehicle to that vehicle trying to arrive in places that do not exist outside of HIM. And then, there are the ones who desire to arrive in Heaven. This isn't right because...well, think of it this way: Would you want someone to do everything they could to make you happy, so they can come and live in your house? But, it's not love that drives them to do right by you; it's because you have that big pretty house that they want. They are trying to use you to get to what you have. GOD said, "If you love ME, keep MY commandments." Not, if you love HIS house.

I was like most people. I wanted to arrive in Heaven and avoid all turns to hell. So, I tried to live right, but the more I got to know the FATHER personally, the more I want to please HIM. Heaven is just the bonus.

Everyone you meet; even your family, has somewhere they are trying to get to. This is called a motive. And when they are not trying to arrive at that divine place in GOD, their destination has been perverted, and they will, without question, use whomever they can to get there. You may say, "Well, she's a user! She likes to use people!" But, what you have to understand is that people are never one thing with you that they aren't with GOD. In other words, they tried to use the FATHER first; you just stepped in and thought that because you were trying to be genuine with them, that they would automatically be genuine with you. And when you saw that after all you did, they still misused you, betrayed you, talked about you and tried to bring you down; you were hurt. But, this pain isn't justifiable. If it were, wouldn't that mean that we could expect people to be better friends to us than they are sons and daughters to GOD? Again, people are never better with you than they are with GOD, that's why you have to pray and ask HIM if they are ALLOWED in your life by HIM, or if they are PROHIBITED from going anywhere near your heart.

GOD made you where people can arrive at certain points in you, but wisdom is like a security guard. It'll let you know when they've come far enough. But, when you disregard GOD and think that you can be better to them than HE is to them, consequentially changing them, you are sadly mistaken. HE is LORD. Whether it's a man who wants to get with you or friendly individual who wants to get close to you and label themselves as a friend, you need to check with FATHER GOD to see if HE is giving them clearance, or if you're doing it according to your understanding.

In the example below, I will tell a story of betrayal from both ends so that you can get a better view of the subject.

Valerie was very adamant about being fit. Her family had a history of heart disease, and being from the South; Valerie knew that a lot of the food she grew up eating was not good for her. So, when she moved to Michigan, she changed the way that she ate and began exercising everyday. Valerie was jogging when she met Larry. Larry saw this beautiful woman running by, and he'd seen her many times on that stretch of highway. So, one Monday morning, he decided to put on his workout gear and jog down that stretch of road so that he could run into Valerie. But, she was late that day, and he wound up jogging an extra 30 minutes, before she finally showed up. When she arrived, she was wearing a white t-shirt, pink stretch pants and pink and white tennis shoes. Larry watched her as she stretched; thinking about how pretty she was.

Like most men, Larry wasn't looking at her to see whether she was his future wife or not. He just saw a pretty woman and wanted to get to know her better. Like most men, he wanted to see where she would fit in his life.

While Valerie was jogging, Larry began to jog beside her. He kept staring at her and jogging along side her, which made her uncomfortable. "I have pepper spray," she said to him before attempting to jog faster. Larry responded, "That would hurt me and it would temporarily blind me. But, at least the last thing I would have seen was your beautiful face." Valerie laughed. As corny as his line was, he was cute, and he looked harmless. I mean, really cute. He was a firefighter, and he looked like a pin up for a firefighter.

They jogged together and stopped at a nearby park to fuel up on some water and chat a little. Valerie was a nice girl. She'd give her number to almost anyone who asked. Not because she wanted to be with them, but because, like Larry, she wanted to see where people fit in her life. She wasn't thinking 'relationship' per-Se, but she's not one to pass up an opportunity.

To top it off, Valerie is Christian. Saved and sanctified! And after talking to Larry, she found out that Larry goes to church sometimes as well. *(Pay attention to what I just said.)*

Months go by and Valerie and Larry are now an item and the relationship is heating up fast. He'd even been to church with her a few times and he was really into public affection. He wanted everyone to see that this beautiful woman was his woman. Six months after the relationship began, Valerie thought it was okay to sleep with Larry. Well, he said he was going to marry her. Isn't that how a lot of women see it? They'd talked about marriage and kids and it just seemed right, so they decided to move in together. He's handsome, a working man and he goes to church....*sometimes*! Plus, he'd told Valerie that a nice Christian woman like him could help him to change and get closer to the LORD. *Sound familiar?*

Valerie worked as a software engineer at a local company, and she earned a pretty decent salary. New associate Nancy took an instant liking to Valerie. Valerie seemed to have it all together, and Nancy felt like they had kindred spirits. So, she'd asked Valerie to lunch with her a few times, and they hit it off well. A few months later, Valerie and Nancy were friends. A year later, they were telling everyone that they were best friends. Nancy's boyfriend Pablo was a little rough around the edges, but he was friendly. Nancy would always try to get Valerie to push Pablo and Larry to be together, because she was hoping that some of Larry's ways would rub off on Pablo. But, Valerie was afraid that some of Pablo's ways would rub off on Larry, so she never did.

One June night, Nancy called Valerie, and she was crying hysterically. She just couldn't take Pablo's antics anymore and had ended the relationship. Pablo kicked her out of the apartment, and she was going to have to quit her job and move back to Texas to live with her family until she got on her feet. Well, Valerie, being the friend that she was, told her to come and live with her for a while. She had an extra bedroom, and Nancy was most welcome. And shortly thereafter, Nancy moved in.

Now, most of you are already saying that this is a no-no and you already know how it's going to end. But, there's a lesson behind it, so keep reading.

While living with Valerie, Nancy noticed that even though Valerie and Larry seemed to have the perfect relationship, they had one major problem. Valerie wanted to get married very soon, and Larry seemed to be agitated when she bought up the conversation. He grown to love the idea of just living together. Other than that, everything seemed to run smoothly in their home. Valerie would talk to Nancy about this sometimes and express the deep hurt she felt that Larry had wanted to marry her at one point, but now, refers to marriage as a piece of paper. He said their relationship was too good now, and he didn't want to ruin it.

The next day, Larry sat in the living room and the conversation started about the situation. Nancy initiated it, of course, to see where Larry's heart was. Valerie was in the shower getting ready for work.

Larry: At first, I wanted to get married, but it's like lately, the thought frightens me. I feel like Valerie and I have a good thing as it is now and I don't know why she wants to mess that up. One of my friends was with his girl seven years and they finally got married just last year. Now, they are going through a divorce. I don't want that.
Nancy: I completely understand, but Valerie loves you and you love her. I think that you two should get married. Whether you have the paper or not though, I can agree, love is love and if you're not ready, I wouldn't pressure you...if I were her.
Larry: Yeah. I keep thinking that the time will come when I'll be ready, but it's like the more and more we're together, the less I think about marriage. I don't want to go through a divorce. When I'm married, I want it to last and Valerie doesn't understand that.
Nancy: Yeah, at first I wanted to marry Pablo, but what changed my mind was seeing how you were with Valerie. He kept pressuring me to marry him as well, but after a year or so with Pablo, I just couldn't imagine being his wife. I guess it's because Pablo couldn't see past getting his next tattoo. That's all he talked about. For me, just to live like you guys lived, would have been sufficient; even without a ring. But, I know that the time will come one day when I can have a decent boyfriend.

Valerie came out of the shower and walked into the living room where the two were sitting. She didn't know what they'd been talking about, but she wanted to strike up the conversation about marriage in the presence of Nancy since when they'd talked in private, Nancy agreed with her.
Valerie: Nancy, I want your take on a matter.

Larry sighs. He knows what's coming.
Valerie: If you love a man and he loves you, would you hesitate to marry him? I mean, like if you two have been together for three years and the relationship has been almost perfect, wouldn't you want to marry him?
Larry: Now is not the time, Val.
Valerie: Hold on; let her speak.
Nancy: I would, but I wouldn't put pressure on him because I would want the feeling to be mutual.
Larry: Thank you!

Valerie is astonished. In the private conversations, Nancy had egged her on, but now, she can empathize with Larry? No time to think about it. Valerie and Nancy had to get off to work. Usually, they rode together in Valerie's car to save gas, but lately Nancy had been taking her own car, saying that she needed to go house hunting on her lunch breaks.

Two weeks later, it was a rainy day and Valerie arrived home before Nancy. Larry was off work and Valerie went to the fridge to look for some carrot sticks to snack on, but there were no more carrots.
Valerie: Did you eat all the carrots, Larry?
Larry: You know I don't eat rabbit food.
Valerie: Well, the carrots were here when Nancy and I left to go to work today. How did they leave?
Larry: I think that's what Nancy was eating on her lunch break.
Valerie: Lunch break? She came here?
Larry: Yeah, she always comes here on her lunch break. I thought that was strange because when you'd take your break, you wouldn't come here, but she always came.
Valerie: What?

Larry: I'm not understanding your question.
Valerie: No, I'm just thinking. She never told me that she came here on her breaks. She said she was going house hunting.
Larry: Well, she told me the same thing, but she'd spend most of her breaks here that I know of. When I'm off, I always see her. She would leave a little early though, so I figured she was stopping in to get something to eat and then looking at houses for the remainder of her break. Maybe she looks at houses from the Internet, checks them out on her break and then heads back to work.
Valerie: Yeah; maybe.

Valerie dismissed the incident and she and Larry went out for their daily jog.

One day, Nancy wasn't feeling too well, so she called in to work. Valerie had spent the day before nursing her and wanted her friend to get better. Nancy said she was suffering from cramps and a stomachache, so Valerie naturally assumed that Nancy had her monthly visitor. Valerie went to work and on her break, she called home to check on Nancy. Larry answered the phone. Puzzled, she asked Larry why he was home. "I'm off on today. Remember? It's Wednesday." Valerie replied, "That's right. Where's Nancy? Is she feeling better?" Valerie was concerned. "She's right here. Hold on...," he answered. Nancy got the phone and sounded horrible. "Hello?" When asked if she was feeling better, she assured Valerie that she was getting better, but needed to go and lay down some more.

After they hung up, Valerie went back to work. Two hours later, something struck her. Wait a minute. Larry's off today and Nancy knew he'd be off because he's always off on Wednesdays, and she conveniently gets sick Tuesday night? Something's not right about all this. Valerie hopes that it's all just paranoia, but she just could not shake the feeling, so she decided to leave work early and go home. If questioned, she planned to say that she left to make sure Nancy was okay.

Valerie pulled into her driveway. Her heart was racing as she anticipated looking like an insecure woman coming home so early, since this was not in her character. Valerie would go to work on her sickest days, so she knew how she'd appear, but she'd rather look insecure than to have those thoughts. When she entered the house, the first thing she noticed was that Larry's shirt was on the couch, and he was nowhere in sight. His pick up truck was in the driveway, however. She went to Nancy's room, which was downstairs in the basement, but there was no Nancy there. Her stomach churned as she quietly tip toed up the stairs. She noticed that the bedroom door was closed, and she didn't want to alarm them by knocking on the door, so she stopped by the other bedroom upstairs and took a wire hanger from the closet. She knew that her bedroom door could be easily unlocked by putting any wire through the hole on the doorknob. She nervously unwrapped the hanger, bringing the edge to an almost perfect straight line before heading to the door. She could hear what sounded like the television going and grunts, or maybe those grunting sounds were coming from the TV. She thought to herself how embarrassing it would be if Nancy was in the downstairs bathroom, which she hadn't checked. Thoughts aside, she put the wire hanger through the door and twisted the door knob slowly. What she saw took her somewhere she'd never been. Neither Larry nor Nancy heard her open the door because she'd opened it so quietly and the television's volume was turned up to the max. They'd turned the volume up, hoping to mask their sounds in case Valerie was to come home, but they did not consider that it would hide the sounds of Valerie coming into the house, going up the stairs and opening the door.

The rest of their clothes were on the floor, and they were in Larry and Valerie's bed having sex. Valerie stood there for a minute in shock. She couldn't move her feet or say a word. She just held onto the doorknob watching in horror. Suddenly, they were finished and Larry happened to look up and see Valerie standing there, obviously in shock. He threw Nancy off him and screamed, "Val!!! What...what are you doing here so early?! Baby...oh my...baby...please, let's talk. What have I done? Baby? Please speak to me. Baby?" Nancy fell to the floor; paralyzed in fear. She couldn't look at Valerie.

Collecting herself, Valerie began to head down the stairs. She didn't know how to feel. It hurt, but the full impact hadn't hit her yet. She was hurt enough; however, to head to the gun case. While unlocking it, she saw Nancy run past her and out of the front door, wearing nothing, but a bra and some shorts. Larry had come down to see if he could smooth things over. In all of his talking, Valerie couldn't understand one word he was saying. She was just standing there, loading the gun and feeling numb. At the last minute, Larry realized that running was essential to his survival. He ran out the door, just as Valerie shot in his direction. Still naked, he felt the full impact of the bullet as it grazed his arm, but he didn't care about that anymore. He just knew that he was running for his life.

Nancy had unwisely decided to hide behind some bushes, but when she saw Valerie standing there about turn in her direction, she took off.

This story ends with the police's arrival. Valerie didn't get a chance to shoot either of them. She was disarmed and taken into custody and Larry decided not to pursue charges in hopes that she would forgive and reconcile with him. Nancy didn't press charges or file a report either because she knew that Valerie knew some of the illegal things that she and Pablo had once done, including stealing over ten thousand dollars in an insurance scam. Of course, Valerie did not reconcile with Larry. Instead, she moved out of the home that her and Larry shared and eventually bought her another home. Nancy quit working for the software company the day she was caught with Larry. She just never showed up again. She was afraid that Valerie would bring a gun to work and finish what she'd started to do.

Months went by and then a year and Larry would always drive by and see Valerie out on the trail doing her daily workout. He'd always wondered how he let her get away and why he didn't marry her when he had the chance. Relationship behind relationship, he'd never found a woman as good as Valerie again. And if you're wondering about Nancy, Larry never pursued a relationship with Nancy; his destination was simply to have sex with her. Once he arrived there, he had no further use for her. It wasn't so easy for Nancy to let Larry go, however. She had been pursuing Valerie's life and wanted what Valerie had, so she stalked Larry for four and a half months; eventually setting his car on fire and causing him to lose his job. Ironically, he had been on duty when she set his car on fire, and he'd retaliated by setting her car on fire. Her stalking was cut short by a brief stint in the county jail and a restraining order. She later returned to Texas and reconciled with Pablo.

Two years later, Larry saw Valerie out on the trail again and he was about to get his nerve up to stop and talk to her, until he noticed a blinding glow that emitted from her left hand. "It couldn't be," he thought. Without warning, a man jogged up beside her and kissed her before they jogged off towards the sunrise.

Now, if you're like some, you wanted to see this story end with Nancy and Larry being tortured more than what they were, but that's not necessary. Or you may have wanted them both to get saved, but this doesn't always happen. We hope for it, but some people just love their evil.

Explanation:

What Valerie had to learn from the incident was that both Larry and Nancy had a point of interest that they wanted to arrive at when they met her. Larry was unsure of his. He wanted to see where the relationship would take him, and he would decide from there. But, because Valerie started acting like a wife before he married her, he lost interest in marrying her. Why would he? He'd reaped the benefits: having sex with her, living with her and sharing the bills with her (roommates) without having to commit himself before GOD as her GOD ordained husband. When he met Nancy initially, he wasn't thinking about her, but Nancy pulled off a lot of schemes, and her destination was to take him from Valerie. She succeeded in ending him and Val's relationship, but his destination with her was not the same as she had. She'd just been flirting with him for so long that he'd allowed his mind to wonder, and he finally went there with her. Valerie's friendship with Nancy was to be her friend, hoping to see the day that she was happily married, and they could all get together and just be the best of friends. Valerie wanted someone around her that was like her and since Nancy wasn't too much like her, she set out to inspire Nancy and help push her to a better way of thinking and living. She succeeded, but she didn't understand that she was and is not Nancy's lord, so she was only resetting Nancy's GPS to destination envy.

Valerie's intention with Larry was to marry him, have his children and live happily ever after. But, you need to be reminded that Larry goes to church....*sometimes!* He's religious. That's it. He's not sanctified or holy. He doesn't read his Bible, and he doesn't pray. He's not concerned with living right. If he were, he wouldn't have been so comfortable sleeping with Valerie knowing that it was against the order of GOD. In Val's conviction, she wanted to make things right, but Larry wanted to continue to have Val as a girlfriend, and if a wife should come along; he wanted to be able to end things with Valerie without the paperwork and fees. When a man convinces a woman to act like a wife without giving her the title of a wife, he has decided that he wants this woman in his life, but he knows that he will more than likely change his mind later. He doesn't want problems ending the relationship. That's basically what he's saying to you if he says that he wants to live with you without marrying you. Translated, he is saying that you make a great decoy of a wife, but you're just not what he wants. So, just in case someone that he believes is worthy of a ring should come along, he doesn't want to have to go through divorcing you to get to her. It's not that he doesn't want to get married; often times, the problem is...he just doesn't want to marry you.

Larry liked Valerie a lot. Initially, he had even thought that maybe she could be the one. But, after having arrived in the fullness of Valerie, there was nothing left to search out about her and the hunter in him needed to hunt fresh prey.

Years later, Val's reinvention of herself landed her as a wife. She began to pay attention to the words people said when they initially met her. She learned that more often than ever, people usually tell you within the first few days what their motives are. And more than that, she learned to pray about everyone and stop thinking that temporary sin would lead her to a permanent blessing. Like most women, she thought she could fornicate and eventually make it holy by marrying the guy. But, even if the guy does marry you, after fornication, you have opened doors into your relationship that will more than likely destroy that marriage. Because, like a thief, you came through the window and took what you wanted, rather than waiting on GOD to open the door for you.

It does not matter how good you were or how good you were trying to be in a relationship (romantic or friendship), everybody that you meet has a point on a map that they are trying to get to in your life. It's up to you to pray that GOD will redirect the enemy's footsteps away from you. If they are trying to arrive in CHRIST in wholeness, GOD may permit you to have a friendship with them or a marriage with them. You were never called to be anyone's girlfriend. If he is a man of GOD and has arrived in GOD, he will know HIS voice enough to hear that you are his wife, or that you are not his wife. As many have learned, you can rescue a scorpion from the mouth of a snake, but that scorpion will still sting you because it's a scorpion.

Remember, let GOD be GOD and let HIM lead you to a place in HIM of wisdom, safety and correction. HE will protect you from evil types, but HE'S where we are to live. If we step outside of HIM, then we are leaving his protection and correction to follow rejection. It's your choice. Be patient and let HIM be your GOD or go the do-it-yourself route and get broken every time.

To Each Day, Its Own

"Holding onto your past is the same as letting go of your future."

Dear Yesterday,
How are you? Today, I was trying to figure out how I can get you to stop calling me. We have had some good times and some rough times, but it never fails....tomorrow you are always calling me asking if you can visit me. Look. We had fun, but today, I'm moving on, and I hope you will too. Besides, tomorrow won't let me take a peek at her schedule, so I'm too busy trying to smooth things over with today so if she calls me tomorrow, we can talk about what a good day she was. Please stop calling me and understand that you are history!
Sincerely,
No Longer Torn

Good days visit you; bad days stalk you.

Most women revisit times in their lives when they were mistreated, mishandled, misused and misunderstood. We love to say, "I'll forgive, but I won't forget." That's because the average woman does not know the definition of "forgiveness." In the original Greek text, forgive (aàfesiv) is defined as pardon of sins; letting one go as if a crime had never been committed. But, how can this be done if we keep in mind what has been done to us? That's not to say that you won't think about it, but that is to treat the person as if they have never sinned against you. Of course, this is done in wisdom. For example, if a man tried to rape you; you wouldn't go hang out with him again. However, to operate in forgiveness towards him is to, for example, give him food if you saw that he was hungry, but to do it in public sight in a group setting.

Today is a new day.

Janell, Janell. Anointed with beauty, and the envy of many. Janell worked at a local news station as a reporter. Janell's skin was flawless and her hair always seemed to fall perfectly into place. Her smile could light up a cave, and her eyes were mystifying. There was hardly a man who did not find Janell attractive. But, of all that she had going for her; Janell wasn't happy. She looked happy, of course. Not many knew the issues that lurked within such a beautiful tent.

Janell was married to Jonathan, and he just could not figure her out. He was in love with her. He couldn't imagine life without her. But, she seemed so distant. Sometimes, she preferred to sleep in the guest bedroom. Sometimes, she'd come to bed and act like she loved Jonathan. Then, there were the times he dreaded the most. When she would come to bed and talk all night long about life before Jonathan.

The problem is: Janell has been married before. Her first husband (Wesley) had been found dead in a hotel room some eight years ago. His mistress's husband was later charged and convicted of his murder. But, the incident didn't just take one life. Janell was two months pregnant at the time and suffered a miscarriage due to the stress brought on by his death. She still had a lot of questions. She'd forgiven him for the affair. In reality, she blamed herself. She'd been so busy trying to build her career that she'd neglected spending time with him. So, in her mind, his affair was in response to that.

Jonathan tried to be understanding. He'd been married to Janell for three years now and didn't want to seem insensitive about the issue. So, he'd let her talk all night about Wesley. After she'd finish going on and on about what her and Wesley used to do, and where they used to go; she'd fall asleep next to Jonathan. By this time, Jonathan would normally have a little over an hour left to sleep before getting up for work the next day. How long could he take this? How long could he sit there and be denied a wife, the children he wanted, have to endure sleepless, and long hours of torture listening to her go on and on about her ex?

Jonathan was a meteorologist, working for the same station that Janell worked for. Co-workers always knew when she'd kept him up because he'd slur his words, be moody and a little on the clumsy side.

For three years, he waited patiently for his wife to become his wife, but his patience was wearing thin and would often be tested.

It was a rainy day in May when Janell sat Jonathan down. Her first husband's brother (Warner) was coming into town for a few weeks; maybe a month. She'd already told him that he could stay there with them until he found an apartment. He'd promised her that if he didn't find a job in a month's time, he'd move anyway.

Jonathan, of course, was not in agreement with the setup and voiced his disapproval. He was met with tears and silence. This combo was too much for him since he adored his wife. So, he agreed to the arrangement, hoping this would mark the end of her infatuation with the days of Wesley. For the rest of the week, she rewarded Jonathan by sleeping in the bed with him and acting like a wife, pretty much.

A week later, Warner arrived. He was about 5'7, a little on the husky side and kind of semi-attractive, but nothing to write home about. Jonathan had imagined what he'd look like and he was off by a landslide. He'd pictured Warner as being dark skinned, tall and strong. But, the man that stood at the door was caramel complexioned and looked like he couldn't hurt a fly. He just looked like he wanted to apologize for everything. One of the things that struck Jonathan immediately was how much luggage Warner was carrying. If this is going to be just a month's stay, why did he bring five huge suitcases and a few boxes? Nevertheless, he dismissed it and let him in.

The first few days were okay. A little uncomfortable for Jonathan, but Warner was okay and Janell was to-the-moon with glee. One of the perks Jonathan found in the ordeal was, she no longer kept him up some nights talking about Wesley. Nope. Poor Warner couldn't get a peep of sleep. She remembered every story of Wesley; things most people would probably forget. Some nights, Warner didn't seem to mind, but there were the nights when he'd give Jonathan the “help me” eye, but Jonathan wasn't a good sport. He'd grin at his unwanted guest, salute him and head off to bed.

For the most part, Jonathan and Wesley got along fine. Two weeks into his stay, however, they had a brush with one another that would change the whole thing.

One morning Jonathan and Janell were getting ready to go to work and Jonathan noticed that Warner was still in the bed asleep. His car hadn't moved since he'd been there. Jonathan decided not to say anything to Janell because, well, Janell's a woman. She's emotional, and she would plead for him to keep quiet. So, rather than riding to work together today, he suggested that Janell go to work in the Blazer, and he would follow up in a few in the Accord. She agreed and after eating breakfast; she left. After he'd made sure his wife was gone, Jonathan went and knocked on Warner's door. When Warner finally got up and answered, the conversation went like this:

Jonathan: Hey man, I noticed that you haven't applied for any jobs since you've been here. I know you said you'd be here a maximum of one month, and it's not that I don't enjoy your company, but you can understand that I want everything to go back to normal around here.

Warner: One month? I thought I could stay here as long as I wanted. I was planning to take a month to rest and then next month, I'd probably go job hunting. I'm sure that within the next two to three months I should be working and be able to help you guys out.

Jonathan: Wait. Janell told me you were staying here one month...maximum!

Warner: Well, looks like you and Janell need to sort that out. But, if you don't mind, I'm going back to bed. I had a late night last night.

He closes the door.

Disrespected and hurt, Jonathan jumps into his car seething with anger. How could his beloved Janell be so treacherous and conniving?! He danced with the idea of confronting her in front of everyone at work, but decided that this matter was best left alone until after hours, and it was very hard keeping it all in. Janell knew something was wrong. She could sense that Jonathan was wrought with her, but she didn't know why. She hoped that he hadn't talked to Warner about his extensive stay, but felt that Jonathan would never go behind her and do such a deed.

On the way home, Jonathan trailed Janell thinking about his conversation with Warner. He felt stupid; like he was her personal doormat. Where was Janell's love and respect for him? Pulling into the driveway, he saw the curtains move and knew it was Warner. Once Janell unlocked the door, Warner met her with his luggage. "Can y'all help me bring this stuff to my car, please?" He looked serious, but Jonathan knew it was just a game. Why hadn't he left earlier? He had all day to pack, and all of a sudden when they come home, he wants to be seen? Yeah, right. Let the games begin.

Janell: What's going on, Warner?
Warner: It seems that I am a bother to you guys, and I don't like to be where I'm not welcome. So, I'm going to stay in my car for the next few months. That way, I'll have my peace, and you'll have yours!
Janell: What do you mean? What...what happened?
Warner: Well, your husband confronted me today about my annoying presence. I thought you two had discussed my stay, but obviously not.
Janell angrily turns to Jonathan.

Janell: What did you say to him?!
Jonathan: I simply and politely asked him why he wasn't out looking for a job and come to find out, you have told him that he can stay here as long as he wants! When were you going to tell

me? I thought this was our house! I thought we discussed these types of things first!

Janell: For what? So you can tell me no?! So you can play the quote on quote man of the house while little ole me just sits back and fiddles with my hair?! You got me confused with your ex! I told him he could stay here as long as he wants...yes! I said that! I don't need your permission!

Jonathan: No, obviously you have ME confused with Wesley! I have tolerated you talking about him on and on for years now, and now you want to pull this stunt, Janell? You're right. It is your house. Your name is on the deed. What was I thinking? Matter of fact, Warner, cut the act! Stay as long as you want, man. I can guarantee you won't hear anything else from me about it! Wait a minute, let's make it official; here is my house key. Keep it. If you need underwear, t-shirts...anything, brother, let me know, and it's all yours!

(Jonathan storms off and goes to their bedroom and slams the door.)

Janell: Good! Warner, go back to your room and unload your bags. I'm going out for a drive to sort some things out in my head. I'll be back later. *She then yells to her husband.* Um, Wes...I mean, Jonathan, try not to be slamming doors around here! Because at the end of the day, you can't fix a thing!

Janell left to go for a ride. She really wanted to head out to the cemetery where Wesley was buried. Every time she had problems with Jonathan; she would go out to Wesley's grave to talk to his headstone. Little did she know that Jonathan was in the bedroom packing his bags and she didn't know that Jonathan had another property. He didn't keep it a secret from her to be malicious or secretive, but he'd just found out about the property a few days after Warner moved in. He decided to keep quiet until Warner had moved out; fearing that Janell would get the bright idea of offering the property to Warner. The house was his mother's old house. His mother was in a nursing home and with Jonathan being her only son, she'd decided to sign the house over to him. She feared that she wouldn't be here too long and wanted to ensure that all of her things were in order. She never really cared too much for Janell, but she'd tolerated her because Jonathan loved her. However, she knew that Janell was bound by something. She always seemed withheld, kind of distant.

After loading his bags into the car, Jonathan sat in the driveway for two minutes, crying and listening to the song that he'd first danced with Janell on. Was he making the biggest mistake of his life? Or was Janell the biggest mistake of his life? He was still very much in love with her, but he'd lived years of her being in love with her dead ex. Midway through the song; he could see Warner peeping out the window again, so he decided to go ahead and leave. He told to himself that he wasn't coming back...ever. It was over.

While driving, he happened to pass the cemetery and saw Janell's Blazer parked on the side of the road. He turned in and parked beside it and took the long walk to Wesley's grave. He knew where it was, since Janell had taken him there several times before.

Janell didn't see her husband approaching. She was too busy crying and talking to the headstone that even the faint sounds of Jonathan's footsteps were muzzled by the sound of her voice. For a moment, Jonathan almost pitied her and felt bad about the incident until he heard her crying out. "Wes, baby, why did you have to leave me like this? Why, baby? I miss you so much. I can't stop thinking about you. You're in my dreams; you're everywhere. I slept in the other room again the other night, baby. I pretended that you were asleep beside me like old times. You held my hand and suddenly everything was alright. It was. I just want to hold you so bad! I can never love any man like I love you and I'm sorry for pushing you here. It's my fault that this happened to you. My fault! I should have paid attention to you. I should have been there for you. I'm going to sleep in the other room tonight or I'll sleep there all this week if you want. I need to feel you there beside me. The other night, I could smell your cologne and I held our picture all night long. Baby, I wish you could come back. I love you more than I can ever love any man. Please come back to me."

After this, she could hear the sound of the leaves crunching behind her. She turned and saw Jonathan walking away. She paused, for a moment, trying to decide if she wanted to go after him or not, but decided that she would talk with him when she got home. She couldn't disrespect Wesley like that. No. She knew how to handle Jonathan. She'd lay on an emotional breakdown act, and he'd be apologizing before the night was done. Or so she thought.

Not to mention, this was the confirmation that Jonathan needed about his marriage to Janell. He would never have her as his wife. He finalized the divorce in his heart and planned to start the legal proceedings on paper.

When she arrived back at the house, she found Jonathan's car still gone. She thought that maybe he was still out cooling down. But, when she came into the house, something felt odd. All of the pictures of her and Jonathan were gone. She hurried to the room and saw that Jonathan's clothes and belongings were gone. Before she could grab her cell, Warner came into the room and told her that Jonathan had packed his bags and left.

Janell ran out of the front door, dialing her cell phone before jumping into her car. Jonathan was too good of a man to let go, and she knew it. His phone didn't ring; instead, his voice mail came on. She hung up and called him again and again. It kept going to his voice mail. “Baby, please come home. I'm sorry. I know that I have been difficult, but if you come home, I will try to be a better wife to you. Please come home. I can't go through this right now. Please Jonathan.” She made this call around eight p.m.

Around 12 a.m., he still hadn't called. By this time, Janell had left him more than 10 desperate messages ranging from sincere, to desperate manipulation. But, no call returns. And this was on a Friday. Jonathan was off work for the next two days, just like Janell. She felt like she couldn't endure those two days without hearing from him.

Saturday came and went. No Jonathan. No calls from him, no text messages from him, and her calls to him just kept going to voice mail. Sunday came and by this time, Janell is in a full-blown state of desperation. She goes to the nursing home to visit his mother, which was the first time she'd ever been there, but the nursing home wouldn't let her see her. The nurse reported to Janell that her name had been on the list, but had been removed on Saturday. At this, she realized that Jonathan did not intend to come back, nevertheless, she went back home, hoping he would pull in the driveway. As the day turned into night, she realized she'd be spending another cold night alone.

While this was going on, Warner was getting frustrated too. Janell hadn't cooked for the last couple of days, and he was tired of eating cold cuts. So, after she got home, he walked up to her and began to say that he had diabetes and the food he'd been eating was making him sick. Frustrated, Janell goes to the kitchen to cook the chicken dumplings, corn on the cob and bake the cake that Warner had requested.

Monday arrived and Janell was at work early. She was looking forward to seeing Jonathan there so she could talk with him. But, he'd called in and Trevon Floyd was sitting in his seat, waiting to go on in his place.

The next day (Tuesday), Jonathan did come to work, but he asked security and management to keep Janell away from him. He explained to the management team that he and Janell were having some personal issues and were no longer a couple. So, when desperate Janell came in, she was met by a note on her desk asking her to come to the manager's office. There, she was warned not to bring her personal problems to work and to stay away from Jonathan while at work. Any violation would be met with immediate termination. It was hard to see him there. Passing by him, this familiar face, the man who'd embraced her for three years now and all of a sudden, he's off limits.

The lunch hour finally came and Janell had to walk pass Jonathan to get to the lounge. She let the tears flow, hoping it would tug on his heart strings, but Jonathan wasn't moved. He walked around her and went into the parking lot to get into his car. Nothing was working.

A week later, a certified letter was delivered to her home. It was the divorce papers that she'd prayed would never come.

Now, we can draw a conclusion as to what we would like to see happen with this story. Most of you are wishing Jonathan would run for the hills and stay there. Some of you are wishing that Janell would put out her manipulative ex-brother in law, turn her life over to GOD, let go of her ex-husband and rekindle the fire between her and Jonathan. If you're hoping that manipulative Janell gets with manipulative Warner, stay away from the marriage altar for now.

Explanation:

What happened with Janell is classic. She lived in the past to the point where she denied herself to one man (her living husband) because she was still in love with the old man (her dead husband.) She kept revisiting the issue of his death and the circumstances surrounding it. It was not impossible for her to carry on a healthy loving relationship with her husband at this stage, because she was in a relationship with her past.

When we are focused on what's behind us, we can't see what's in front of us. Janell had a good husband, but she threw it away for a stroll down memory lane. That road is a dead end! There is so much evil that we open our doors to when we refuse to walk into the presence of today. When we live in the past, we are surrounded by witchcraft. You see; Janell kept using manipulation on her husband because she was growing increasingly evil by the day. We are called to adjust our lives to fit the WORD of GOD and live in HIS infinite wisdom. When one is focused on yesterday, they can't fit into the WORD because GOD is focused on what we are to do, not what we should have done. HE makes things new again! We just have to repent.

When Janell began manipulating her husband, she opened a demonic door where every evil thing could come into her home. When a man is there, that man has to be bound before a devil can take his home. Janell clearly had a Delilah spirit on her, as she knew her husband's weakness and exposed it. Once she exposed it, she let the devil in. And because this door was open, Warner came in and began manipulating her. She set her home up to be chaotic and Jonathan's error was letting her play on his feelings, rather than standing up and covering his wife by disallowing her to con him.

If you want to go forward, you have to stop looking behind you. Whether it's somebody that hurt you or someone you hurt, you are prohibiting yourself from going to the next level when you are standing in today fighting with yesterday's devil.

Today is filled with opportunities that will set in motion what will happen for you tomorrow. But, life has no rewind button. To get a better tomorrow, learn to sow seeds of obedience today so that tomorrow's harvest will be blessed. Sometimes, we don't want what's growing up for us because we gave GOD seeds that HE didn't want. And when HE allowed them to grow and we saw the fruits thereof, we began to cry out that we were under attack, when in truth, our harvest was simply upon us. Many hear these words, but just think it's all religious babble. The truth is, every time you open your mouth; seeds fly out. Every time you do something; seeds are sent out. That's why so many things in your life have to be uprooted so that you can live the life that GOD has aligned you for.

Today is today. Yesterday is like an abusive ex-boyfriend. It'll keep trying to court you, beat you down with who you were and deny who you are.

Let go of your dead past and grab on to your living future! You cannot resurrect the pass, but you can breathe life into your tomorrow!

Witchcraft You May Unknowingly Be Using

"If it ain't a miracle, it must be a mirage."

Most of us know that manipulation is a form of witchcraft. Why? Because we have learned that manipulation is the use of a wile or a tactic to get one's desired results, when GOD said let your yes be yes and your no be no. Anything else is of the devil. But, when we try to con a 'yes' or a 'no' out of someone, we are no longer operating in faith and trusting GOD to work that thing out, but we are using the devices of the devil and trying to force that thing out.

There is a lot of witchcraft that many believers participate in unknowingly. Most of it involves manipulation and trickery. Rather than list a story, I will give you some examples of witchcraft that you may find you are involved in. This is so that you will come out of it.

1. **Casting Shadows.** I heard this in my spirit one day. I don't remember what was going on, but I think I was talking on the phone, and the person was casting shadows. It sounded 'witchy' and I later found out just what it

meant. Casting shadows is portraying yourself or someone else to be bigger than they are for the purpose of intimidating, seducing or encouraging someone to do as you'd like them to do. For example, someone gets angry with you and tells you that they are well-known, and that they could easily destroy your name. Another example would be someone with a little experience pretending to have a lot of experience to get a job or a seat in a ministry. This is actually very common and most people that do it don't realize what they are doing. Casting shadows is an attempt to seduce the mind into seeing what is not there.

2. **Pity.** Ladies, please stop this. We learned this as children. Men don't like to see crying, so many of us cry when things don't go our way. It's manipulation, of course. And some of you may not cry, but will put on a sad face when, for example, husband tells you no about something. When he asks you to tell him what's wrong, you just clean the house and humbly say, "Nothing." This is witchcraft. I had to be delivered from it. Most of you use it on your friends and family as well. Even your own children! You may, for example, call your friend and ask her if she'd like to accompany you to the mall. When she says no, you sigh and say, "Well, okay. I guess I'll go alone." Stop it! Stop it! It's witchcraft! Or, you may tell your children that you want to spend Christmas with them, but you know they want to spend it with their dad. So, you go on to tell them how good you've been to them and how you're going to have to spend Christmas alone. Witchcraft! Anytime you use witchcraft; you are standing in a congregation of demons and subjecting or attempting to subject whomever you are trying to use it on to those demons. Let people say no! It is their right!

3. **Salesman Witchcraft.** You want someone to do

something for you or with you and you spend all day trying to sell that idea by dressing it up all over. Your poor friends or husband has to sit there through long hours of discussions, stories and so on. It's point on point witchcraft. ***"In the multitude of words there lacks not sin: but he that refrains his lips is wise." (Proverbs 10:19)*** You don't have to sell something. Let them say yes or no and let that be that. It's not the end of the world. When you are right, for example, and your husband is wrong, pray on it and let GOD do what GOD needs to do to make him a wiser man.

4. **Using Sex.** This is mainly done by wives. You get angry because hubby says no to you or does not do what you want him to do and now you're withholding sex. That's a Delilah spirit. How so? What you are doing is binding up your husband by exploiting his weakness. When doing this, you are binding up the strongman (hubby) and letting the devil come in and take siege of him, your children and all that you have. ***"No man can enter into a strong man's house, and spoil his goods, except he will first bind the strong man; and then he will spoil his house." (Mark 3:27)*** A lot of women use this on men who are not married to them, as well. She may want a new car and know that the older and richer man that's been flirting with her is determined to have her to the point where he'd spend greatly for her. So, she flirts with him, dropping in his hearing the fact that she wants a new car. Before or after doing this, she has sex with him or seduces him into believing that sex with her is going to happen if he would only buy this car.

5. **Using Adornment.** Many women adorn themselves with apparel, accessories, makeup and so on for the sole purpose of catching a man or getting a man to do

something for them. Some even wear the shortest of skirts, the tightest of jeans and the sexiest of shirts to seduce a man's eyes and his flesh. This is witchcraft. Don't get me wrong. It is not sin for a woman to look good, but the sin is when the motive behind your looking good is to entice another human being. We didn't have to know that Jezebel painted her eyes when Jehu came to the castle, but GOD told us anyway to demonstrate to us how we should and should not conduct ourselves as women. We are to adorn the inner 'me' and not the outer 'me' so that we could be that Proverbs 31 woman to our husbands, but when you spend so much time and money working on the outer 'me,' when the inner woman is broken; you are wrapping a bomb in a box with pretty gift wrap. Timothy spoke what he was against, and this was because the women were so obsessed with attracting men that they were distracted from what they should have been doing. When you go to put on your makeup, ask yourself this. Am I doing it to attract a man? Witchcraft. Am I doing it because I like the way I look when I wear it? That's fine. Am I doing it to get an A in Geometry because our math teacher is on the flirtatious side? Witchcraft. Your motive will always display what's in your heart. ***"And you, O desolate one, what do you mean that you dress in scarlet, that you adorn yourself with ornaments of gold, that you enlarge your eyes with paint? In vain you beautify yourself. Your lovers despise you; they seek your life." (Jeremiah 4:30)***

6. **Divide and Conquer.** Have you ever known a woman who had a mutual friend with you, and she tells you all of the bad things about this friend so that you'd leave her alone? Then she continues on being friends with the 'bad girl,' telling her all of what's wrong with you? Women often do this when they want you to themselves. You may

notice that your best friend's friends don't like you. It's because your best friend said something to them about you that made them want to steer clear of you. Or what about the man who doesn't like your friends or family? The man who gets women to disassociate themselves from people he believes to be a threat to what he wants to do in and with their lives. In most cases, he's the abusive guy who usually starts off emotionally abusing his prey and then graduates to physically abusing her. GOD has called us to realize a thing through revelation or discernment. No one has to shove it into your head, but when they do, it is because there is a motive behind them or a spirit in them. Satan likes to divide first and then conquer his prey because unity is a bond that is too strong for him. ***"For where two or three are gathered together in my name, there am I in the middle of them." (Matthew 18:20)***

7. **Using the Bible or Conviction.** You will find this form of witchcraft mostly among believers. Of course, it's used by a tare and not a true plant of GOD. Someone may come and tell you to join their church, for example. When you refuse, they go on to tell you what happens to people that go outside of the will of GOD. Or someone may ask you to sow a seed, <u>and when you refuse</u>, they throw scriptures at you or tell you what happened to the last guy or girl who was blessed with this opportunity to sow into them; but refused. This form of witchcraft is particularly sad when you see a mother or a father use it on their children. I have seen leaders do this with their followers as well. In particular, one thing I've seen, that is common is, a follower will challenge or disagree with something their leader does or says. The leader responds by sharply rebuking them and declaring that a curse would come upon them for questioning him or her. Afraid, the follower repents to the leader (not GOD) and dares not to

question the man or woman anymore. Yes, I have actually seen this, and it's raw witchcraft.

8. **Hinting.** This is trying to convey a message to someone without directly speaking what it is that you want to say. Someone who hints, for example, may decide that they don't like the way you dress. So, they may take you to a clothing store and try to get you to purchase new clothes. They may say, "Girl, I think this would look good on you, and it won't make you look fat." This is witchcraft. JESUS is bold, and HE called a hypocrite what he was to his face. When GOD calls us to tell someone something, we have to speak it out loud and not under our breath. The purpose of a parable was to speak to the believer, but be hidden from the unbeliever.
   This is also familiar on today's most visited website 'Facebook.' I've been guilty of this until the LORD corrected me and told me what I was doing. You have to be direct with your sisters and brothers, and if you're afraid to do so, simply pray for them. Talking about them or hinting to them is witchcraft because you're using a tactic, instead of sharpening your sister or brother. Hinting is very common with Christians, many of them using social media as their platform. Sometimes you know who a person is directing their messages at, based on what that person just said. This is not of GOD; it's the witchcraft of cowards. All things are done in love. Therefore, if Joanne put a post up that was misleading, instead of Erica hinting that the post was wrong and talking about false prophets misleading people, Erica should have sent a message to Joanne. It could be that GOD allowed Erica to see the post so that she could clarify some things to Joanne. This could make Joanne go back and reword the post, or it may teach her something. It doesn't mean that she's a false prophet, but it could

mean that she, like all of us, needs to be sharpened daily.

9. **Sowing With Motive.** Everybody that sows into your ministry is not doing it because GOD told them to, or because they want to bless you. Sometimes people sow into you because you are fertile ground. This is good if they are trusting GOD for the increase. Some people sow into you because they want to be your "friend," but you have to first understand what that word "friend" means to them. Everyone has his or her own definition of what a friend is, so they often size you up to see if you could fit into their yokes. There are times when people sow into someone because they covet something that person has. That's witchcraft. Everything should be directed at being obedient to GOD and growing HIS Kingdom here on earth, but when the motive is selfish and fleshly motivated, it roots itself in witchcraft.

10. **Excessive Talking/ Arguing.** Boy, did I have this one bad! Ladies, sometimes, we act like the attorney, judge and a hung jury! We want to talk, talk, and talk some more until our mates understand what we are trying to say and feels convicted enough to sentence himself to doing what we want. Women often do this to their friends as well, but many have this bad, when it comes to their relationships. You want, for example, your husband to stop hanging with Peter. So, you tell him about Peter, what Peter has done, why you don't like Peter; you conjure up stories about men like Peter, what you've heard about Peter and so on. Every time you get a chance; it's Peter this and Peter that. Or, let's say you have told your husband again and again that you don't like it when he grins at the neighbor or chats with her. So, you badger him every chance you get, trying to wear him down. It's witchcraft. The right way works like this....you say what

you want, pray about it and let GOD bring the fruition of it. But, when you try to make a thing happen yourself using wiles and tactics; you are no different than the women who pay or solicit witches to cast spells on their husbands.

And please stop trying to convince your children to do as you think they ought to do. Trying to convince anyone of anything is error. You lay the truth in their hands and let the truth do the work! But, when we try to convince someone of something, we try to force our thinking patterns upon them. In doing so, you are trying to force them to think with your brain, when GOD designed all mankind to seek and find the truth on his and her own. You're basically saying to GOD that your children or the people that you are using this witchcraft on are your very own projects, and HE doesn't need to intervene. When you try to force feed someone, they often regurgitate what was fed to them. But, when you tell them the truth, pray for them and allow them to make their own mistakes; you are saying to GOD that you trust HIM with your children and your relationships. Control is a spirit of witchcraft. Anytime you try to get into someone's head and rearrange their way of thinking; you are in the will of the devil, for this is what he wanted, when GOD gave us the ability to choose right from wrong.

11. **Using Others.** I have seen parents do this to their children; wives do this to their husbands; leaders do this to the flock and so on. It's okay to ask someone to reiterate what you've been trying to get your child, husband, friend or family member to see. But, first, the person needs to will your words in and they must want what you are sharing with them. Otherwise, if you're trying to force it in, you are actually triggering rebellion. Rebellion will come out and entice your child and tell them that they are

grown and to prove it, they must stop listening to you. So, your words are having an opposite affect!
There are those that will use others to promote themselves or their own agendas. For example, a mother doesn't want her son to date a particular girl, even though he's a grown man. So, she calls around and tells her friends and family what she believes and why she believes it. Everyone who doesn't support her beliefs, she'll get angry with and consciously try to keep them and their ideas away from her son. But everyone who agrees with her; she will ask them to speak to her son or badger her son. It's witchcraft. Mankind is designed to fall and get back up again. Our mistakes teach us what we refused to learn through wisdom and direction. Our falls will teach us to watch our steps.
Another more detailed example is a wife who wants, for example, a new room added onto their house and hubby disagrees. She then gets upset with him and calls his mother or anyone she believes could persuade her husband. This is witchcraft. You are to let your yes be yes and your no be no and in the same, you have to let his yes be yes and his no be no. Don't get me wrong, it's okay if you talked to, for example, your pastor about your husband being controlling and asked him to bring you guys in for counseling. But, you have to be willing to let the pastor tell you what you may not want to hear. Don't try to tell him or her what you want him or her to say or how to say it. It is better to say that you want a session without telling the pastor what the session is about. That way, your husband will have a fair chance to say what he feels or believes or to schedule the session in the presence of your husband.

The End of a Thing

"Every sentence ends with a period or a closing mark. When you don't know where your mark should end, you can't start a new sentence in your life."

Most of us know that manipulation is a form of witchcraft. Why? Because we have learned that manipulation is the use of a wile or a tactic to get one's desired results, when GOD said let your yes be yes and your no be no. Anything else is of the devil. But, when we try to con a 'yes' or a 'no' out of someone, we are no longer operating in faith and trusting GOD to work that thing out, but we are using the devices of the devil and trying to force that thing out.

But, there is a lot of witchcraft that many believers participate in unknowingly. Most of it involves manipulation and trickery. Rather than list a story, I will give you some examples of witchcraft that you may find you are involved in. This is so that you will come out of it.

Imagine this. Donna was incarcerated for three years for check forgery. It wasn't her first brush with the law or her second. At the end of the term, would Donna refuse to leave from behind the bars, so she can continue the sentence even though it has ended? If so, they would probably commit Donna to a psycho ward, so she could start a sentence and end it there.

Tamar met and married a man who was not anointed to be her husband. Why? Because she started a sentence that she was not to write, but she wrote it anyway. When we don't know CHRIST or when we are young in HIM, we tend to, like children, start sentences that don't make sense. Now, her husband, the unbeliever wants to abandon her and their children. Tamar has done all she could do to hold on to him, but he just wants to leave. And he does. GOD tells us that if the unbelieving wants to part (or leave), let him go. But, instead of letting him go; Tamar keeps calling him, keeps coming by his apartment and keeps on crying about him. Why? Because she started a sentence that she was not called to write, and she doesn't want to accept that her husband put a period where she now has a question mark. Now, she is serving sentences in misery, unforgiveness, strife, slander and all of the curses associated with disobedience.

When you start a sentence that you were not supposed to write, you wound up having to write other sentences to finish the story. Now, Tamar is in the club, half naked trying to reel a new fish in because her story did not end in her reality the way it did in her imagination. Her life's story is being read by GOD and HE has already determined how sin ends.

How about Christa? Christa and Lea were friends for the last seven years. But, Christa, who is now closer to GOD, cannot find it in herself to let go of Lea, who wants no part of GOD. When the friendship started, they were both unsaved. But, Christa gave herself to GOD a few years back, and she did the right thing by trying to get Lea to give her life to the LORD. However, when Lea rejected HIM, it is the same as rejecting Christa, since we

(GOD'S sons and daughters) are the temple of the HOLY SPIRIT. Nevertheless, Christa elected to continue the friendship and as a result, Christa kept finding herself going from blessing the Name of the LORD to cursing. She found herself going from the club to the church trying to hold on to that friendship. Therefore, Christa will serve time in tribulations and trials by fire to get her to understand that the tares, and the wheat were planted by two different forces. Christa is trying to place a comma where the LORD wants a period.

Explanation:

Try to read this sentence. "Taylor gave her life to GOD, but in the midst of her giving her life to HIM, she did not want to let go of her sin and her husband got tired of her straddling the fence her children were also in love with the idea of staying in a sinful lifestyle Taylor was in love with the wrong things even though the season came for her to divorce those things and walk with GOD so as a result Taylor lost all that she had so that she could be made new again to start afresh and hopefully this time make the right decisions about her life so that her children could see and understand that GOD will not accept a lukewarm believer they did not want to get it, but life happens so we can understand it more"

We call that a run on sentence because I was trying to connect several messages without stopping to start a new sentence or inform you when a new sentence is being formed. So, the sentence doesn't make sense. What about your life? Many times, women complain that their lives don't make sense, but could it be that you haven't ended many of the sentences that you started? And now you want to start a new one and can't figure out why the old sentence is affecting the new one?

What about Tamar in the club hunting for a new man to start a sentence with? She hasn't yet caught on to the "why" of it all. Why did her first husband leave? Ask her and she'll say that he's a dog. And like many women, she's out at the club looking for a puppy or a man she can train. But, all puppies grow up to be dogs and every relationship that Tamar starts will run into the ones that she never ended in her heart. She didn't put a period at the end of her marriage, therefore, starting a new relationship does not make sense.

The message here is know when the season is over and know when and how to end that season on the right tone. Every sentence started in GOD should read in a way that glorifies GOD and end before the start of a new sentence. Every sentence started in sin will read that way, but in the end, it will glorify GOD because what HE has already declared about the sinner will manifest and ring true that HIS WORD is everlasting and will not return to HIM void. And every sentence started in sin will involve a sinner and end in death.

When you wake up this morning, pay attention to what you are beginning to speak during the day, through your actions. Be sure to keep that sentence holy and acceptable as you should be keeping yourself. Whatever your life speaks is a witness to where you will spend your eternity, and none of us wants to end up in hell with a period behind us.

How to Know When You're Ready For Marriage

"Being a woman does not make you a wife. It just means you look like one."

So, you think you're ready for marriage? That's only normal, but many women do not understand: A man will marry a woman, but a husband will marry a wife. The difference will make a difference in how the marriage plays out, whether it has staying power, or if it's just a spark that will be extinguished by the first storm or a series of storms that comes along.

Knowing when you have graduated from being a woman to being a wife is essential to knowing when the husband has arrived. A woman does not know the difference between a man and a husband, but a wife does. And all too often, wives marry men, and husbands marry women. This is when you discover that being the right woman for the wrong man is like taking a pig to a five-star restaurant and then having the nerve to be embarrassed when he pigs out. Serve him with the best, but at the end of the day, he's still a pig and will act as such. Below are some tips to let you know if you are ready, on your way to being ready, or if you're just not a wife...yet.

Review the scenarios and choose which way you would handle each situation. Please don't say what sounds good because you know it's the right answer. Imagine yourself in the situation and answer truthfully how you would handle the situation. Jot down your answers.

1. Your husband comes home from work with lipstick on his collar. He says he saw an old high school friend today and hugged her and that's probably how her lipstick got on his collar.
You would:
A. Scream and yell at him. No man is going to cheat on you and get away with it!
B. Put him out of the house. No need for explanations; he's cheated. How dare he lie about it!
C. Ask him to explain himself and then put him out based on his answers.
D. Ask him again and again to tell you who "she" is. Tell him you're not going to get mad.
E. Keep your eyes peeled and investigate the matter.
F. I wouldn't say he was lying or telling the truth. I would just drop it, pray about it and continue to treat him with respect. GOD will deal with him if he's cheating.
G. Well, you know he's cheated if lipstick is on his collar. Right now, you want him to just tell the truth so you both can deal with it.

2. In the heat of an argument, your husband raises his hand like he wants to strike you, but he doesn't. How would you handle this?
A. Call my brothers, cousins or uncles. If he wants to hit someone, he's about to get his chance.
B. Beat last night's dinner out of him before putting him out.

C. Put him out. He's going to hit a woman eventually and it won't be you.
D. Go for Christian counseling. It's bad what he did, but we will work through it and hopefully, it'll never happen again.
E. Just put him out; no questions asked.
G. Talk to him about the situation until you can pull out of him why he thinks it's okay to hit a woman.

3. Your brother needs somewhere to stay, but your husband says no. You want your brother to stay with you; after all, you have an extra room, but husband is adamant that he's not going for it. What would you do?

A. Tell your brother to come on. You pay rent too and hubby don't run the show.
B. Listen to your husband and tell your brother he'd have to go elsewhere.
C. Tell your husband that his family can't stay there if your brother can't stay there.
D. Leave your husband or put him out. Cause he's obviously got the wrong woman!
E. Cry and try to talk him into it. After all, that's your brother!
F. Beat the ignorance out of him and then move your brother in.
G. Talk to your pastor or someone you feel could influence your husband to reconsider.

4. Your best friend used to hang out with you when she was married. But, now she's divorced and she wants to hang out with you more. But, your husband doesn't like her and tells you that he'd prefer if you stayed away from her. How would you handle the matter?

A. Hang out with her anyway. One good deed deserves another.
B. Your husband is being insecure and you are not feeding his ignorance. Time to put on the gloves!
C. Sneak and hang out with her. What he doesn't know, won't hurt him.

D. Ask him why, try to talk to him about it and then if he insists, stop hanging out with her.
E. Tell him that he has to stop hanging out with his best friend first!
F. I don't know what I'd do. I'd probably try to talk with him again and again until he understands me.
G. Pray and ask GOD to change his mind.

5. Your ex boyfriend is in town and wants to talk with you. You know your husband would be against this, but you don't plan to cheat! You just want to catch up and see how he's doing. What would you do?
A. Say no way! I don't even have to ask my husband if that's okay. That's a no-no!
B. Ask my husband to see how he feels about it, and if he says yes, I'll go forward. If no, I guess I have to honor that.
C. What my husband doesn't know, won't hurt him. After all, he's already talked to one of his exes, or you know that he would if the situation was presented to him.
D. Call my ex with my husband on three-way.
E. Talk to the ex and then tell the husband about it. It's no secret!
F. Send messages to your ex through a mutual friend. That way, you're not guilty of speaking directly to him!
G. Try to convince your husband that it's all innocent because you want to talk to him.

6. Your mother never liked your husband. And she calls to talk about him to you. What would you do?
A. Listen. He doesn't have to know how she feels or what she's saying about him. As long as she doesn't show it when he's around, we're good.
B. Agree with her if she's telling the truth. It's just girl-talk.
C. Defend your husband and tell her that if she doesn't respect him, you will have to cut her loose even though you love her. No

one has the right to stand between you and your husband.
D. Talk to your dad and ask him to talk with her about it. But, keep it from your husband so he won't feel uncomfortable going over there.
E. Tell her to tell your husband how she feels. How they handle it is between her and him; not you.
F. Leave your husband. Mommy's always right!
G. Ask your mother for advice. She may know how to handle his type.

7. You have children from a previous relationship, but your husband wants to discipline them. How would you handle this?
A. Tell your husband that when the children are wrong, he needs to talk with you, and you will discipline them. After all, they are your children, not his.
B. Let him discipline them, but in your presence only.
C. Neither you nor your husband will discipline them to keep down confusion. You'll both just talk with them.
D. Ask your pastor what he thinks is best.
E. It depends on my husband's relationship with my children. I don't mind him disciplining them, but I have to be sure that he loves them and it's just discipline, not animosity.
F. Talk to their dad to see if he will give his permission. If he says no, the answer is no.
G. Let him discipline them, but after we've talked about it first to make sure we are on the same page.

Now, you may have found that many of these questions have several answers that you have considered. But, I urge you to choose the one that you are most likely to do. After you've completed the questions, compare your answers with the best answers below. And write down if you are wife-material, have wife-potential or if you're still a woman waiting for your wife's badge.

Answers:

1. The best answer would have been F. It is very very easy to have a situation that escalates to the point of no return that was sparked by a simple misunderstanding. Sometimes, accidents happen and if an old friend did put lipstick on his collar accidentally or intentionally, you could pay a great price for your insisting that he is guilty of having an affair. If you have been seeing other signs that he's cheating, it's not okay to let this situation steer you to the left or the right. GOD likes to be GOD because HE is GOD alone. Therefore, you have to **be still** and trust HIM. When you try to discover the answers on your own, you will find things that look like he's guilty and send you into an emotional spiral. And you won't be easy to live with. Satan knows how to make a pear look like an apple when you keep staring at it. If you chose to keep your eyes peeled and investigate the matter, you are only opening a door for hurt to come in. Because when we look for something, we tend to find evidence to support what we believe. If you answered F, give yourself one point.

2. If you chose D, bravo for you. We like to listen to things people say that sound right, but in truth, are just right-sounding wrongs. This could be the first time he has ever raised his hand at a woman and the last time. You should seek Christian counseling to get him to understand and denounce whatever is in him that makes him feel that he needs to go in that direction. Talking with him is good, but it doesn't deal with the spirit that lies within. If you chose D, give yourself one point.

3. B is the correct answer. We were not called to be sisters and brothers by blood. It is the covenant relationship with our spouses that reflects our relationship with GOD. If your brother

is a good man, he will understand and won't take it personal. If he's a bad man, he's going to be angry and want to harm your husband or your relationship with your husband. If that becomes the case, your husband was right to say he didn't want him there. Using your pastor or anyone else as a tool of manipulation isn't good because you are using people to force him into doing something he doesn't want to do. Who knows? Maybe the LORD has hardened your husband's heart for a reason. If you chose B, give yourself one point.
4. If you choose D; bingo. We would all want to know why and the flesh's reaction is to roll your head and 'handle him.' But, sometimes, the LORD will use our husbands to protect us from what we refuse to see. Even if it's a case of him being insecure, the LORD has to show him this and change him. You can't lord yourself over him. Asking GOD to change his mind is error. What if GOD put that on his heart because GOD saw envy in her for you? If GOD changed that man's mind, you may find yourself losing your marriage and all that you have because of a woman you felt you owed something to. Sure, you can pray and ask the LORD to change your husband's mind if he is wrong, but if he's not, to change your mind. If you chose D, give yourself another point.
5. If you chose A, you're wife material. All too often, women get married and try to force their past on their future. This means the soul of that man is still present in her, which renders her a woman and not a wife. Your husband should never have to feel threatened in his position as your husband or vice versa.
6. If you chose C, you should hear a ringing sound in your head. You were right. No mother, daddy, sister, brother, cousin, uncle, aunt, grandparent, pastor or anyone has the right to divide your marriage. GOD said what HE put together, LET NO **MAN** PUT ASUNDER. You are one with your husband and anyone that tries to come between this is operating under demonic assignment. I can understand if your mother knows somethings

about your husband that gives her pause, but you should have never told her this anyway. What happens in the house stays in the house unless you are planning to get out of the house. Leaving him to fight it out with her or talk to her about it is giving her permission to try to manipulate your husband into being what she thinks a man should be. That means you're giving your mother permission to Jezebel your husband. Say no. If he's a bad man, GOD knows how to deliver you from him or change him. Mommy doesn't! If you chose C, give yourself a point.
7. G is the correct answer. A house divided will not stand. If you chose E, I understand you, but if you're scared of how he may be with your children, then you didn't use discernment in marrying him. When GOD sends the real husband, you won't have anything to worry about, but if you marry a simple man, you have plenty to stress over. If you chose G, give yourself a point. If you chose E, give yourself a half of a point. (.5)

Now, if you've got 7 points, bravo! You're a wife in waiting. If you got 5 or 6 points, you're wife material. GOD is still working on you in that field. You may want to get around more married women who have been happily married five plus years. If you've got 3 to 4 points, you are leaning both ways and there is no telling which way you'll tip over. Just keep on learning more about the WORD of GOD and get around some Christian wives who are happily married to learn what you need to learn about being a wife and what to expect in a marriage. If you've only got 1 or 2, it doesn't mean you won't be a wife one day, it's just that right now, you're still a woman. Ask GOD to change you into being a wife. If you didn't get any right, just pray. What looks impossible to you isn't impossible for GOD.

Being a wife means you have to be a woman that can easily forgive. Because in marriage, a husband will often step on your flesh and you'll find yourself wanting to react. I have listened to women put me on hold and go and chew their husband's manhood up and spit it out. I was once one of these women, but I asked GOD to make me a better wife to my husband and the first thing HE did was teach me to first be a better daughter to HIM. As such, I automatically transitioned into a better wife for my husband. Sometimes your husband may be having a bad day and he may attempt to take it out on you. He may, for example, be snippy in speech and not act like the loving husband that he ordinarily is. You can get in the flesh with him and take him up toe to toe, but this does not glorify GOD and will not solve your issues. Sometimes, you have to get over yourself to show him how to get over himself.

The Man That GOD Drove Away From You

"GOD may say 'no' to the man you chose because HE has already said 'yes' to the man HE chose."

I'm a woman. I don't have to say that. I have dealt with an adulterous affair and had a marriage to end because of it; but I survived because I chose to love, forgive, and to move forward. This was a decision that I had to make during the transition so that I wouldn't be held back. In the midst of my pain, I asked the LORD to put forgiveness in my heart towards the people I felt had wronged me. HIS response set me free and helped me to understand just how these things come into play. HE told me that they hadn't wronged me at all. I wronged myself by failing to follow the order that HE has in place to keep and protect HIS sons and daughters. I chose to skip the seasons, ignore the WORD, come in through the window, and pursue the imaginations of my own heart. Therefore, what happened wasn't the result of a man betraying me; it was the result of me betraying myself. I chose to believe that sin would take me to this blessed place that my imagination had shown me; I chose not to believe that the WORD of GOD was true for me. Like most people, I thought I was exempt because I thought I could follow my sin up with a prayer, and GOD would take my wrongs and make them all right. Therefore, to not forgive them for what they did was to not be forgiven by HIM for what I did. My wrongs set everything in motion that happened to me in my adult life. And with that lesson, love met me and unforgiveness could not come near me. I wanted no part of unforgiveness because I understood what it would do to me, and I made a choice to stand on the WORD of GOD and move forward. I saw what unforgiveness did to other women and men. It is a cancer that destroys them from the inside out. It even begins to take a toll on their health and their physical appearance. Sometimes, when a man or woman speaks, you can hear unforgiveness in their lungs! It rattles like smoker's phlegm, and it isn't attractive at all. Unforgiveness is a curse! Remember, Satan did not force Eve to eat that fruit; Eve listened to Satan and bit it herself. He simply lied to her, but she picked the fruit with her hands, and she bit the fruit with her teeth. And if she wasn't wrong enough, she then took it to her husband, and he chose to bite it as well.

So, when I meet women who have endured or are enduring a breakup from a man because of an adulterous affair, my heart goes out to them. Nevertheless, I am often surprised at the amount of venom and hate that these women retain for the man and his mistress. Many of them sit back and wait on the day that GOD'S vengeance would visit these people because they believe that this will bring closure to them. (And to think like that is pure evil.) What is even more surprising is the amount of time that these women retain this hate and unforgiveness. I have literally met people who are still nursing wounds from breakups that occurred more than twenty years ago! Seriously. Of course, this means that they have not forgiven the man or the other woman, and until they do so, they can't move past yesterday and embrace the blessings of today. Which means, they could not be found by their GOD ordained husbands

~~because they haven't divorced their pasts.~~ Therefore, they are found in their pain by broken men who, in turn, give them a few more problems to deal with.

"Grab that microphone for me!" The voice was loud and the woman who it came from stood 5'7 with long brown hair, wearing this beautiful shimmery green dress. Her beautiful brown skin was accented by her chestnut colored eyes and full face. She was on stage, a few hours away from the celebration where she was to sing for the LORD. She'd waited years for this moment and it finally came.

Her name is Iyana. She'd just begun to understand her walk, her trials and now, here she was about to sing in front of a stadium of believers who'd gathered together to celebrate the LORD. And in that stadium was a person she'd never thought she'd see there. So, she was ready to worship and praise the LORD like she'd never done before.

Five years ago, Iyana met Mario at a church function. Well, not EXACTLY at the function itself. When she'd come out to go to her car, he was there picking up his mother. Driving a gold Lexus and quite a looker, Iyana could not resist his request to hand over her phone number. He jokingly said to her, "This is a stick up. I want your phone number and your heart. Don't make any sudden moves, or I'll be forced to start crying in front of all these people." Iyana laughed. He was so cute! Even though he'd told her that he'd just left a party where a few celebrity rappers were, Iyana did not hesitate to give him her number. He was obviously worldly. But, he was so cute! And who can resist a cute face? (A wise woman is the answer, if you're wondering.)

Mario lived a couple of hours away in Daytona Beach, Florida, whereas Iyana lived in Gainesville, Florida. Mario's mother also lived in Gainesville, so he came to see her once or twice a month. He was a momma's boy, and Iyana liked that. She believed that because he seemed to adore his mother so much, that he could and would adore her just as much, if not more.

The distance between Iyana and Mario seemed to bring them closer together. Mario was enamored by the beautiful GOD-fearing woman who'd admittedly been with only one other man in her whole 27 years of life. The kind of women he was used to, by the time they'd reached 27, were already in their double digits in relation to sleeping partners. Plus, Iyana was very much like his mother; a church-going woman and Mario could always depend on his mother. Iyana was in love with the fact that Mario was a business man. He'd bragged on making thousands as an A&R agent for up-and-coming hip hop artists. He would then take some of the money he earned and buy houses to flip. Yep. He was coming up on the financial end pretty fast. The only thing that was missing was GOD in his life. Iyana felt like she could and would be the one to help his mother lead him to CHRIST. *A lesson insert here, women: a woman is and was never called to lead a man. So, you can't lead him anywhere.*

A few months into the relationship, both Iyana and Mario had a sexual tension building up between them, and that pressure was both intense and somewhat bothersome. Iyana believed without a shadow of a doubt that Mario was her husband. And oh, what a great prize she believed him to be! And Mario often said to her that he believed that she would be the woman who could help him get his life right with CHRIST. *(Let's stop here for a moment of silence. If you heard this before...run from the man whose mouth it came from.)* Again, back to the story. Mario made it known to Iyana that he planned to marry her.

Iyana tried hard to remain celibate. She wanted the relationship to be blessed by GOD. But, 10 months later, she found herself in a hotel room with Mario. She'd promised herself that while he was in town, she'd go and visit him for a while and then leave. But, Iyana...why did Mario get a hotel room when he could have easily stayed with his mother? The answer is obvious.

At the hotel, Mario said all of the right things, touched all of the right places, and it happened. They fornicated and even though it was wrong, it felt so right. Iyana was smitten. There was no going back for her. She now wanted Mario more than she wanted the LORD. But, she didn't see it that way at the time.

After the rendezvous, Iyana gave the typical hypocritical church-girl speech. "I know what I did was wrong, and I feel so bad about it. I don't ordinarily do this. It's just that there is something so special about you that it just feels right to me. I don't usually do this with any man. I hope this doesn't come back to bite me. I don't usually do this." But, this didn't move Mario. He was in love with the fact that he was the second man to have her and again; she was like his mother. Plus, she'd made him wait 10 months?! That was longer than any girl had made him wait. So, the sexual encounter didn't sway him.

Mario started coming to Gainesville more often, even though sometimes Iyana was having one of her "religious" spells and would not sleep with him and other times, she would easily give in.

Thirteen months into the relationship, he decided to pop the question. After all, Iyana kept going on and on about how she felt convicted; she couldn't sing right on Sundays anymore, and she needed to be married to make it all right. Of course, after Mario proposed, Iyana accepted.

The wedding was huge. They held the ceremony in Gainesville and almost everyone from Iyana's church home came. The women stood by in awe of the tall, handsome brown skinned, muscular man who stood with military authority as he awaited his bride. He was beautiful to look upon. A real treat to the eyes. Mario's mother was happy because Mario was marrying a girl who was in the church. She too felt like Iyana could lead her son to CHRIST. *(Again, women weren't called to lead their husbands.)*

After the wedding, the newlyweds went to Athens, Greece for their honeymoon before settling down in Daytona Beach. Iyana was so very happy. This handsome, successful man wanted to spend his life with her, give her children, and share what he had with her. Mario was happy because he felt like he'd accomplished another feat. Not only was his career on track, but he had this beautiful trophy wife whom none of his friends or the people he knew had ever had or been with. She'd kept herself well.

Like any other relationship where the spouses are unequally yoked, Iyana found herself going between gospel and secular. There was no way Mario was going to let her slide by with that beautiful voice of hers. And slowly, she began to come out of the church.

They seemed to have it all. They had the big house, the beautiful cars, they traveled the world, and did things most people have never done and will never do. Nevertheless, Iyana found herself falling into this 'heaviness.' She didn't know what it was, but it was some sort of depressing that had come over her often and for no apparent reason. *(Joy is found in the LORD, but outside of HIM, you will have to settle for occasional bouts of happiness.)*

After Iyana gave birth to Mariana, the couple's first child, she began to notice a change in Mario. He seemed to go out more, but bring in less. And when he was home, he was distant. That passion fueled look that he used to gaze at her with had somehow run out of gas. He was more "short" with Iyana, getting irritated by even the most loving gestures. Once she'd offered to massage him, and he'd yelled, "If I want a massage, I'll ask for a massage! That's your problem. Always trying to fix what ain't broken. Sit down sometimes! Man!" Iyana began to pray against that devil. The devil was attacking her marriage! That's what she believed, anyways. *(Satan wasn't attacking, but was claiming what belonged to him.)*

Feeling her marriage was in danger, Iyana decided to try to give Mario a son. She didn't tell him about her plans, since he'd voiced that he didn't want anymore kids. However, Iyana felt this was the cure for their troubled marriage. So, one night, when he did come to bed, Iyana went after him, and it worked. Nine and a half months later, she gave birth to a son, Mario Winston, Jr. Despite the birth of his son; the relationship continued to get worse. There were nights when Mario didn't even come home, citing that a party for one of his artists had gone over into the next day. And he basically dared Iyana to question him by giving her a look that told her that if she made a big deal of the issue, she'd pay for it. So, Iyana quietly sat by and cried when he was not around. She was always in prayer about him. At the same time, she knew that there was the possibility of an affair.

One day, while Mario was supposedly out of town on business, someone called Iyana's cellphone. The voice on the other end was a woman. She sounded very seductive and whatever devils she had could be heard whispering in her vocals. “I know Mario is your husband,” she said, “but I've been sleeping with him for the last five months, and now he is messing around with a girl they call Passion. She lives in Rochelle, but she dances in South Daytona. Since he messed over me, I just thought you should know. By the way, my name is Tyisha.” Before Iyana could respond, Tyisha hung up. This explained it all. He always said he had to go to Rochelle to promote this new artist called Passion, but Iyana had never considered that Mario was two-timing her, or worse than that, three-timing her. She called his cellphone and as usual, got no answer from him. Hurt, confused and hoping it was all a bad joke; she left him a voice message telling him about what this girl had said. It was easy to hear that she was crying.

A few hours later, Mario called her back and unleashed a fury of words on her that would leave her in a state of shock. “Look, don't be calling my phone talking about what some prostitute has told you! What you don't know, you don't need to know, but if you must know, Tyisha is a prostitute, and she comes to the parties sometimes and sleeps with a lot of the men there. But, when she came at me, I told her I was happily married! Me and Passion are business partners! That's it! But, if you don't like what I do, you know what you can do. Head back to Gainesville and find yourself a church boy!”

Iyana began to apologize. Even though he'd thrown some pretty harsh words her way, she felt comforted that he said he was not having an affair. Those harsh words seemed like cookies to her, and she ate them all up. But, while apologizing, Mario hung up the phone on her.

The next day, Iyana went out to purchase a few things to prepare for a romantic night. Hubby was coming back today, and this was her way of apologizing. She'd taken the children to his mother's house two hours away, so that she could keep them for the weekend. And when she went home, she moved the furniture around, cooked, ran a bubble bath for her and Mario and waited for her husband to come home. But, he didn't. Around 11 p.m., she called Mario, but he didn't answer. A few minutes later, a text came in. "See you tomorrow. Meetings ran over. ~Mario." Heartbroken, Iyana retreated to her bedroom to cry and to pray. She was beginning to feel like GOD wasn't listening to her. Why was HE letting Mario do all of these wicked things to her? Deep down in her heart, she knew he was having an affair, but she wouldn't accept it as her reality because she thought it would run her crazy. She got up, blew out the candles and fell asleep on the bed, surrounded by tissues.

The morning came and Iyana was awakened by Mario. "You sick or something? Why are all these tissues on the bed?" Afraid to tell him that she'd been crying the night before, Iyana replied, "No; my sinus was draining last night." After that, Mario told Iyana to get the tissues off the bed because he was tired. It was a long night, and he didn't feel like talking right now. "The good thing was he didn't go take a shower," Iyana thought. "Because when a man is cheating, he always showers." ~~But, when she laid close to him, she noticed that he smelled like Dove when she~~

~~knew they only used Irish Springs~~. He always took a bar of soap to the hotels with him to shower with because he said that hotel soaps were cheap and broke him out. Iyana didn't bother to ask. She didn't want the argument that she knew would follow. She just tried to lay her head on his chest, but Mario immediately snipped, “Move. It's hot, Iyana! All this bed and you need to lay this close to me?! Move, Iyana!” Iyana moved over and turned her back to Mario so that he wouldn't see her cry. She tried not to be loud with it, but her sniffles and the movement of her body made it evident that she was crying. Mario let out a loud sigh before retreating to the living room to lay down. He was cold. Oh, so cold. ~~Unemotional ice.~~ ~~There was no warmth in him; no empathy; no love.~~

Later that day, Iyana decided to shake it all off and try to ignite the night the way she'd tried the day before. She went and showered and put on a nice satin gown. She lit the candles and turned on some old romantic slow songs to bring in the mood. When she walked into the living room, Mario was laying on the couch, watching television. When he saw Iyana, his face didn't change. He looked serious, and he made it clear that he wanted to be left alone. “Can you move? I'm trying to watch the game, please. Anyway...after you called me the other day acting stupid about what some hooker told you and then today, you want to cry because I said I was hot...no, Iyana...get away from me. Move out the way. You can't expect me to act like our marriage is good. Go read your Bible and pray or something.”

Have you ever had a moment where situations and words shocked and hurt you so intensely that all you could do was to stand there and fight off thoughts of violence? One of those moments that you thought you would react violently, but instead, all you could do was stand there...frozen, not knowing how to respond? Well, this was Iyana's moment. Mario was getting colder and colder and now; he'd ruined the weekend. He brought her even lower when he looked at her and said, “Oh, by the way, I'm going out tonight. Don't be calling my phone either. I don't try to track your whereabouts, and I don't want a wife who acts like a police issued ankle bracelet.” Numb, Iyana walked into the kitchen and stared at a large knife. She thought about plunging it into her husband, but decided against it. She then went to the bathroom and picked up a bottle of aspirin. She thought about taking all of them, daydreaming of how sorry Mario would feel at her funeral or how people would criticize him as she recovered. In her imagination, he'd humble himself and realize how horrible he had been and try to do better.

She walked into the living room and told Mario that she didn't want to live anymore, and that she was thinking about taking her own life. She could see Mario's frown lines as he sharply formed his words. “Stupid, ignorant woman! You waste of skin and teeth! And you wonder why I don't come home, and I don't touch you! Cause you're stupid! Do you want to kill yourself? Then do it! What's stopping you?! Oh. Would you like me to open the bottle for you?!” Mario snatches the bottle of aspirin from Iyana's hand and pours them out in his own hand. He then heads to the kitchen and runs water into a glass and brings it to Iyana. “Here you go. Knock yourself out! I don't know why I married such a dumb...let me stop. I'm out!” At this, he throws the aspirin at Iyana, dashes the water into her face, and throws down the glass; shattering it. He then grabs his keys and leaves; slamming the door so hard that their picture fell off the wall. This was one of the many unforgettable moments that Iyana had to endure. She cried so loudly and violently that the neighbors could hear her. She tried to muffle the sounds of her screams by crying into a pillow, but her hurt and sore rage could be heard and felt.

The next day, Iyana prepared to go and pick up her children. It was seven a.m. on a Sunday morning, and her eyes were still red and puffy. One of her neighbors who'd heard the crying and arguing the night before was heading out to go to church. When he saw Iyana, he stopped to speak. She tried to greet him back, but her voice was hoarse. She sounded almost like a frog. The man came over to formally introduce himself. He was carrying a Bible and immediately, Iyana thought he was coming to flirt. But, how could he? She'd seen him so many times with his wife and daughter. Men! She fixed her face in a rude way to express her disdain for what she believed he was coming to do. "I'm Pastor Parlow," he said. "I just wanted to come and encourage you and tell you that GOD has not forgotten you. If you ever need someone to talk to, my wife is at home, and she doesn't mind. She doesn't work, so she's home most of the time. I won't hand you my business card because that may seem out of order. I just came to tell you that our door is open because I can see that you have an anointing on your life, and daughter, you can't run from that anointing. You can't sell it, market it or prostitute it. You were created to serve the LORD, and anytime you come out of serving HIM; the devil will have his way with you."

Iyana thanked the pastor, but said that she had to leave. She felt ashamed and convicted. What did he see? Or better yet, what did he hear? She got into her car quickly and started it up, waving at the pastor as he waved and went back towards his car.

Two hours later, she arrived at her mother in law's house. She went up and knocked on the door and Phoebe, her mother in law, answered the door. "Hey baby!" She reached and hugged Iyana, but she could see that Iyana looked run down. She looked older and drained. She knew where it was coming from. "Come in and sit down," she said to Iyana. "Let me talk to you."

Phoebe: I know you're a private person, and I try to stay out of you and Mario's business, but daughter; you cannot let this man kill you. Mario is my son and I love him dearly, but I won't excuse what he is doing. Iyana, if you have to leave my son; do it! Don't you die trying to breathe life into a marriage that GOD never called to live.

Iyana: Momma, I understand, but it hurts so bad. It hurts so so bad. I have never felt this kind of pain before, and I don't know what to do with it. I have done everything that he has asked me to do, and it's never enough. It's never enough! I even go outside of what he expects of me, hoping that he will see how I love him, and that I'm here for him, but it's like, everything I do irritates him.

Phoebe: You know, Iyana, when you first got with my son, I was happy. I thought, here is this girl that GOD has sent to win my son's soul. But, since you've been with him, I have seen him bring you down. You don't go to church anymore. Now, you're singing all that devil's music, and I had to spank Jr. a couple of times for cursing and carrying on. You've got to come back to CHRIST, baby girl, before it's too late. It's not working out because it was never called to work. Satan did what he wanted to do with you and now, he wants to break you down and destroy you. Get back to CHRIST, baby. HE is your safety tower.
Iyana: I want to, but how can HE accept me? Look at me. You know the last CD Mario had me to make was all about sex. He got me singing on all of these rapper's CDs, and I have never seen a dime from it even though he claims the albums are doing so well.

Phoebe: Why didn't you just tell him no?

Iyana: Cause, sometimes it's easier to just do what Mario wants then to have to hear his mouth or deal with his tantrums.

Phoebe: ~~Oh. So, you'd rather comfort Mario by sinning against GOD than to stand up for what you believe in and offend Mario? Sweetie, you can't drag him to GOD. He came here the other day, and I had to make him leave....he wasn't bringing that thing into my house! No way!~~

Iyana: He came the other day? Down here to Gainesville? For what?

Phoebe: I don't know; he said that he was down here for some concert and he had one of those hip hop artists in his car. I think she said her name was Passion. Sounds like a stripper to me. Anyhow, he wanted me to let him and Passion stay the night, talking about his credit card was maxed out so he couldn't get a room. And I wasn't having that because he's married. He said that she was just one of his artists, but I saw the devil on that girl, and she wasn't coming into my house. No way! Plus, you are his wife. You are the only woman he can bring to my house.

Iyana felt sick to her stomach. There goes that name again. Passion!

Iyana: Momma, don't tell him that you told me about Passion. I heard about her from some girl that called me and said that she had an affair with Mario. But, apparently he must have left her for Passion, and she called to tell me about it. Don't say to him that you've told me, okay?

Phoebe: Why not? I'm not scared of him and neither should you be! Wrong is wrong and I told him that I was going to tell you.

Iyana: And what did he say?

Phoebe: He shrugged his shoulders and said "Tell her." Baby, he has grown cold and callous towards you. I can see that. But, you gotta find your way back into the warmth and comfort of GOD'S arms. ~~If you don't, that man is going to destroy you. But, I'm praying that GOD'S will be done. And Iyana, sometimes HIS will isn't what we want, but it is what we need. Just trust HIM.~~

After a long conversation, Iyana decided to leave the kids with their grandmother for a few more days. This was all too much, and she didn't want her kids to see the torment she was going through. When she got back home, Mario was already there, packing up his clothes.

Iyana: Mario, where are you going? You don't have to do this!

Mario: Yes, I do! I'm tired of you. You're always complaining! You're always crying! Obviously, I don't make you happy, so I'm going to free you up so you can find happiness and maybe find yourself a church boy.

Iyana: Mario, I know about Passion. So, this is what you want?! To leave your wife for a stripper slash prostitute?! Do you really believe it's going to work?! Seriously, Mario?!

Mario: See, that's what I'm talking about. You're too stupid for words. You know that? You're just a waste of breath, and I can't stand looking at you. I wish I would have been out of here before you got back. Now I have to hear this stupidity! Iyana, please just let me leave without having to look at you or listen to you. Can you do that for me? Can you spare me this ugly moment?

Iyana: Why are you doing this to me? I have done nothing, but loved you. Why, baby? Why? Please, look at me! I'm your wife. Look at me! Why do you hate me?

Mario: Move, Iyana! Man! When a man says that he doesn't want you, let him go! Get some sort of dignity! What? Do you think you can force me to want you?! What are you going to do?

Wear one of your boring gowns, cook one of those dry dishes, or try to pray over me when you ain't even right yourself?! Please! Get off me!

At this, he pushed Iyana so hard that she fell down and slid across the floor. She sat there against the wall, covered her ears and began to let out intense cries of hurt and anguish. Her painful screams made Mario grab what he had and leave suddenly. He wasn't sure if he'd hurt her physically. He didn't care. He hated her. She disgusted him. He went immediately and changed his cell number so Iyana wouldn't have it, and he moved in with Passion.

It wasn't long before Iyana saw him with Passion. Two weeks to the day, to be exact. He hadn't called to check on his kids nor had he filed for divorce like he claimed he would. Iyana went to the mall to purchase some coats for her children. The winter was rapidly approaching, and she wanted to prepare the kids. In the children's store, she saw her husband. He was walking behind this tall caramel colored woman who wore a blonde wig that was cut into a bob. She was wearing a black midriff top with a leopard-print mini skirt. Her stilettos were red with a leopard-print tip. She accessorized her outfit with a red purse, black and red choker and fire red lipstick. Her fingernails were so long, she could barely grip the clothing she was looking at. Of course, this woman was Passion.

Following up behind her were two little girls. They looked like they hadn't been bathed or had their hair combed in months. Her honey blonde wig was perfect for her slender face. She wore gray contact lenses and had somewhat of a Northern accent. A tattoo of a vine wrapped around her belly and went down into her skirt. Mario was dressed to impress as well. Who wears sunglasses in the store, though? Mario does. He was wearing all black. His black muscle shirt seemed to fit his every muscle. Tattoos covered his arm, and his combat boots made him look as if he was preparing for war. His wedding ring was off. When he looked over and spotted Iyana standing there and staring at him, he tossed his head back and sighed. "Here we go," he said aloud. At that, Passion looked over and recognized Iyana. She'd seen Iyana at one of the hip hop parties that Mario had thrown. She knew everything there was to know about Iyana, including the fact that she was a "church-girl." So, she didn't worry about her. Instead, she stopped and winked at Iyana before saying aloud, "Baby, how much is my allowance again? Because my kids need some more shoes and some coats. It's getting cold outside." Iyana's eyes filled with tears as she formed her hands into fists. She stared at Passion with such rage that when she felt that life-changing tap on her shoulder, she turned around angrily. It was the pastor from next door. "Hey, woman of GOD," he said. "This is the wife that I was telling you about. Barbara, this is the neighbor...I think your name was...yeah...Iyana!" Seeing the tears welding up in Iyana's eyes, Barbara (the pastor's wife) said to him, "Baby, would you mind if I spoke with Iyana alone? You can go ahead to some of those stores and look at some suits, and if I can't find you, I'll call your phone, okay?" At this, he agreed and walked away.

Iyana was still standing there with tears in her eyes. Her rage had caused her to tremble and her fists were still balled up, but suddenly, she felt a calming peace come over her. Like someone warm was holding her. "Take a walk with me," Barbara said to her. For about five minutes, they walked without saying a word. During this walk, Iyana began to weep. On the way, Barbara passed by the store that her husband was in. Spotting her, he came out. He knew that because these were two women, he'd probably be in the mall until next summer, while they spoke. So, he said, "Baby, take your time." Before he could finish, his wife said to him, "I already know. Finish your shopping and I'll meet you at home. I will ride home with Iyana because I refuse to let her drive right now." He placed his hand on Iyana's shoulder and said, "Daughter; it's going to be okay. You're in good hands." At this, he walked away and Iyana began to break. She began to tremble and cry so much that Barbara felt the need to get her out of the public eye. So, she hugged her and said, "Let's go to your car." As they broke the embrace, Iyana could see Mario and Passion standing in the distance. His words could be heard from afar. "Just stupid!," he exclaimed. Passion began to laugh and put her arms around him and then put her leg up around him. "Don't pay them any attention," said Barbara. "The devil already has them, but what's not going to happen is that he gets you. Let's go. Some people were created to testify while others were created to be a testimony. Let's get you out of here." She grabbed Iyana's hand and began to pull her towards the door. Iyana kept looking back at the meddling duo as they began to kiss passionately, even though Passion's kids were standing there looking lost.

When they got to the car, Barbara asked Iyana for the keys and she gave them to her. She began the long drive home and she ministered to Iyana. At the moment, the conversation was soothing and was what Iyana needed to hear, but because the soul tie was still present, Iyana was still angry and grieving. Through her tears, Iyana told her about her life before, during, and now after Mario.

Barbara: I know what you've been going through, and I know that you are in a place of grief. It's like going to a funeral; you feel helpless. You wish there was something you could do, but you can't. That marriage is dead and now, you've got to say your good-byes and bury it. But, you will come out of it with a testimony. Don't give up. That man was never called to be your husband. I knew that the first time I saw you together. He's not a wheat, sweetie. He's a tare, sent by the enemy to distract you and bring you to a place so the enemy could murder your purpose by perverting it.

Iyana: Mrs. Barbara, the Bible says that I could win him by my chaste behavior. I tried that and it didn't work. I have done everything right! I gave him all of me and it wasn't enough.

Barbara interrupts.

Barbara: The WORD says this would work on a husband, and it had to be coupled with fear. There is a difference between a husband and a married man. A husband is sent by GOD to his wife, and because he is of GOD, when he went away from GOD, you could win him back to GOD by your chaste behavior and your fear of GOD. You can never win him back when sin has you in its grips. A married man is just a man that someone went and married. There is no fear of GOD in him. Baby, you did like most women. You went into the world trying to bring him out. You'd be amazed how many women fall into this trap because we like to buy the lies that the Devil sells to our imaginations. So, we ignore the signs that the object of our affections could never rightfully or legally have us as wives. Did you sleep with him before the marriage?
Iyana: Yes, ma'am.

Barbara: Do you know why you did this? In every relationship, Satan needs an entry point. He can't come between what GOD has put together; he can only come against it. But, when a relationship is illegal, he can come between it because he has rights to one or both of the parties involved. Satan has no rights to you, but because you fornicated; you gave him rights to the relationship. He used it to twist you, pervert you and corrupt you. His plan was to kill you in it, but GOD wasn't having it. Had you not fornicated, that man would have never married you. Believe me. He would have went away from you because of your obedience to GOD. James 4:7 says, ***"Submit yourselves therefore to God. Resist the devil, and he will flee from you."*** You didn't resist him, so he stayed with you. Now, you have to take back the parts of you that Satan has scattered around. He took your faith and tossed it into the left winds. He took your identity and tossed it into the right winds. He took your anointing and perverted it for himself. He took your purity and drowned it in the ocean. But, if you will just let this hurt run its course and trust GOD; HE will restore you. Let that woman have that man. Don't worry about a man now. Right now, get your kids and submerge them in the WORD of GOD.

The discussion was revealing and comforting to Iyana. They talked for four hours before Barbara went home. "Come by anytime," she said as she exited Iyana's car. "We are here for you if you need us."

Iyana did as sister Barbara told her. She took it day by day, trying not to think about tomorrow. It was also relieving not to have to endure Mario's harsh words or that agonizing hurt and fear that she would feel when he wouldn't come home. She knew this was the start of her journey back to GOD. She just needed to heal.

A month later, Mario sent the divorce papers to Iyana. It hurt her to see them, but she signed them anyway; unintentionally dropping a tear-drop onto the papers as she signed her name.

Iyana wasn't working, but the house she was living in belonged to her and Mario. She had plenty of money (that she'd stashed) in her accounts, so she was able to keep up with the bills. It was stressful, however, to explain to her children why their daddy wasn't coming around anymore. Junior was okay with it. He was only a year old at the time, so he didn't ask too many questions. But, Mariana was four years old and was obviously heartbroken. Nevertheless, Iyana did not speak evil of her dad, but told her to just pray for him.

Day by day, it got a little easier. Some days were hard and on those days, Iyana would go by Sister Barbara's house for an encouraging word. And then, on some days, she decided to tough it out and let the pain run its course. She began to read her Bible again, and she began to attend services at Pastor Parlow's church. It always felt like the message was custom tailored just for her. And when the time was right, she got up to sing. The anointing on this girl was so intense that not one soul was left undelivered.

A year later, the divorce had been finalized, and Iyana was a lot better. Her face had a glow about it that had once been stolen. She'd kept in touch with Mario's mother, who was so proud of her progress. Iyana asked her ex mother-in-law not to tell her anything about Mario. She just said that she was praying for him, and that was that. But, Phoebe could not resist. She would began every call with, “He's still with that ole nasty girl.” At this, Iyana would always giggle and say, “But we're praying for them, right?”

She always wondered why he'd stuck with this Passion girl for over a year. She was supposed to be a toy. Nevertheless, she would always shrug it off and keep living.

Iyana's prayers often included Mario. ~~She would pray that he would turn his life around and give himself to CHRIST. She also prayed for Passion, but the LORD works on those that want to be worked on. Meaning, HE gave us will, so if we don't want HIM, HE won't force HIMSELF into our lives.~~

A year and a half after the divorce, Iyana was out at the mall again. She was with one of the church members named Phara, and they were shopping for their kids. Phara's sons trailed behind her as Iyana's children stood by her shopping. While she was shopping, Iyana heard this familiar loud baby like voice. Yep. It was Passion in the same store shopping and yelling at her kids. But, this time, Mario wasn't with her. Iyana looked up at her and at the same time; Passion looked at her, and their eyes met. Passion grinned and began to say to her children, "Come on. We gotta hurry up cause your daddy is taking us out on the town....AGAIN!" Iyana didn't feel anger towards her. Just love. She turned her head and continued to shop.

Three years went by and Iyana was doing pretty good for herself. She'd healed and learned from her mistakes. Still no husband yet, but she was content as she was and didn't care to have one. She focused on GOD, her kids and her new career as an interior designer.

Mr. and Mrs. Parlow adored Iyana. She was so very anointed and loving. She was like a daughter to them, even though they were only about 10 years older than her. Mrs. Parlow asked Iyana if she would sing at this year's annual gospel celebration. Every year, tens of thousands of souls would fill the stadium, and thousands were saved. This event had become such a worldwide stir that if you didn't buy your tickets at least six months in advance, you probably weren't getting in. Iyana had been to a couple of these celebrations, but she'd never imagined that she would be one of the singers to grace the stage. But, there was something about this year that she knew she had to sing.

As that day approached, Iyana searched high and low for the perfect dress to wear. She remembered that there was a new store in the downtown area that a lot of people were raving about. So, she went. When she arrived there, it was almost dark out. As she pulled into the parking lot, she could see the silhouette of two people fighting. A man was pulling a woman out of her car and punching the back of her head as she kept trying to enter the car. She immediately recognized them. It was Mario and Passion. Mario was yelling obscenities at Passion and all she could do was scream and beg for mercy. Iyana thought to herself, "They stayed together because they are just alike. Shame. GOD moved me because this foolishness is not my portion." Love and empathy for Passion filled her heart again, and she dialed 911 from her cellular phone. The police arrived three minutes later and by this time, Mario had Passion leaned over the hood of the car and was trying to choke her out. The police were pulling in as Iyana ran over, tapped Mario on the shoulder, and when he turned around; she sprayed him with pepper spray. Passion, dazed and confused; fell to the ground, crawling and trying to catch her breath.

The police came and immediately restrained Mario as he lay on the ground screaming and holding his eyes. He was crying and begging for an ambulance. Ten minutes later, Passion sat on the ground by the car, smoking a cigarette and crying as she gave the officer the report. She listened and watched intently as Iyana gave her side of the story. Because Mario had lied and said that

Passion had attacked him so the officers were considering arresting both of them, but Iyana told them what she'd seen. So, the officers took their reports, arrested Mario and left. Iyana stood there and asked Passion if she was okay.

Passion: Thank you. You didn't have to help me. I'm actually very surprised that you did. Thank you.

Iyana: You don't have to thank me. You don't deserve that. I couldn't sit by and watch him kill you.

Passion: Do you know what's funny? I have two friends who came out here with me. Neither one of them stopped to help me. They saw when he started attacking me and they went back inside. They heard me screaming that he was trying to kill me and they heard me ask them to call the police. But, it was the woman who I did wrong that turned out to be the woman who saved my life. For that, I say thank you and I am so so sorry about what I did to you. Please forgive me.

Iyana: I didn't save your life. GOD did. GOD knew you needed help at this hour. HE wanted you to see that the people around you did not love you. I can look at you and tell you that you don't belong in this lifestyle. I can sense that you are running from GOD. Why are you running, Alexis?

Passion began to cry. No one had called her by her real name 'Alexis' for years. And she knew it to be true. She took a long puff of her cigarette before answering.

Alexis: I don't know. I guess I'm scared. I've known this lifestyle since I was 14. I was angry at GOD for a long time because I felt like HE let my daddy rape me again and again. I don't know why I'm telling you these things, but it's true. I have been praying a lot lately though and I noticed that the more I prayed; the more violent Mario got towards me and my children. It's like; he isn't there any more. I know this makes you happy because of what we did to you. But, I deserved this. I'm not mad because I deserved it.

Iyana: No beautiful. You don't deserve to be abused or mistreated. I forgave you a long time ago and I have been praying for you to come back to CHRIST. What your dad did was wrong, but he is not your FATHER. GOD is. Satan adopted you when you ran away from GOD. But, now HE is calling you back, prodigal daughter.

Alexis: You know what I don't understand? Why would HE want me after all the mess I've done? A man walked up to me in the supermarket the other day and said GOD was calling me back and I was thinking...yeah right. I figured HE wasn't listening to my prayers because of the stuff I did.

Iyana smiles.

Iyana: I said the same thing. I turned from HIM to follow behind that same man. But, you know what? The LORD will never leave HIS daughters with men that are not HIS sons. It won't be easy, but you'll make it through and I'll be here if you need me; GOD willing.

She lowered her hand to help Alexis off of the ground.

Iyana: You're not Passion anymore. You are who GOD called you; not what Satan nicknamed you.

Alexis reached for Iyana's hand and when she stood up off the ground, she hugged her with such intensity that Iyana almost thought, for a second, that Alexis was a man. They both hugged, and Iyana forgot what she'd come to the store to get. She said to Alexis, "I'm not letting you drive home in your condition. I'll take you home and tomorrow; I'll bring you back to get your car."

Alexis smiled and got into the car with Iyana. When Iyana started the car, Alexis spotted her two friends coming into the parking lot. “I know you're Christian and all, but you gotta know that I have a long way to go. I know GOD sent you cause if I was behind the wheel at THIS very moment, those two would be licking my tires.” Iyana laughed and said, “Nope. That's why I got the keys. Let GOD deal with them, sweetie. Right now, you've got a journey ahead of you.” And they drove away.

During the next few weeks, Iyana would pick up Alexis for church on Wednesdays (Bible Study) and Sundays. She also gave her a coveted front row ticket to the gospel celebration, but she didn't expect her to come since she would put up such a fuss about going to church so often.

Three weeks later, at the gospel celebration, Iyana was the last to come out and sing. Pastor Parlow had given a life-altering message, and all of the singers were there in true worship fashion. There were no 'concert' types. Everyone was there to worship. As Iyana went onto the stage wearing her sequenced green dress, she hugged First Lady Parlow and began to weep before receiving the microphone from her. She blew a kiss at the First Lady as she exited the stage and the music began. Just when she was about to sing, she looked out into the audience and saw this bright yellow dress that was similar to hers. It was Alexis. Alexis blew a kiss and formed the words “I love you” with her lips as she held her heart. Iyana smiled and began to bless the Name of the LORD with such intensity that not a soul was left in that building undelivered.

It was a long journey for Alexis. She was delivered, but her way of thinking had to be changed. Slowly, but surely, Alexis rose from the ashes of who she was not and began to find who she was as she journeyed further into GOD.

Two years later, Alexis was waiting outside of strip bars, ministering to the men and women who went in, and many were saved. Iyana continued her walk in CHRIST, never ever looking at another man with her eyes. When her husband finally came, she looked at him with her heart and six years after her divorce from Mario, she was found by the man that was anointed to be her husband. Even though Mario continued in his life of sin, he was finally converted 11 years after Iyana got married. He had a car accident that almost took his life, but a pedestrian, seeing him on the ground after being thrown from his vehicle prayed over him. Even though he was now confined to a wheelchair, he gave himself to GOD and began to have a relationship with his children, who were now adults. And his mother Phoebe lived to see this day.

Seven years after the accident, he went to a church where he was healed. He got up and walked. He had to walk off all of the accusations that Satan had placed against him. When he was 55, he was ordained a pastor. Who knew? What looked like a lost cause to most was GOD'S opportunity to glorify HIS Name.

And one of Mario's sermons to the ladies:

"A man will serve himself, even if that means he will use you as an offering. A man who worships himself cannot be with a woman, unless she is serving him because he is his own god, and a god needs servants. You can't get with a man and expect to serve the LORD. It just doesn't happen. That man won't have it. He will get with you and expose the sin in you, feed it, nurture it and love it. But, when you try to get back to GOD, that man will hate you because you have chosen GOD over him. Many of you in here are in relationships that GOD isn't in. And you're trying to make them right when GOD called them wrong. A leaf can't dance with the wind because wherever the wind blows, the leaf goes. The wind is too powerful for it. That's why you have to let the LORD root you in the WORD as a fruit-bearing tree so that you won't be carried away by the winds of doctrine, lust and lies.

You can pray all day, fast until you fall out, and anoint that man with oils from all over the world. You can pour water on him from the Red Sea, but what that man is; he is. GOD created us and gave us will. And when that man has willed himself to sin...listen to that word again...'willed.' When he has willed himself to sin, he is saying that he is giving all that he has, even after death to that sin. You can keep praying for him, and GOD may give him a life-altering encounter that will bring him to CHRIST, but you are not to marry this man. You are to pray for him, and that's it! Sharpen him when it's needed. You don't know how much this man has to go through, and how long he has to go through it before he finally surrenders. I've seen men wait until the last hour of their lives to call upon the Name of the LORD! Do you want to have spent your whole life being called out of your name, disrespected, cheated on, beat up, beat down, spit on and brought low waiting on this day to come? Only to have it happen when you're too old and too tired to appreciate it?! GOD called you to be the wife of a husband. A husband is a living man who is in CHRIST. Now, if he's waiting until his last hour, that means, you've got 59 minutes to enjoy his newfound salvation! So you'd better squeeze everything that you have ever wanted to do in that 59 minutes! Will you waste your life for an hour? Sure, you want him to come to CHRIST. That's a part of who you are. But, you are not women; you are women of GOD. You are wives! You are to be led of your husband, not dragged to death by a man!

When you go out and try to force a relationship that was not meant to be, you are in that same hour saying that you will serve that relationship and the one who established it. But, remember, it wasn't brought together by GOD so now you're over there having to do satanic things to try to keep this man. He got you over there watching porn, cursing and fulfilling his lusts and in the end; he'll still toss you out like a used paper towel. If he left to be with someone else, applaud! He couldn't stay with you because your FATHER and his father did not agree about what they wanted to do with you. But, he may stay with that other woman because they have the same daddy! That is unless she gets up one day and decides she wants to be saved, and now she has to face them devils in him. An evil man needs an evil woman, but an evil man is drawn to what he does not recognize, and that is a saved woman. He thinks there is something in that woman that will birth something in him, but when he sees that she is just another woman, he will begin to hate her. Because, in a way, he feels like she betrayed him by making him think that she was someone she was not. She never told him that. But, the Devil led him to believe that by seducing a woman of GOD, he would be able to continue in his sin and have this trophy of a beautiful, GOD fearing wife at home to boast about. As time goes along, she gets uglier and uglier to him. Her voice is irritating. Her thoughts, to him, are stupid. The way she chews bothers him. Even touching her becomes disgusting to him. Why? Is it because she's ugly, stupid, retarded or nasty? No! It's because he is no longer blinded by the lustful idea that you'll be his holy, but freaky housewife and let him go out and have what he wants in the world. No. Now, his eyes are open, and he sees this woman before him that keeps on talking about...GOD this and GOD that. He doesn't want to be changed, even though he told you that to get you. He wanted to change you. Pick yourself back up again and reclaim your anointed places! Stop giving yourself to men who don't want GOD! How can they want you when they don't want your FATHER?! I know. I was once one of these men, and I saw my friends dying; refusing to know who HE was. They treated whatever woman that was in their lives like toilet seats. They'd do their business on them and get up when they were finished, only coming back when they had crap coming out of them. Is this what you want to be?"

Explanation:

It is common for a woman to cry and talk about how good she was to the man who broke her heart. But, then he left her for another woman, and he's settled down with that woman and is trying to make a life with her. Think about this. Maybe you were good to him because you are a good person and maybe he was bad to you because he wasn't a good person. We are who we choose to be. But, a man can never be for you what he isn't for GOD.

You should never be distracted by your past because it only came to dress you for your future; not to be worn in your future. The past should not be a part of your wardrobe. At the same time, each lesson comes to bear witness to GOD'S WORD, so it should build on your faith, rather than tear you down.

A lot of women of GOD don't realize that when you are the daughter of the KING, HE will say no to any union not put together by HIM. We put it together, but GOD'S "no" will tear it apart; not to break your heart, but to repair your faith. Because the wrong man cannot do the right things to or for you. He doesn't understand your build because he's not a part of it. You don't have his rib. You're trying to force yourself into his life, and you wonder why you're like a thorn in his side.

And then...there's the question...How does she get to keep him when you were better for him? That's easy. He wasn't better for you. A man will only be attracted to a woman who is like him, but a little lower. Now, this isn't something to go and smudge in the other woman's face because she may be in her lost 'hour.' Who knows? GOD may want to use you to show her the way out. Because you weren't always right either. Admit it so you can forgive her and move on. We often hold other women accountable for their sins against us, forgetting about what we have done to others. Sure, you probably have never played the other woman, but are you sin free? Have you never hurt someone before? That's why you are to confess your sins to one another! So that you can hear yourself and know that you are not perfect. Believe me; knowing your imperfections will help you to overlook the imperfections of others. Confessions are moments of healing because they bleed the unforgiveness out of you. Think about that picture of you when you were younger and not so cute. Maybe you had no front teeth, or you were sporting a hairdo that made your head look way too big for your body. And you try to hide those photos because you don't want anyone to see the old you. You keep the pictures because they have sentimental value, and you have no choice but to show them off from time to time. That's how a confession works. It's like showing people that old ugly picture of what you once were, but once you put it away; they can see the beautiful and anointed creature that you have grown to be.

You will find that a man can be with a believing wife and leave her for a woman who drinks, curses, cheats and bounces her butt around for everyone to see. He can relate to her whereas, he probably could not relate to you. Again, you are called to pray for them and pray that GOD cleans you up so that you won't seek anymore relationships outside of HIM, but you will learn to stay in HIM as HIS daughter. What's ahead for you in CHRIST is far greater than what is behind you. Love the sinner, but not the sin.

You need to:

- Understand your sin.
- Forgive the sinner.
- Move forward.
- And sin no more.

Humble Me...Humble He (A Wifely Encounter)

"Humility isn't a disease, but it is worth catching."

A man is built to be stronger than a woman. A man is a warrior, built to war and built to love. Against an opposing nation, men had to go to war. Against a devil, men of GOD have to war in the spirit. With a wife, a man is built to love, protect and cover. But, when the wife stands in warrior stance, a man often defaults to the warrior in him, and a warrior likes the thrill of the win. On the other hand, women were built to love and to be loved. We were created as help-mates to our husbands. We have some 'warrior' blood in us, but this is only to come out if our husbands were bound up or unable to fight; then we'd stand up to protect our homes.

Evelyn believed that her mother in law (Helen) was the devil's adviser. This woman was an undiluted evil force who was bent on one thing; controlling her son (Jim), even if that meant destroying his marriage to do so.

WISE HER STILL

Jim and Evelyn's marriage had initially felt like a marriage made in Heaven. He'd showered her with love and affection, and he treated her like royalty. Evelyn was smitten and could not wait to be Mrs. Moretti, but there was one problem. The other Ms. Moretti was obsessed with her son's day to day. She called him several times a day, took lunch up to his job almost everyday, and was always asking him to come over to do something for her. Little things that she could have done herself; for example, once she'd called him over to change a light bulb....in a floor lamp! She was needy and to her, Jim was her son, her husband and her slave. Helen's husband, Jim Moretti, Sr. had passed away when Jim Jr. was only 11. Since then, it was just her and Jim. She'd even tried to stop him from going to college, saying she could take care of him and when that didn't work; she insisted that he take online classes from home. But Jim, tired of his mother's controlling ways, decided to go to college and live on campus. This is where he met Evelyn.

In the beginning of their courtship, Jim didn't talk much about his mother to Evelyn. He loved her, but he knew the evil that lurked in her, and he kept Evelyn away from her as much as he could. He didn't even tell his mother about Evelyn until after he'd proposed to her. He was afraid that she'd run Evelyn away, like she'd done so many of his previous girlfriends, and he was right.

While preparing for the wedding, Evelyn got her first whiff of Helen's venom. Against his better judgment, Jim went ahead and gave in to his mother's pleas to let her go along with Evelyn and her mother to pick out Evelyn's wedding gown. He asked Evelyn and she happily agreed, thinking this meant that her new mother-in-law-to-be could use this time to bond.

At the bridal shop, Evelyn tried on a total of 12 gowns. She really liked three of the gowns and there were four that she absolutely detested. The other five were okay. Helen hated the ones that Evelyn picked out, and she voiced it over and over again. Evelyn's mother was bothered by Helen's obvious attempt to control her daughter and the wedding. She did not want to pressure Evelyn and wanted her to be happy with **her** choice. So, when Helen would say idiocies to Evelyn like "That gown makes you look fat," or "My son wouldn't like that," Angelica would simply respond by saying, "Well, I think she looks beautiful, and I'm sure he'll like it."

Evelyn had narrowed it down to three gowns and Helen's face was riddled with disapproval. The saleswoman hung up the three gowns and placed them on hooks side by side to help Evelyn make the final choice, but Helen decided not to stay around for it. She was angry that Evelyn would not consider the gown that she'd chosen. Helen got up suddenly and stormed out of the door without saying a word. Her exit was so dramatic that everyone in the store took notice.

Another incident came along during the rehearsal dinner. Helen came to the dinner and told Evelyn that she had went back and purchased the wedding gown that she'd chosen for Evelyn because she just did not like the one that Evelyn chose for herself. "I paid a lot of money for that gown," she said. "And I'll be really disappointed if you don't wear it. You can just take the other dress back to the store and keep the money. I also bought you some accessories. Just trust me on this." Of course, Evelyn politely, but firmly declined her offer, stating that she would be wearing the gown and the accessories that she'd chosen for herself. That's when Helen showed the height of her venom. She pulled a catalog from her purse and attempted to show the gowns to her son. She said that she wanted him to choose the one that he would prefer his wife to wear. In reality, she knew that if Jim Jr. saw the gown; Evelyn wouldn't want to wear it because every bride wants her husband to see her in the gown for the first time when she walks down the aisle to marry him. But, Jim turned his head and Evelyn's mother; Angelica snatched the catalog and left the room with it. At this, Helen got up and left, but not before saying that their marriage would never work.

The final straw, for Evelyn came when she realized that Helen didn't even show up for their wedding. Instead, she tried to disrupt the wedding by making a frantic call to Jim right before the ceremony. She said that she was in the hospital and probably wasn't going to make it out alive. She claimed that the doctor said that she was having a heart attack, but Jim didn't fall for it. He knew his mother all too well. He'd responded by telling her to just listen to the doctors and he'd come to check in on her after the honeymoon.

Yes, you've probably guessed it by now. Helen has a Jezebel spirit. How so? What are the signs? She is trying to usurp the power from a man (her son) and is manipulative, controlling, religious and so on. She is hungry for power and when she doesn't get it; she erupts with rage, jealousy and tantrums. She wants to control his home, when he is supposed to be the head of his house. She wants him to listen to her, but JESUS is the head of a man. She wants to disrupt the order in his life because Jezebel hates order.

Eight months later, Evelyn was ready to walk out on her marriage. She was tired of the frequent visits, the frequent calls and Helen's desperate attention ploys. Jim, who was an ordained pastor, knew his mother had some issues, but he didn't want to offend her. He couldn't bring himself to tell her that coming to his house every day was too much or calling his house three and four times a day was too much. Plus, Evelyn was now two months pregnant and when Helen heard about the pregnancy, the first thing she did was urged Jim to get a paternity test. She'd said, "I have a friend with a son who married a girl who looks just like Evelyn. She (his wife) had two children and told her husband that they were his children, but he's just finding out that neither one of those kids are his. I'm just trying to look out for you. Evelyn is okay, but to tell you the truth; I don't trust her." Jim's error was; he let this go on. Evelyn's error was; she would not humble herself. Instead, Evelyn kept yelling at her husband about his evil mother and trying to get him to put her in her place, but Jim was afraid that if he said the wrong thing or said the right thing the wrong way, he could hurt his mother so bad that she would die of a broken heart. This is what she'd been feeding him for years. So, Evelyn took it upon herself to go and find a lawyer to discuss the cost of a divorce and her rights as a soon to be mother. But, a miracle stopped Evelyn from leaving. One that would set off a chain of events, destined to knock Jezebel off her wall yet again.

Angelica (Evelyn's mother) came to visit Evelyn one Monday morning. She knew that her son in law would be at work and she knew that Evelyn would be home alone because the doctor had put her on bed rest. She also knew what her daughter was going through. She'd battled a Jezebel and won through the application of the WORD of GOD and she wanted to see her daughter get through this without divorcing her husband. Angelica knew that Jim was a nice guy. He just didn't understand how to balance two women without losing one of them, and even though he was a pastor, he could not bring himself to believe that his mother was inhabited by a devil.

She'd found an old video tape of Evelyn playing with her now-deceased dad, Antonio. Angelica's brother recorded the video back in 1979 at Evelyn's second birthday party. Evelyn could be seen on the video refusing to go to anyone, but her dad. The love between them was so powerful; it could be felt just by watching the video. She adored her dad, and he cherished her. While watching the video, Evelyn was tearing up and began to cry. Her dad had passed away a couple of years ago, and she missed him dearly. When the video stopped, she was crying and laughing at the same time. All of the pain in her surfaced. Not just from her dad's death, but the pain from what she was going through in her marriage, and her mother saw this was the time to speak with her about her situation.

Angelica: You know; your grandmother had that same spirit. A Jezebel, that is. She hated me with everything in her. She felt like I'd stolen her son from her and when you were born, she said she didn't want anything to do with you because I refused to name you after her. She was a mess. And your daddy couldn't see how evil she was at first. After all, she was his mother. And that's what he saw. He saw his mother acting up. He only hoped she'd realize what she was doing and stop, but she wouldn't. I was ready to leave him, but you are what stopped me. The love the two of you had for one another...I couldn't separate that. You had this beautiful two-toothed grin when you were about nine months old, and I don't care what happened to you that day, how upset you were...when your dad would walk into the room, you'd light up and show those two teeth. When the doctors would give you a shot, he'd tear up and have to leave the room. I decided to stay because I didn't want to rob you of the joy I saw living in you.
Evelyn: Mom, what are you saying? That I should stay with Jim just because I'm pregnant? Do you know what happened the

other day? His mother called here and told me that she was moving in when I had the baby, whether I liked it or not. She told me that Jim had already given her his approval. Mom, he hasn't talked to me about anything, and I'd rather be alone, divorced with my daughter living in a tent than to live in this big house, married and miserable with her.

Angelica: I understand that, but have you turned it over to GOD?

Evelyn: I have prayed and I have prayed, and it seems like the more I pray, the worse it gets. She even said to my husband that she knew I'd been praying, but that my prayers wouldn't do anything because I was an evil witch. Do you know what he did? He sat there and just said, "Mom, don't call her out of her name. Be respectful please." That's it?! I'm his wife, and he is letting his mother call me a witch?

Angelica: I understand. Your grandmother called me everything from a floozy to a druggie, even though I have never done drugs and your dad was my first and only. And your dad was like a scared little boy. She would scream and yell at him until he'd sit down and look like he was ready to wet himself. And when that didn't work, she'd manipulate him; claiming to be sick, hurt, injured or going crazy. She actually did destroy your uncle Timothy's marriage. She ran that girl off, and I felt like she'd been granted early parole. I actually envied your uncle's ex-wife because she got out. I wanted out too, but I couldn't do that to you.

Evelyn: Mom, I am a woman of GOD, but I would fight her. That's why I want to leave. Because I have visions of me slapping her dancing in my head and instead of counting sheep at night, I'm counting the punches that I want to give her.

Angelica: That's because you took your eyes off of the spirit in her and started focusing on the outer shell of the woman. You're not warring against flesh, my dear; that is a spirit. And that spirit has gotten through the first line of defense, which is your husband and now; it's attempting to further take your home by running you away from it. What if Jim got into a fight with a man who was trying to break into your home, and Jim got knocked unconscious? Would you lay there and let him take it or would you fight him yourself?

Evelyn: I'd fight. That's my house too! Especially if I had children.

Angelica: Bingo. He's unconscious, sweetie. And you have to fight until he wakes up. You have to stand in for him to protect your home. Don't rob your daughter of the opportunity to have what you had. Jim's going to be a great dad.

Evelyn: Mom, you don't know if it's a girl or a boy. So, it could be my son.

Angelica: No; it's a girl. I know it. I saw her in a dream, and she is beautiful. She looks just like Jim, but she has your eyes and your daddy's smile.

Evelyn: But, how do I fight against that spirit in her? I'm tired, Mom. Really tired and that woman is a half mile past crazy right before you get to insane.

Angelica: Your weapon against a spirit is the WORD of GOD. It is the only weapon that will work. A devil will laugh at you when you come at it swinging your flesh, but when you pick up the Sword of GOD; devils flee. What I urge you to do is read Ephesians 6 every day, several times a day if you have to. Read it and apply it. Don't stop reading it and don't stop praying until you see your breakthrough. Ask GOD to give you what you really want. I know you Evelyn; you want your marriage to work, but you just feel cornered and defeated. Remember, you have to submit yourself to GOD and resist the devil; and he will flee from you. When you prayed, the situation looked like it was getting worse because you were being brought through the center of the battle. That means, you are on your way out. But, you kept retreating back by trying to win the fight with your own hands. You are prolonging the process. If you want to really see the hand of GOD move; you have to be still. You want to know how your grandmother's evil reign stopped? One of the mothers of the church had been ministering to me about the situation and she told me to sit still, be quiet, and make my request known to the LORD. She told me to anoint the door of my home and bind up every devil in my home and cast it into the pit until the day of Judgment. She also told me to pray for your dad, pray with your dad, and stop trying to convince him of how evil his mother was. I was blocking GOD from showing him. He is a man, and a man is designed to war. But, because I was taking your dad to war, he drew his sword against me, while his mother just kept on manipulating him by buying him things and playing the victim. There were times when I wanted to hold your dad's head underwater until his legs stopped kicking, and he saw the light of Heaven; but that's illegal. *(Laughs)* So, I opted to keep quiet and spare his life. And it did seem to get worse for a while. She would call my house and scream, “Put my son on the phone!” Then she'd mumble something. It wasn't easy; believe me. I grew up fighting with the flesh, and I wanted to fight her with my flesh, but I would hand over the phone to him. Sometimes, he was sitting near me and could hear her yelling, but I said nothing. When I was too angry, I'd go to the other room and silently cry. To me, I was bleeding myself of the rage. I would pray and do like mother Mildred told me. Don't try to force him to see what GOD has to reveal to him.

She would even come to my house and be downright disrespectful. One day she even came there and tried to move my furniture around, but it was too heavy for her. I kept praying, day after day...month to month until it broke! Oh, it broke! I wasn't warring with your dad, so he could see the toll it had taken on me. I was no longer a guilty party in the ordeal. I was the victim and when he realized that; he went to war. He banned her from coming to our house and completely disassociated himself from her. She tried everything in her power to manipulate him. She'd knock at the door and when we wouldn't answer, she would fall out on our front steps so that our nosy neighbors could call the ambulance. She was a resourceful woman… knew how to use the people around her. *(Laughs.)* Sad to say, she eventually got sick and passed away without a soul around her. All of her children disassociated themselves from her because of her narcissism, but I prayed for her soul. She was an evil woman, but I knew that no matter how evil she was...she was still a soul and GOD loved her. I encourage you to be quiet. Talk to your husband one day in a calm tone and tell him what his mother is doing. Say it in love. Don't wake up the warrior in him. Don't talk for hours, complaining and definitely don't try to force his eyes open. After you talk with him, pray with your husband. Ask him to pray so that you won't end up praying from your flesh. It will get harder first. I know that. But, GOD said you will win him by your chaste behavior coupled with fear. It worked for me. And I know it will work for you. Humble yourself, daughter. A warrior will always try to show himself more powerful than his opponent, and if you are acting like his opponent, he will oppose you strongly.

These words blessed Evelyn. She was at the end of her rope and could not comprehend any other direction to go in with the situation, but her mother's words opened up another door of hope for her.

When Jim came home, he expected the normal, dry Evelyn that

he'd gotten used to fighting with. But, Evelyn wasn't home. This was unusual, but her clothes were there and surprisingly enough; she'd cooked. So, he knew she hadn't left him...yet. He took off his shoes and put them away and walked into the bathroom for a shower. He felt like he needed to shower again and again throughout the day. He just felt dirty, but he did not understand that his soul was crying out for purification. He was surprised to see that Evelyn had cooked. He could smell the food. He was expecting her to serve him with divorce papers at any given moment, and he'd been praying that the LORD would repair and restore his marriage. His prayers coupled with his wife's prayers, and her chaste behavior would be his mother's undoing.

He showered and he prayed from within the shower. The tears began to well up in his eyes again. He needed to cry, but lately, he had been surrounded by the people at work, the people at church, his wife, his mother and complete strangers; so he didn't have time to cry much. So, in his alone time, he would cry and pray.

Evelyn was out buying a surprise for him. She knew he'd always wanted a digital voice recorder to record his notes for church, so she purchased one. She also bought him a greeting card, some tools and a small tub. She'd prayed and gotten this idea divinely. When she came home, Jim was sitting at the table eating. He was relieved to see the Wal-Mart bags. He thought she was out getting moving boxes or looking for a storage unit. At this time, Evelyn was six months pregnant and her belly was beginning to show more and more. She looked like she was four months pregnant, but he noticed how the bulge had grown as she put the bags down. She took the tub into the bathroom and proceeded to fill it with water. Curious as to what she was doing, Jim followed her into the bathroom, but stood by quietly as she filled the tub with water and put bubble bath in it. She filled it halfway and then asked Jim if he would pick it up and take it into the living room for her. He did and she had him put it in front of his favorite chair. Jim's heart filled with hope. He knew what she was doing. Evelyn asked him to sit down on the chair, take off his socks and place his feet in the water.

"You're not going to throw the radio in the water, are you?" he joked. Evelyn laughed and shook her head. For the first time in months, Jim could see his wife again. She didn't look like the fighter who'd been wearing him down. She looked like this beautiful angel that came out of nowhere. She had a beautiful glow to her skin. Maybe it was the pregnancy. Maybe it was GOD in her. It didn't matter at this point. He sat down and put his feet in the water while Evelyn went to the other room to retrieve the greeting card and the tools. She sat the tools on the table next to him and handed him the card. After giving him the card, she began to wash his feet. The card read:
"My dear husband, I love you with all of my heart. I know that I haven't been easy to live with, but today that is about to change. You are my husband, my head, and I understand that CHRIST is your head. I am sorry for stepping from under your authority. It has been very hard on me, but I now understand that I made it harder by not trusting the GOD in you. If you will have me, I would like to continue being your wife. GOD has given you the tools to fix what needs to be fixed. Sometimes we try to fix things with the wrong tools, so I bought you this tool set to demonstrate something. The wrench was not designed to act as the screwdriver and the hammer can't saw down a tree. I was using the wrong tools trying to fix our marriage and when I saw that it wasn't working, I was ready to walk away. But, upon further review of my contract (in the Bible), I was never supposed to try to fix it. I was only to remind you of the tools that were in you,

but instead, I cut you down, and I'm sorry. For this, I wash your feet to demonstrate my humbleness and my meekness being restored upon me like a crown to the Queen. I love you, and I know that you will make a great Father, and I know that all will be well. Just ask the LORD what to do, baby, and HE will lead you.

Your wife.... FOREVER AND A DAY
Mrs. *Evelyn Meyers."*

Now, Jim was ordinarily a man's man. Wouldn't cry in front of anyone, but he couldn't hold back the tears. He opened his mouth to speak to his wife, but the only words that would come out were praises to GOD. He had wanted a chance to make it right, but feared that it was too late. But, GOD had answered his prayers, and his wife was restored. In that hour, he was restored as well.

Later that day, sensing something was out of place for her, Jim's mother called. That demon knew it had been overcome, so his mother felt sad and desperate and didn't know why. She called Jim and asked him if he would come over so that he could help her put together her last will and testament. Jim replied, "I'm busy with my wife. Can't do it. Talk with you later." After the call, he turned off the ringer because he knew his mother would call back again and again.

Days turned into months, and Evelyn continued to be humble despite the evil things Jim's mother kept doing. And Jim grew to adore his wife all the more, but he got weary of his mother's antics.

One day, he got a call from Los Angeles, California. It was the call he'd been waiting for. His loan had been approved. He was able to purchase the property that he wanted to start a new church. He didn't plan to close the one in Texas, where he was living. Instead, he had already ordained another pastor (Pastor Henry Norman) to head up the Texas chapter of his ministry, and he was going to go to California to pastor the new church. He'd also gotten pre-approved for a loan to purchase a home, but he wanted to travel to California with his wife first so that they could shop for their home together. He was ecstatic and when Evelyn heard the news, she was overjoyed. She was now eight months pregnant, so they decided that it would be best for Jim to go ahead and move to California to get things in order. They would go house shopping after the baby was born.

When Jim's mother heard the news, she was horrified. She blamed Evelyn for this move and called her son to demand that he leave Evelyn. She was tired of Evelyn "playing games" as she called it. But, Jim let out some words that would haunt her day in and day out. "Mother, I love you and I will always love you. But, I'm done with you. You don't like my wife because you don't love me. I have let you almost destroy my family and drive me to the brink of insanity; but no more. Just know that I will always love you, but you won't have my phone number nor will you have my address when I move to California. Save your heart attacks, asthma attacks and all of your manipulations. If you pass away, I now know it was not my fault and I won't hold myself accountable. You need to forgive the people that have hurt you, but I won't let you take it out on my wife anymore. With these words, I request that you stop calling me, and I'll do the same for you. I pray that you get the help you need so that one day you can be a part of your grandchild's life. But, as of today, your witchcraft stops! I'll be praying for your deliverance, but remember; deliverance comes to those that want it."

At this, Jim hung up the phone and refused to answer anymore calls. He left that day to head to California to prepare for his wife and his unborn child. Evelyn stayed behind, moving into her mother's house to prepare for the new baby.

When their daughter was born, Jim flew down and came to the hospital to see little Deja. She was eight pounds of beauty. He went directly to the nursery to see his daughter, and his life changed all the more as he put his finger in her hand, and she gripped it with her tiny fingers. He was still wearing his priestly robe because when he'd gotten the news, he grabbed his already prepared suitcase and went directly to the airport.

When he entered Evelyn's room, his heart felt overwhelmed from what he saw. On one side of the hospital bed was Angelica, Evelyn's mother, holding her hand. On the other side sat his mother holding Evelyn's hand. He wondered who'd called her. Knowing his thoughts, Evelyn said, "I called her. The two of you need to go to the hall to talk." And they did. Helen wasted no time trying to hug her son, but he didn't return the hug. He'd forgiven her, but he didn't know what she was up to.

Helen: I went to your church back here and that pastor you ordained is no joke. I wanted to find a way to contact you. I tried to go by your old house, but it was empty, and I didn't know how to reach you or Evelyn, so I went to the church. Please hear me out. At first, I was planning to go there and humiliate Evelyn. I was hell-bent on destroying her because I was sick. That pastor you ordained is no joke at all; I tell you the truth. Well, I went in and sat down. It was the middle of his sermon and when he saw me, he called me to the front. I felt this fear rise up in me. I wanted to run, but I couldn't understand why. I'd been in church almost all of my life. Why did I want to get up and run from this one? Anyhow, I mustered up the strength to go, and he began to tell me things about me that he couldn't have known. He told me that if I didn't change, I would be dead in two months. He asked me if I wanted to be free of that generational curse of witchcraft. Baby, I cried and cried. Yes, I wanted to be free. I was always worried, always scared, always angry...who doesn't want to be free of that? Anyhow, he asked me to stretch out my hands, and I did. I don't remember much after that, but when I saw the video of what happened, I was taken aback. A voice came out of me that was not my own. It was angry. My...my, it was hateful! But, I was set free that day. I was set free!

Jim reached to hug his mother, but she grabbed his hands so that she could finish saying what she wanted to say.

Helen: I apologized to Evelyn the following Sunday. I didn't realize what I was doing. I was just so scared of losing you that everything and everyone who stood in my way; I wanted to be destroyed. But, it wasn't me; it was a spirit and I now know it. Pastor Norman has been counseling me, and I have been going to bible study twice a week. He still doesn't know that I am your mother, though. Evelyn is a good woman, and I knew that even when I was sick. I just couldn't see past myself, but I am committed to loving her as much as I love you. And my grand baby? I want to be in her life every step of the way. I don't plan to move to California. You guys don't have to worry about that. *(Laughs.)* But, I would love to come and visit you all at least once or twice a year. I ask for your forgiveness, my son and I ask this of you. Never let me or anyone come between what GOD has put together. I am free now. I ask that you pray that I remain free. I never want to go back to that place again. It's a process, learning how to undo what I have done in my dark hours, but I will get through it in JESUS. I'm still a work in progress, but I know I am restored. Keep praying for me, son.

Jim: Mom, I don't know what to say. My heart is so full of joy. This is truly the best day of my life and I bless GOD. GOD is more than just a good GOD; HE is the only true living GOD. I am amazed; however, that I did not come against that spirit that was in you. I'm wondering if I was blind. Why didn't I see it at first?

Helen: Because you didn't want to see it. It was a familiar spirit and it was in someone you were familiar with. Plus, a prophet is not without honor, except in his own country so it would have been very hard for me to receive from you anyway.

Not only was his daughter born on this day, but Jim's relationship with his mother was reborn because she'd been reborn. He and Evelyn went on to have three more children and to be examples and role models in their communities.

Explanation:

What made this possible? The obedient heart of Evelyn, of course. She listened to wise counsel. A husband who has stepped from under the authority of the CHRIST, often times, is trying to catch up with the wife who has stepped from under his (the husband's) authority. And all too often, a wife who has exalted herself against her husband has stepped from under his lead because she knows that he has stopped following CHRIST and has begun to follow his own understanding. In order for her husband to return to his place under CHRIST, Evelyn had to return to hers. That way, in order to cover her, he had to come back into place. Men are designed to fall, but not fail. Their falls aren't a break in the man, but a tool designed to repair that break in the man and to teach them to stand on the WORD of GOD. Sometimes, they take longer than we want them to take to get the message, but long-suffering is a blessed gift that is essential to a lasting, loving and happy marriage.

What have you believed GOD for today? What have you struggled with believing GOD for? As a wife, you cannot lord yourself over your husband. When you do, you expose your head to witchcraft and this is when you will feel like you're going crazy. Stay covered, stay in faith and let GOD be GOD...even in your husband's life. A silent prayer is more effective than a loud rebuke.

Wealthy Wisdom

"Wealth without wisdom is like walking around Afghanistan naked; wearing an American flag."

GOD has commanded everything to line up in accordance with HIS will. This includes the wealth of the earth. Nowadays, it is the norm for people to chase money, but ignore wisdom. This is a fatal flaw in their thinking, as wealth without wisdom is deadly.

"Come on! Come on! Lucky seven?! Where are you?!" Phyllis was anxious to win! She had to win. This was her grocery money, and she was hoping to at least double it. The machine finally finished its spin to reveal that, once again; Phyllis had lost.

She was at the Lucky Fox Casino, and she'd just played her last dollar. Her friend, Yvette stood beside her shaking her head in disappointment. She knew that Phyllis would now have to borrow the money from her for groceries, and she'd been planning to take her kids to the county fair this weekend. She hoped that Phyllis would ask her dad for the money, but just in case she asked; Yvette already fashioned a lie in her mind.

Yvette used to gamble right along with Phyllis, but lately Yvette's been different. She's been trying to get her life right with the LORD, but she doesn't want to turn her back on her friend of seventeen years. So, she comes along to a lot of the old places that they used to frequent together. She always tries to minister to her lost friend; hoping to get her to see the light of truth, but her attempts have been in vain. She did, however, manage to get Phyllis to come to church with her a couple of times, but this wasn't really out of Phyllis' character. She went to her own church often, but she rarely caught on to what the pastor was saying because she would be text messaging or dozing off during service.

As they got up to leave, Phyllis did her usual complaining about the machines allegedly being rigged.

Yvette went along with her; hoping that she'd learned her lesson this time, but it wasn't likely because Phyllis believed that she would win millions of dollars one day. She had more faith in this than she had in GOD.

Yvette worked at the casino, but today was her day off. She didn't want to come into that place on her off day, but Phyllis had begged her; promising to give her a few dollars to play with, even though she was no longer a gambler. As usual, Phyllis felt strongly that this night was the night that she was going to get her million-dollar breakthrough. She kept seeing the number seven all day, plus her hands were itching. Not to mention, her horoscope said that she would be very fortunate today, so Phyllis was anxious to get out and try her luck. *(The mind of witchcraft.)*

As they drove out of the parking lot, Yvette began to speak with Phyllis again about her lifestyle. Yvette is the daughter of a preacher. She met Phyllis seventeen years ago while she was in the world, but now that she has found her way back to CHRIST, she isn't into the things that she was once into. She continued her friendship with Yvette because she didn't want to walk away from her friend. After all, Phyllis has been there for her through some pretty hard times in her life. So, she tried to reason with herself to stay and try to bring her friend to the perfect knowledge of CHRIST.

Yvette wanted to go directly home after the casino. She was tired and planned to go to church in the morning, but Phyllis was still feeling animated. She had taken down a few drinks at the casino and wanted to stop by a night club to burn off some of that fuel. Yvette protested, but her words fell upon deaf ears as Phyllis pulled into Equilibrium; a new night club that wasn't too far from the casino. Phyllis wasn't so downtrodden after having lost over a hundred dollars because the alcohol had taken its effect, and she was numb to the fact that she didn't have money to feed her kids this week. Plus, she felt like tonight was still her lucky night. Maybe...just maybe, she'd pull a decent man. She was getting tired of Drew, her live-in boyfriend, because he wasn't bringing in enough money. Plus, he was too quiet and reserved. Phyllis liked bad boys, and Drew wasn't bad enough for her.

Yvette, of course, was angry with Phyllis. Yet, she often went along with whatever Phyllis did because she was used to putting herself second. As they stood in line, Phyllis could sense that Yvette wasn't happy with her. She wasn't her talkative self so Phyllis turned and began to stare at Yvette. After a two minute stare, she broke her silence.

Phyllis: You're not angry, are you? Because if you are; just tell me, and I'll take you home. I don't want to force anyone to hang out with me.

Yvette: I'm fine, but I can't be here too long. I need to go home and make sure my kids are okay, and I have to go to church in the morning.
Phyllis: No problem. Calm down and let's have some fun! We'll stay here an hour; no more than two hours, okay?

Yvette shrugs as they approach the cashier.

Phyllis: You're not mad, right?

Yvette: I said I was okay.
Phyllis: Would you be mad if I told you to foot the bill because my money seems to have been kidnapped by angry slot machines?

Yvette: I figured you'd want me to pay. It's okay. I'm used to it.

Phyllis: Calm down and let's have some fun, girl! Seriously. You need to get a drink! As soon as we get in, we're going straight to the bar!

In the club, Yvette found a seat and sat there, clutching her purse as Phyllis danced the night away. One hour quickly turned into two hours, and it was now 3:24 a.m.; thirty-six minutes before closing. Yvette's cell phone vibrated, so she walked to the bathroom to answer. It was Phyllis' boyfriend, Drew.
Drew: Yvette? Is Phyllis with you? Because I've been calling her phone all night.
Yvette: Yeah. We're over at the Equilibrium, but we should be leaving in about 30 minutes.

Drew: Okay. Tell her to call me. Wait! Did you guys go to the casino? Please say no.

Yvette: You already know the answer to that one. Yes, we went.

Drew: Yvette, please tell me that Phyllis didn't gamble off that money I gave her. That's for groceries, and that's all we have left.
Yvette: I'll let Phyllis explain that one, but let me go. I can barely hear you.

Drew: (*Sighs*) Okay. Later.

The night passed without further incident and the next day, Yvette got a call from Phyllis. She'd called a few times, but initially, Yvette didn't answer. After a few missed calls, however, she began to worry about Phyllis. This was out of her character, to call again and again. So, she decided to answer this time. She could barely recognize her friend's voice as she sobbed uncontrollably.

Phyllis: He left me.

Phyllis could be heard sobbing and trying to catch her breath.

Yvette: What? Who left you? Drew?

Phyllis: Yeah. We fought all night about the money. I lied to him and told him that I loaned it to you, but he didn't believe me.

Yvette: Phyllis, I told you not bring up my name when y'all had problems.

Phyllis: He left me, Yvette. I don't know what I'm going to do. There is no food for the kids, and I don't even have a dollar to buy a loaf of bread.

Yvette: Just let him cool off. He'll be back. Stop crying and stop worrying yourself.

Phyllis: He's not coming back.

Yvette: Yes, he is. He's just mad. That's just how men are. He

just needs a little cooling time.
Phyllis: No. He said a lot of hurtful things. We are done for real this time. He's not coming back, and I don't know what I'm going to do. Can I borrow about a hundred dollars from you until Thursday?

Yvette: Phyllis, I was planning on taking Roger and Dylan to the fair this weekend. I already told them.

Phyllis: You'll have it back before then. Don't worry. Please, Yvette. If I never needed you; I need you now.

Yvette: You need JESUS, but okay. Come by the house and pick it up.

After picking up the money, Phyllis went by the store to pick up groceries. As she was standing in line, she couldn't resist picking up one of those California lottery tickets. The winner would be announced within a few hours, so the tickets were almost gone.

After arriving home, Phyllis prepared dinner for her kids before retreating to her bedroom to watch the lottery announcement. The winner would be getting over 10 million dollars, and Phyllis danced with the idea of what life would be like if she won.

As the numbers were called out, Phyllis found herself getting more and more numb. She began to tense up as they called out the numbers, and finally; it happened. She'd won! She couldn't move. She couldn't think. She'd even forgotten how to walk. She was so overcome with shock that it took a little over five minutes before she was able to contain herself and call the number.

Months later, Phyllis was living the American dream. She had more money than she'd ever dreamed of having. She was still single, however. After learning of her win, Drew tried to come back, but she wouldn't let him.

Now, she had a house in the suburbs of Beverly Hills and a Porsche parked in her driveway. Everything didn't change, however. You see, the more money you have, the more money you want. People often think that once they are rich, they will be settled in the mind, but the mind is funny because no matter how far up it goes; it always sees itself at the bottom and desires to climb higher. Plus, if you're not adding to your funds; you're subtracting from them. A rich man can stay rich for only so long if he doesn't earn more than what he spends.

So, Phyllis was still going to the casino and still hanging around a few of her old friends. She'd promised them that she wouldn't let money change her. She still dropped her sons off at her aunt Justine's house, which was in a run-down neighborhood, but she had slacked hanging around with Yvette. They talked from time to time, but not often because Phyllis felt like Yvette had changed too much since she started going to church.

It's a year later, and the news flashed across the television screen. Phyllis had been waiting for the lottery to come on, but instead the news came on about some guy being shot. They reported that the police had found the body of a young man laying near a dumpster on 42nd Street. That wasn't too far from her aunt's house. He'd been shot at point blank range; an apparent robbery attempt gone wrong. As the police described his clothing, Phyllis felt her guts wanting to explode. It couldn't be her son, Roman. The young man's body was on a stretcher and was covered up, but his shoes were in plain sight. They looked like Roman's shoes, and he matched Roman's description. Phyllis rushed over to the phone to call her aunt Justine, but there was no answer. Feeling sick, she called Justine's cell phone. Still, no answer. Finally, when she was attempting to dial Justine's husband; her phone started to ring. It was coming from Justine's cell phone.

Justine: Phyllis; they killed him! They killed him, Phyllis! My baby! They killed him!
Phyllis: What do you mean?! What do you mean?! Aunt Justine?! Who did they kill, Aunt Justine?! Who did they kill?! Not my baby! No, not my baby!!!

Justine: They killed him over some dope! They thought he had dope on him and they tried to rob him!

Phyllis: I'm coming over there! They made a mistake. That's not my baby on the television. I'm coming over! And my baby better be safe! No, GOD! Please! He has to be safe!

Explanation:

We could continue with this story from here, but it's too heartbreaking. To tell you the truth, I didn't want to write this one because I knew it wouldn't end well. But, I have to convey the message that GOD wants me to share with you, because it just may save someone from this heartache or something more tragic.

GOD designed wealth to follow the wise. There is a step by step, season by season process that we must undergo before HE will place us in our wealthy places. During this transition, old mindsets pass away. During this transition, old friends go away. Wisdom, knowledge and understanding take their places, and we begin to understand why wealthy people don't hang out with certain groups of people or have too many friends. Sure, some of them exalt themselves; which, of course, is sinful thinking. Then again, a wealthy man could never hang out with a man who wasn't wealthy because the poor man would more than likely kill or rob him one day. Or he'd brag to his friends about his "rich buddy", and they'd go after him.

Imagine your best friend now. The one that has been there for you for decades through thick and thin. Do you truthfully believe that you could continue the friendship, should you become wealthy? The only way that you could do that would be through the sharing of your wealth. You would have to make her wealthy and continually provide income to her for the rest of her life or the life of your wealth. Or you'd have to develop an income source for her for the rest of her life, which would prove expensive and trying, since GOD designed her to only walk in a certain place in HIM. Otherwise, she wouldn't see that familiar best buddy face that she had grown to love. Instead, she would see a millionaire, and this would undoubtedly place you in harm's way. And if you shared your wealth with her, chances are, she'd still go after your life because now you aren't her best friend. You have provided her wealth when she wasn't wearing the wealthy-suit of wisdom! You are now her supplier, and you owe her this money. If you dare to be late or threaten to take it away, you could pay for it with your life. That's why GOD won't give you wealth until HE knows that you won't distribute it amongst the people that HE has withheld it from. He wants to protect them from this exposure as well.

Wealth was never designed to come before wisdom. Any man or woman who comes in contact with wealth must be wearing a wealthy-suit. Let me explain. Wisdom is your wealthy-suit. It's like when someone walks into a room full of radiation. They have to wear a special uniform to protect themselves from the radiation, otherwise they will die from exposure.

Wealth is the same way! Many people have died from exposure to wealth outside of their wealthy-suits. Because people believe that money will make them happy, when it is not true.

Again, I didn't want to tell this story, but the reality is, there are many people who have lost loved ones because of wealth without wisdom. Any and every method of getting money without getting wisdom is spiritually illegal. The seasons have to play out. You have to bud and transition day by day to get into your wealthy place, and you have to be willing to let go of dead things. This includes friendships, family relationships, romantic relationships and old ways. GOD will never give you the stuff without giving you the stuffing. That stuffing is wisdom, knowledge and understanding. They all go hand in hand and form a protective circle around you. Anytime you see a man or woman striving to get money, they are in error and out of season!

GOD said to seek ye **<u>first</u>** the Kingdom of GOD and all its righteousness and everything else will be added to you. What GOD is instructing us to do is stay in line and stay in season! If you removed a seed during the rainy season and placed it in the sunny season, it would die of exposure. It would be scorched! Do what you were created to do and wealth will follow. The reason why you see so many religious people living in lack is because they never acquired the knowledge that they needed to get wealth, nor did they seek wisdom. Why? Because people generally fear success and what it brings. So, people tend to find comfort zones and stay there. And, the ones that want success are often seeking it outside of GOD; not understanding that anything that is given outside of GOD is received in Satan.

When GOD holds back riches from you, it is because HE is protecting you! HE releases it to you as you grow in HIM. When

HE opens up the windows of Heaven, HE doesn't just pour out wealth on you all of a sudden. Often times, you'll get a drizzle of wealth, but a shower of wisdom until you can handle the pour.

Money and material things are vanity, and they cannot make you happy. Look at some of the wealthy souls who have fallen today. Look at the scandals they fall into. It's because many of them got the wealth before getting the wisdom. Sure, we may sit back and say, "Wow, that was stupid. Why did she do that? Why did he fall for that? I wouldn't have done that." That's because we have been down so deep that we had to learn to watch our steps to survive! In your depth, you cried out and GOD picked you up and taught you how to avoid that fall again. Many of them did not learn this. They had to focus on their crafts while we were learning the ins and outs of lack. We had no choice, but to trust GOD and our challenges were like professors, sent to teach us what we needed to know to get to the next level.

The strains and struggles of today are setting you up for a greater tomorrow. However, the devil will tell you that money could solve your problems. Oh, if you only had a few million to kick you off! You could quit your job, move into that big house of your dreams and never have to worry again. This isn't true. The wealthy have their fair share of problems; just not the same types of problems that you have. For example, they have to worry about the people in their circles. They deal with family members that see them as human ATMs. They deal with accountants, the IRS and legalities. Someone is always looking for a way to sue them. They can't go to many of the places that you and I can because, if it is public knowledge that they are rich, they are always at risk of being robbed or kidnapped for ransom. They have to watch what they say and who they say it to, otherwise, their words could be front-page news. However, you and I can say something to someone, and it might get back to a few people, and we end up having those people laughing at us or mad at us, but we can simply strive to avoid them. Problem solved. It doesn't affect our lives because we can walk away from these people and not be recognized by others. Wealthy folks can't do that. Once their words or deeds have been aired to the public, they have to deal with public ridicule by the masses. They have to deal with a world who feels like they owe them an explanation for every choice that they make and every word that they utter. So, problems don't go away with the presence of wealth; they just weigh in on a larger scale.

Your imagination has no limitations. It's like window shopping. Your imagination lets you see what you can have; only you have to come back with the faith to pay for it. But, let your desire to have wisdom override your lust to have wealth. Remember, Solomon did not ask for wealth; he asked for wisdom, and this pleased the LORD. What Solomon did not know was that with wisdom, comes wealth. They come hand in hand.

Phyllis put her children and herself in danger every time she stepped into that casino, but Satan didn't tell her that part. Why would he? His desire is to kill, steal and destroy. GOD would have given her the desires of her heart and added no sorrow to it, but any and everything that Satan hands out is like a charming; poisonous snake. It'll dance for you for a while and then, all of a sudden and out of nowhere...it'll strike.

Yvette seemed like a good friend, but she wasn't. Yvette was an enabler. She refused to say “no” to Phyllis, and she allowed

Phyllis to convince her to go against the will of GOD. Any time you have to offend GOD to please your friends, it's time for new friends or to just be alone with the LORD. You can never drag a soul to salvation. Yvette should have continued to serve the LORD and stopped the evil communications with Phyllis. She was supposed to minister to her and let that be that! Nothing else outside of blessed communicating. If Yvette would have lived her life in accordance with the WORD of GOD and absolutely, without apology, refused to sin; Phyllis would have distanced herself from her before she arrived at her wealthy place. Sinners like to sin! They are drawn to it like a moth to a flame. So, when you refuse to sin, they are repelled from you. Yvette's new life and blessings would have ministered to Phyllis, and she probably would have turned her life over to GOD as a result. It happens! Sometimes, it's not our words that people listen to...it's our life.

Don't chase the wealth of this world because you just might catch it and everything else that's associated with it. Seek the wisdom of GOD and the Kingdom of GOD. When you do, this earth will have no choice, but to treat you like the royalty that you are and there will be no sorrow added to your blessings!

Wisdom is as essential to our existence as water. That's why so many people outside of GOD are thirsty. They indulge in gambling, drugs, alcohol, promiscuity and every imaginable sin around; trying to fill that void in them. Problem is....no one and no thing can fit that GOD shaped hole in their hearts! They find idols to try and replace the LORD, but nothing works. Their idols are people, drugs, money, attention and ideas. They serve them faithfully; hoping that one day, the great payout will come. In the rare chance that it does, the payment will not match what Satan listed for them in the contract, but instead all sin has death attached to it! The wages of sin is death!

The Bible is our instruction manual, and it tells us how we are to operate so that we may live. There are no replacement parts for a broken heart. There are no boot-legged mechanics that can fix what has been broken in you. Only GOD can fix us because HE is our Manufacturer, and HE designed us in such a way that no man can repair us!

Wait on wisdom. Pray for wisdom. Seek wisdom. And evict the foolish things of this world from your heart. Call Satan what he is...a liar!

And the next time Satan tempts you with the idea of quick wealth...ask him this question and command that he answer it truthfully: What is it going to cost me?

Then remind him that GOD already answered that question. ***"For the wages of sin is death; but the gift of God is eternal life through Jesus Christ our Lord." (Romans 6:23)***

What A Soul Tie Looks Like

"You will only have to forgive a man when you need GOD to forgive you."

When we sin against GOD, man sins against us. When we are hurting and finding ourselves searching for a way to forgive the man who has wronged us, it is often because we have hurt GOD and in turn, we need HIS forgiveness. If you never go outside of GOD, you won't struggle with ungodly soul ties that were established in sin. You will be found by your husband, and you will turn away any other man who tries to impersonate him.

Soul ties are very easy to spot on a woman. They show in the way she dresses, can be heard in her speech and even seen in her walk. You can even witness a woman's soul ties through the music she chooses to listen to or the way she dances. You're probably saying, "That's not true! When I was a virgin, I used to love myself, this or that artist and I wasn't having sex with anyone! But, I did dance sexy!"
Soul ties are not just established through sex. Soul ties are established through associations or communications. Anyone who listens to a certain artist will develop a soul tie with that artist. Now, if the artist is GODLY; your connection is brotherly or sisterly. But, if the artist is full of demons; your soul tie is one of demonic nature and his or her words will seduce you to act, think, dance and believe a certain way. After all, that's what

a soul tie does. It engages the mind to change! Observe how you act when you are in the presence of that artist that you love to listen to. Does your heart beat faster than normal? That's a soul tie! Do you pass out or beg for their autograph? Soul tie! Do you tremble and beg for their autograph? Soul tie!

What if your ex passes by you? How do you respond? If your heart flutters, that is evidence of an existing soul tie. Always pay attention to the heart itself. The heart in your chest cavity isn't your real heart, in relation to the Bible. When the Bible refers to your heart; it is referring to your mind. But, our natural heart responds to what is in our biblical heart.

She heads off to the racetrack for a moment of fresh air. After many restless nights and questions from her children, she has opted to take a moment to herself and just relax. So, she drops her children off at school and off she goes to watch the races, clutching her cell phone in her hand. Maybe...just maybe, he'll call. After a few weeks of being apart, he should be feeling what she's feeling, right? Nevertheless, today her hopes are high. Why would anyone want to break up just because of an argument? All couples argue, but he didn't like the taste of arguing. So, he moved out and went to live at his brother's house.

After arriving at the racetrack, her phone begins to ring. Feeling her heart thumping, she raises it to see the number that is calling. Bummer! It's a telemarketer. They always seem to call at the most inconvenient times! She pushes the button to hang up the call; frustrated that they'd taken her through a gut wrenching few seconds. But, he'll call hopefully. After those voice mails that she left, he should see that she meant no harm in talking about getting married. She wanted to make it official, and he wanted to continue as things were.

Explanation:

Let's stop here. This is a common scene that plays in the life of many believers. Who is 'she?' She is the many women that have developed soul ties outside of GOD and tried to bring them into right-standing with HIM; only to have the devil to take back what was his. Understand that any relationship birthed in sin is headed by the devil, and he can do whatever he wants with it. When she was fornicating and shacking with a man who was not her husband, Satan was the connecting tie between the two of them. But, her desire to take her relationship and give it to GOD left the enemy wrought with her. So, what he could control; he did control, and what was in his hands was the switch to that relationship. When we step into sin to carry on a relationship, Satan has the right to that relationship's power-switch. Your sin granted him the rights to turn that relationship on or off. And sometimes, he likes to flick the switch on and off. On again, off again relationships are great examples.

Believers and non-believers do not share the same convictions. When a believer sins, it weighs upon his or her heart and their love for GOD and fear of GOD often drives them to repentance. But, a non-believer isn't convicted in sin because they've been a prisoner of sin for as far back as they can remember, and it is all they know.

A woman is designed to one day become a wife. CHRIST is the head of man, and man is the head of the woman. Head represents the leading authority or covering. When a man sleeps with a woman, he illegally becomes her husband because the two shall be one. What makes it fornication is the fact that he did not bring GOD into the equation, and he has no intention of covering that woman for life, as he was supposed to. He was driven by lust and not love. GOD is love, but lust is of the flesh. So, the man leaves her uncovered and exposed to all manners of evil. She too was instructed by GOD to guard her heart (mind.) But when she had sex with that man, she opened up her heart (mind), which is why she can't stop thinking about him. She is **not** his covering, so his thoughts are far from her. He takes life one day at a time; entertaining his flesh, while she is living hour to hour in total misery.

He wants the things of the world because he is a man of the world. He sees riches, and he chases them. He sees women, and he goes after them. He saw her, and he pursued her until she had been caught and spent. After there was nothing left in her to spend, he wanted to be free of her. But for her, she has given him all that she has and doesn't know how to live without him. So, she waits and waits for her investment to pay off. Hurt and confusion slowly simmer and thicken to become bitterness.

He hasn't called. He doesn't plan to call, and she can't stop thinking about him. So, she goes to the salon to get beautified. She stops by the mall and picks up a short skirt to grace her figure. She has a plan. She's going to get dressed up on Saturday and go hang out with her old friend who lives close to his brother's house, in hopes that he will see her.

Saturday comes, and her plan is put into motion. She heads over to her friend's house and asks her to come outside. After all, the weather is perfect. From there, she could see his brother's house. And his car isn't there, but what does that mean? He could be in the house, and his brother is probably driving his car around. She is conscious about everything. She laughs at her friend's every word, even though there was nothing funny about what she said. She poses a lot while her friend talks; hoping that he sees her. A few minutes later, his car pulls into his brother's driveway, but the first door to open is the passenger's side door. And out comes this woman. A new woman. And he slowly steps from his car. He is laughing until he spots her, who, by now is running towards him in tears and anguish.

This could have been avoided had she listened to GOD. But, she didn't. Like many female believers, she thought that she could go into sin, bring out a sinner and usher him towards repentance, but she was wrong. Instead, that man took her into sin. Why is that? Because a husband is designed to lead his wife; not follow her.

When women are imprisoned by soul ties, it shows. They spend time in confusion, hurt, anger, disappointment, unforgiveness and vengeful thinking. They also spend time creating new soul ties trying to drown out the pain of the last soul tie. Her head was designed to be covered, but instead, it is exposed to devils who waste no time toying with it. She has given him her mind, body and soul. Thank GOD she couldn't give away her spirit, or she would have done so and been lost without a remedy. When she slept with him, what she was speaking in the spirit realm was that she no longer needed the direct covering of the LORD, but now, she had a husband who was covered by the LORD, and he would cover her. When he opened her body, he was in the same, opening her heart and soul. And devils love an open woman with no covering because a woman is a man's weakest point.

But, what if this is you? How do you get back under the protective covering of the LORD to reside in peace? That's easy; you repent. Repent doesn't mean to say, “I'm sorry,” as many religious prisoners would have you to believe. To repent is to turn away from the sin itself, meaning, you won't go back; you've changed your mind. Saying that you won't return avails you nothing if your heart is saying otherwise. GOD pays more attention to what your heart is saying than what your mouth is saying because we are all found to be liars, but our hearts are like that little black box in an airplane. They will only play back what was recorded.

Here are a few tips to help you through the process.

1. Repent and <u>re</u>dedicate your life to the LORD. Stay there!
2. Refuse to go into sin with anyone. When a person has been delivered from a soul tie and the demons that came with it; they are, in a sense...marked. Any demon that has been cast out will always try to find its way back to what it sees as its property. This is why you may all of a sudden become a 'hot item' with men.
3. Be aware of the devil and his antics. He's crafty enough to send the man you really want back into your life. This man now has a “change of heart.” And he wants to get back into your heart. He had a sudden awakening! You are the one! For now, that is. When the enemy can't use other men, he'll use the man whom you want the most. And of course, we know what happens when a demon comes back in. It brings seven demons more evil than itself, and you'll end up worse than before.
4. Stay focused. Refuse to come from under HIS covering.
5. Forgive your assailant. What he did was wrong, but you have to understand that he may serve a completely different god than you do. Sure, he may go to church, but that doesn't make him a 'man of GOD.' That makes him a man who went into a building and sat down. Even if he's a leader in the church, please know that all leaders aren't from GOD'S fold. Period. You will know them by their fruit. If he wanted to fornicate with you...guess whose tree that fell from?

6. Come out of familiarity. Sure, you and your old beau used to love to go to the ice cream shop and share whatever you ordered, but you're not together anymore! That's why you tear up when you pull into the parking lot listening to what you refer to as "our song." You are holding yourself hostage and refusing to let yourself go until GOD gives you what you want. You can't bribe the LORD, and HE definitely doesn't reward emotional tantrums. Find new things to do and to get into. For example, you could go and take real estate courses. What you are doing is broadening your understanding and engaging your mind. In addition, get away from friends who entertain the lies that Satan told you. Understand that when someone is a messenger of GOD, they will say what HE said; but when someone is not of GOD, they will always entertain your flesh and the lies that Satan once told you.
7. Avoid idle time. Idle time gives you too much time to ponder, and you will find that this is often your hour of heartbreak. Find something constructive to do with your time. Don't just sit and watch videos, learn something new.
8. Build on your financial success by building onto your wisdom. Make your request known to GOD and learn some new trades. The more you learn; the more you'll earn. And the more you know; the more you'll grow. After you have grown to a certain height in your knowledge and in your finances, that same ole man whom you once saw as a gift from GOD will look like a poorly wrapped joke. A successful woman is less likely to accept a man who does not excel above her. This is why GOD wants you to wait and get to know HIM first. As HE grows you up in wisdom, knowledge and understanding; your eyes will be opened. Most of the men that you once desired in your blindness will suddenly look to you the

way they look to GOD. And you will bless the Name of the LORD for deliverance!

9. Go on a journey in your imagination. Often times, soul ties leave residue. You pictured this guy as your loving husband and the doting father of your children, but GOD saw the truth. HE knew what this man would do to you. So, now that GOD has finally severed the soul tie; you still find yourself thinking about this man. Why is that? It's called residue. You have to be changed by the renewing of your mind. I used to tell women to just imagine another man being there, but I found this to be error, as it sets them up for the next wrong man. Imagine you and the LORD and the contentment that you'd receive in HIM. Sure, that's hard and it's definitely a stretch of faith, but that's what we want, isn't it? To stretch your faith. Imagine yourself doing what you have always dreamed of doing. Try to find your way back to the whole heart of GOD without feeling like you need to be hand in hand with a man first.
10. Get to know GOD more. The more you know HIM, the more you'll understand. A man should NEVER be your number-one purpose in life. That's idolatry! Idolatry is spiritual adultery. Idolatry is when you try to serve two gods, when there is only one true living GOD. Anything and anyone that we exalt as number one is what we have chosen as a god.

The Unveiling Of The Real You

From here, I won't tell you anymore stories, but I will share some advice with you as the LORD has taught me.

Who you are is a mystery even when you look in the mirror. Because the woman that is 'you' is not found in the skin's identity, but is found in CHRIST. Know more about HIM and you'll know more about you.

As we grow up in CHRIST, we learn to put together the pieces of what we know about ourselves and it is in HIM that we are able to form the whole picture. GOD created us in a way that we have to search HIM out to find ourselves. Without doing so, we find only clues of who we are, but live our lives not knowing the truth behind the woman in the mirror.

Sure, as a child, you may have loved to talk more than most people. Or you may have been excessively quiet and very observant. Our childhood personalities gave us and others the first few clues as to who we are.

Then there are the habits that we have picked up along the way. They aren't always clues to our identities, but are the symptoms that identify what types of spirits or mindsets dwell in or with us. Whatever evil rides with us is illegally there and feeds off of our fears, words and beliefs. For example, a woman who believes that all men are cheaters is infected by and inhabited by lies. This is what she received; whether she learned it from her mother or just chose the wrong men and developed her own theory. Her habitual thoughts bear witness to what inhabits her. If she picked up this lie through her own experiences with men, the question is; why did she choose the men that she chose? What was it about them that she was attracted to? The answer could be many things, but the root of her thinking is a lack of knowledge. And because we were created to require answers, she replaced the truth with a lie and accepted it. Her heart was infected, and one of the symptoms of an infected heart is blurred vision or blindness. She saw only her results and tried to make them the realities of everyone else. Because it is easier for her to accept this lie and just tolerate men who cheat on her than it is for her to accept the truth; she keeps attracting the wrong men because she is inhabited by the wrong things.

Most of us have an idea as to what type of life we want to live. But, here's the problem. Who you want to be often battles with who you were called to be. Who you want to be is a lust that has shaped because of what you have experienced in life. Who you are called to be was given to you before you were even conceived. The two cannot be merged; however, when the LORD cleans us up, opens our eyes and sends us out; our will begins to match GOD'S will for us. Our imaginations and desires are no longer shaped by the crafty hands of the devil. Instead, without the rust and build up of wrongful thinking, we stand polished; knowing how to accept the rain for what it is; the LORD watering us for growth. That is, we get excited and joyful about serving GOD and doing what HE has called us to do.

How do we get to this place of who we are? Matthew 6:33 reads, ***"But seek you first the kingdom of God, and his righteousness; and all these things shall be added unto you."*** That has been the answer all along. Look at the scripture again. Often times, when we read it in religiousness, it sounds like another wise quote to speak, but nothing more. However, we were built by GOD, and the Bible is our instruction manual. It tells us how to operate ourselves in the earth realm. When we operate differently, we break down easily and will eventually retire ourselves to an early grave if we do not let the oil of GOD come in and wax us new again. Who you are is not found in that face starring back at you from the mirror. No, who you are is found in CHRIST. Unfortunately, the average Christian does not discover the entirety of who they are because they get so wrapped up in living that they go to their graves knowing nothing more than a few scriptures, their own names, the people's names around them and their job requirements. The average person doesn't read their Bibles everyday or pray to the LORD everyday. They may talk to HIM and ask HIM to bless their food. They may religiously quote their prayers at night. They may head to church every Sunday, but that's it. That's not knowing HIM, however. Our leaders can tell us only what they know about HIM, but the answers are found deep within the heart of GOD. Your leader has only went so far in HIM, but you have to be willing and determined to go further. That means, as you grow older in CHRIST, the leadership that has fed you may change.

Sure, we all have dreams. We want the big houses, the cars, the wonderful families, the travels and the money to afford all of this. But, the things of life are not high enough to be enough for who we really are. Material possessions are only accessories. They may make us look better to others, but in reality, we are defined in who we are without those things. Nevertheless, on average, most women want nothing more than what they can have here on earth. In Matthews 6:19-21, CHRIST instructs us, ***"Lay not up for yourselves treasures upon earth, where moth and rust does corrupt, and where thieves break through and steal: But lay up for yourselves treasures in heaven, where neither moth nor rust does corrupt, and where thieves do not break through nor steal: For where your treasure is, there will your heart be also."***

Yet, most search out things, situations and relationships that can go no higher than the skies and no deeper than the grave. And if earth is where your heart is found; earth is where you condemn your soul. GOD'S Word is true, and nothing that HE has said will ever come back to HIM void. Therefore, condemnation is found in everyone not found in CHRIST JESUS. And to be found in HIM is not just to be found saying HIS Name or claiming to be Christian. Being found in CHRIST is being found in obedience. You obey the Truth and seek out the Truth, for CHRIST is the Truth. You cannot live a life filling yourself up with lies and lusts and expect to enter Heaven. Lukewarm Christians aren't found in CHRIST because they've been spat out. They are, instead, found in their sins.

Jonah had purpose, but Jonah did not want to honor that purpose. He wanted to live life the way that he saw right. But, he could not escape who he was and in the belly of the whale, he found that he could not outrun who he was. So, Jonah had a choice. Serve GOD as he was called to do or die right there. Because there were many souls that could have been lost if Jonah decided to lord himself over his purpose. Instead, Jonah was birthed in purpose, called to purpose and had to live in purpose. Just like a television set was created to operate as a television and nothing else. If it begins to ring; how could you answer it, seeing that it is not a phone and does not have a receiver? You and I were created by the WORD of GOD, sculpted with HIS hands and sent out in HIS image. We were given 'will,' just as our FATHER in Heaven has. We get to will what we want to do and will what we do not want to do. But, when your will does not match HIS Will, you are cut out from HIS Will and cannot seek an inheritance in HIM; seeing that you chose to divorce GOD and marry Satan. You are to will yourself to obey HIM and be led by HIM and in doing so, HE will unveil who you are.

Wisdom cries out and calls on everyone who comes by. Proverbs tells us that wisdom is looking for those who are willing to dine with her. Problem is, most people pass along the way. Wisdom's dishes are too costly for them. It would require them to give up their foolish ways, evil deeds and lives of ungodliness to walk in the pure holiness of GOD. People are led of their own lusts. They have allowed wealth and power to lord itself over them, and they serve these things faithfully. They desire the Throne of GOD as Satan did. They want all that GOD has to offer, without having to go to or through HIM for it. So, they try to remove GOD from the equation, but a life without GOD is a minus and does not add up to anything, but an eternity in hell.

If you really want to know who you are, you have to get so lost in CHRIST that you don't recognize yourself anymore. Why? Because what you see isn't you. What you see is the camouflaged suit that you've been wearing all of these years, but the joy and the peace that you so desire is found in the depths of the knowledge of HIM. Nowhere else will you find peace or joy. Sure, you can find happiness, but happiness and joy are not the same. Happiness is triggered by an external situation that has caused you to feel a sense of joy, but joy comes from the inside and radiates outwardly. Joy is only found in CHRIST and is not diluted with sin. Joy is pure and it internalizes itself in the believer, but happiness is a counterfeit that visits the ungodly in their sins. Often happiness has to be triggered by alcohol use, drug use, relationships and external situations that are often times ungodly. Joy can be activated without a external remote. Someone who has joy can be alone and still feel more than happy. And when we are found in CHRIST, we are surrounded by the heartbeat of joy.

There are a few things you need to do everyday to get back to you and find out those mysteries that have plagued you all of your life. You could pray all day, but without the works, your faith is dead. Willing yourself to do the will of GOD is the same as willing yourself to live forever with HIM. Here is what you need to do to find you:

1. Repent of your sins everyday before coming to the LORD in prayer. The Levites couldn't just walk into the temple and talk to HIM; they had to be purified. Thank GOD, we don't need bulls and goats anymore, but we need only to repent and plead the precious Blood of JESUS over ourselves.
2. Talk to HIM and tell HIM your struggles. Sure, HE already knows, but when you tell HIM about them and ask HIM to cure you of them; you are in the same hour acknowledging that HE is GOD alone.
3. Stay in obedience. I see so many women who never ever get to their blessed places, even in the church, because they are downright rebellious. They believe by going to church often and shouting all over the place that they have somehow rendered themselves righteous. GOD is looking for your fruit and whatever you yield will bear witness to what you really are; evil or righteous.
4. Cut all evil communications. Sure, she's been your friend for

most of your life, but if you plan to grow; she may have to go. That is, if she is serving sin. Even those friends that are religiously going to church, but can't seem to break it off with gossip, slander and complaining cannot be found in your midst. Sometimes, we have to cut people off; not because we want to, but because we have to. It's not just for our sakes, but for theirs. We want them to go into HIM and grow in HIM.

5. Live everyday as if it were your last day. Don't lie, cheat or steal. Worship the LORD and do HIS will.

6. You are the temple of the HOLY SPIRIT; not that building! Realize that cursing, lying and speaking perversions are evil even when you are not in the building!

7. Stop listening to secular music. Okay, this is where many of you get off the bus because many like to believe that some music is okay to listen to. Everything that is birthed has a spirit behind it. The singers that you love to listen to all have a spirit behind them or in them. I don't care how much they thank GOD on stage; if their music does not reflect HIM, the spirit behind them is one of idolatry. It doesn't matter if they have one gospel song on their CD, or if you only listen to their positive songs. If they are ministers of Satan...they are ministers for Satan; point blank! You can't listen to what goes from their mouth because it is contaminated. If the singer sings or raps any songs that go against the LORD, and they are unrepentant and still singing this type of music; point blank, you cannot listen to their music, no matter how much you like it. It has polluted your life and perverted your ways. Okay. Let's think of it this way. If Satan threw a concert, and today he was singing gospel; would you go? No!!! Because he is the devil, himself. Why is it that when he uses people to sing music for him that you spend the money that GOD blessed you with to go and hear what the devil is saying through that vessel of his? Seriously? If you want to be in right standing with HIM, you have to be an enemy of the world. It is written! Hey, I'm just the messenger; put the religious guns away.

8. Stop listening to some of that gospel music you listen to. And some of it is just for listening...don't sing it though....your words have power. But, wait! It's gospel! No, it isn't. Some of it is secular music with gospel lyrics. GOD said that when we worship HIM, we must do it in spirit and in truth. That means...no lies please! And we worship HIM in spirit...from the inside! Not just a few cute words that you have learned. Did you really die and wake up again? If not, don't sing it into your life! If that's the singer's testimony; that's great! Listen to it and learn from it, but watch your mouth! Some of those lyrics sound good, but get to know GOD and you will find that many of it results in you you singing yourself into situations that you were not called to enter. There is a spirit behind everything and everyone! You will know them by their fruit!
9. Forget about befriending everyone. Try asking the LORD to remove the people from your life that HE doesn't want in it and to add people to your life that HE wants in it. A lot of women are held back because of their associations. You have to get an attitude about your blessings and refuse to be hindered just because this woman or that man doesn't want to do right.
10. Don't strive for anything, but to please GOD. HE said to ask for everything you want and need. Your stride and strive should be to arrive further and further into the perfect knowledge of GOD. That's it and that's all! Everything else will be added to you.
11. Intercede for others daily, but be wise in your prayers! Someone may come along and say, “Will you ask the LORD to give me everything I have been praying for?” Well, would you? No way! First off, you don't know what they've been asking for. They could be asking for someone to fall off a mountain and drown in the sea. Then there's the fact that you don't know where they are. What if it is a woman living with her boyfriend asking the LORD to give them a child? Would you stand in agreement if you knew that you would stand in judgment? Don't use your

prayers to promote or bless evil. Instead, ask the LORD if HE would open her eyes and show her what needs to be done to get her into a better place in HIM. Now, if it is a husband and a wife saying they want to have a child together, by all means, pray for them! But, also pray that they will see what is hindering them and pray that their faith is made whole.

12. Beware of false leadership and prophets. Some prophets aren't GOD'S Prophets; they are psychics or diviners, operating through the use of familiar spirits. There are people that can tell you the color of your bathroom curtains without having ever been in your bathroom. Does this make them GOD'S Prophet? No way! They can be false prophets! Were Pharaoh's magicians men of GOD? After all, they were able to mimic many of the miracles that Moses did. What about the slave girl with the spirit of divination on her that followed around Paul, Timothy and Silas proclaiming who they were? Was she a Prophetess? No. They used familiar spirits.

Never step foot into a church unless the LORD has told you or pulled on you to go there. And never let someone pray over you and for you if you are unsure of the spirit in operation.

13. Cancel every evil word that you have spoken and every evil word that's been spoken against you every day. People like to create roads for us to walk on with their mouths. Roads that lead to destruction, chaos and hindrance. Of course, it is what GOD speaks that will take dominion over us, but evil communication gives people rights to speak into our lives because in evil communication, we are outside of the Will of GOD. And this is not a safe place. Be careful.

14. Be who you know you are and not who have you learned to be. Often times, we develop personalities to fit the people around us. After a while, we lose touch with who we are because we have to keep up the act for the people who have grown to love our shows. We morph into what people want in their lives; disregarding who we really are. This woman wants a protective friend, and you're there with your dukes up, willing to fight for her. That woman wants a friend that she can control, and here you are being her puppet. People won't like you, and that's okay. Some will even hate you. That's their issue. But, you need to be who you were called by GOD to be and not what or who they call you.

15. GOD first. Never ever ever put a person, place, material thing, thought or situation higher than
GOD. Pay attention to yourself every day. What is at the forefront of your thoughts? Who do you find yourself striving to please? If it's not GOD; ask GOD to reorder your steps in HIS Word.

16. Rebuke yourself and pray for yourself. We see our own issues more than anyone else sees them. A woman that corrects herself is a woman that doesn't need correcting.

17. Date GOD and let HIM to take you out. That is, you need to get used to not being surrounded by people, but only by GOD. In this, what you are doing is refusing to let loneliness become a part of your life; should the people around you choose to disappear for a while. People should not have that kind of power over you. So, it's good to spend some time alone; just you and the LORD.

18. Never get too comfortable in any situation or too comfortable around people for long periods of time. You have to be willing to get up when GOD says to get up and to let go when GOD says to let go. Let HIM lead you in your relationships and in everything, and you will find just what the seasons mean and how they work. GOD will bring people in and GOD will take people out, but you have to be willing to let go when HE says to release them. Sometimes, HE may take them away for a season and a reason. And HE may bring them back at some point. But, HE'S GOD...you just be you.

19. Get an attitude about your relationship with GOD. Seriously, you have to be stubborn in and for HIM so that nothing and no one can pull you away, drive you away or run you away from what HE has for you. You have to stand up and know that everyone that walks in HIM is challenged on every side, even by the people that profess to love them. But, stand firm in HIM and refuse to come out of HIM.

20. Have faith in GOD. GOD cannot tell a lie, and HE will not fail you. Some situations look hard, and it seems easier to just go back to what you know, but you have to stand firm in HIM and refused to be moved by anything or anyone that is not GOD.

Random Quotes

"Wisdom is like a beautiful woman and wealth is like a wise man seeking his bride. Wealth always chases wisdom, but runs away from a foolish woman that chases it."

We all know that a man will evade capture by a woman who is chasing him. It is because he was created to be the chaser. GOD designed women to attract their husbands; just as HE designed wisdom to attract wealth.
And wealth comes as a whole; it cannot be torn apart, limb by limb. Wealth is a wealth of peace, a sound mind, wholeness (in body and spirit), the absence of debt and living in the presence and righteousness of GOD.

"If your flesh is your enemy, why do you believe another person's flesh could be your friend?"

Sure, we all want 'friends' or have wanted 'friends' at some point in our lives. But, I have found that the closer one gets to GOD; the less people they want around them. Why? Because we all deal with our own struggles. Sometimes, we are up and sometimes we are down. But, having a friend is having to deal with her struggles as well; even if one of her struggles is to not be able to listen to or empathize with your struggles, yet want to share her load with you. Sharpening one another is great, but when a friend becomes a crutch or views you as a crutch; the friendship is in the flesh, of the flesh and by the flesh!

The further we go into GOD, the less we feel the need to "pair up" or "buddy up" with people. We want simply to pray for one another, sharpen one another and give one another the space to live their lives without constant interruptions. After all, when you're in CHRIST and living there, you don't have much time to spare for idleness or idle conversation. Abraham didn't have time to fight with Lot. He loved him enough to send him away and to come back to his aid when he needed help.

A friend that sticks closer than a brother? What a blessing, right? What's the difference?
A friend of the flesh: Is there for you most times and expects you to be there for them all the time. A friend of the flesh will lift you up <u>where you are</u>, but hold you down when you try to get to a better place. A friend of the flesh expects to talk with you every day or every other day to share her life's events with you and hear what's going on in your life. A friend of the flesh is a hindrance because the two of you cannot move forward on your paths because you are trying to pair up on a journey that you were called to walk alone. A friend of the flesh is driven by motive.
A friend that sticks closer than a brother: Is there for you and knows you will be there for them, when the time arrives. A friend anointed by GOD does not weigh you down with the yoke of expectation. Don't call her for her birthday? No big deal. You probably forgot or were busy. Say 'no' to her and she understands, but say no to a friend of the flesh, and you've got some explaining to do! A friend anointed by GOD can go months without hearing from you or calling you and still know that you are their friend. But, a friend of the flesh is offended in

the flesh when you miss a day or a week of talking to them and/or sharing with them. A friend, anointed to be your friend does not need to know everything going on in your life because they have their own lives to live. However, a friend who needs to know where you are and when you're going is someone who's attempting to make sure that you don't go too far without them; and that's not your friend.
When we know the difference, we can be the difference!

"If the rib doesn't fit; you need to quit!"

"And the LORD God caused a deep sleep to fall upon Adam, and he slept: and he took one of his ribs, and closed up its place with flesh; And from the rib, which the LORD God had taken from man, made he a woman, and brought her unto the man. And Adam said, This is now bone of my bones, and flesh of my flesh: she shall be called Woman, because she was taken out of Man. Therefore shall a man leave his father and his mother, and shall cleave unto his wife: and they shall be one flesh. And they were both naked, the man and his wife, and were not ashamed.

If a man can leave you easily; it's probably because you are not his pre-ordained wife! He did not cleave to you because his rib was not found in you!

Ladies. Beautiful sisters. Why are you trying to hold on to men that were not anointed to be your husbands? You want to laugh and talk about the women who go to the prisons marrying prisoners, but you yourself keep going into the prisons of sin and marrying prisoners of sin. Slaves. Men who worship their flesh and blindly serve Satan. Men who are shackled to their demons; who serve money and their flesh, but want no part of GOD.

Then you get with this man, and you CAN CLEARLY SEE that he is not the one that GOD sent for you, but you keep trying to force his rib into place, and it hurts! And guess how he addresses you? He says you keep trying to imprison him! He says that you are acting like a warden! Because you are trying to make him a prisoner of love, and he's already serving a sentence elsewhere. So, he keeps on acting up. You have to live in his prison to keep him. Your children have to be prisoners to please him. He's a thief, taking on a woman who is anointed as another man's wife. Sure, you haven't gotten married yet, but your husband is in GOD; not prison. And this man knows that you are not his wife, and he does not intend on marrying you; unless he can find a way that the marriage will benefit him. But, you keep trying to match who you are to his missing rib and wondering why you're always in pain. It doesn't fit!

"Believing in the Word of God and acting out in faith is more than a reflection of who I am, but it is a rejection of who I was."

We reject the flesh. We reject the past and we are to embrace who, what, and where GOD has called us to be. Our acts of faith will not and cannot be understood by people because faith supersedes the thoughts of a man. Stay in faith, for there, you are under the wings of the LORD.

"A good woman deserves a better man."

Women love to complain about being mistreated after having been good to the man they chose to give their lives to. But, the facts and the truth are not the same. The facts are what can be proven in the realm of the natural, but the Truth is what has been proven in the realm of the spirit; or what GOD has already declared. Fact is, you were good to him, and he didn't reward you with the love and respect you feel you deserved. Truth is, you were being the right woman for the wrong man. How can a man appreciate a woman who was not created to be his wife? But, the man who is anointed for a particular woman has to walk at a greater height than she; therefore, he will know how to love and appreciate her because he will know how to lead her. A man's wife is created by GOD for him. She is cut from his fabric and therefore, cannot be successfully interwoven with another man and when she tries, she will find herself always hurt, disappointed, rejected, used and eventually cut out. As good as you are, your husband has to be better.

"Life writes us a check to pay us for what we've done. Don't like your check? Quit your sin."

Many of us complain about the manifestations of troubles in our lives. We like to go to the pastor, rebuke the devil, and cry our eyes out. But, in reality, most of what is coming up against us came as a result of our disobedience to the LORD. We like to walk to the left when GOD called us to the right. On the left, there is something like a beautiful river that looks inviting. Left alone, it sits dormant. But, when you go to the left, you pour who you are into that river and the fumes of disobedience rise up and knock the wind out of you. Sometimes, we have to come against ourselves and our own selfish desires, rather than trying to introduce our wrongs to our rights, hoping that they would form a healthy relationship.

"Only the blind would dance with a wasp's nest and get mad when they get stung."

Have you ever met a married woman who had a single friend

that liked to sleep with married men? And the married woman feels 'safe' because she has befriended the woman. Because she's a friend, she thinks that this woman won't come after her husband. Unfortunately, there are a lot of women out there like that. I was once in the world, so let me explain it this way. You may hang around with a woman and keep her as a friend for years, and she has never went after any man that you had. Is it because she is your friend? No. That particular man, to her, was not worth it. But, get a man that she feels is too good for you and too good to be true; and she will go there.

This goes for romantic relationships as well. I once met a woman who carried on an affair with a married man. When she got him away from his wife, full-time to herself, and he cheated on her; she didn't know how to handle it. Because she did not understand that he was an adulterer, and an adulterer does what? He commits adultery! Whether you're his legal wife through GOD or his illegal wife through fornication, he will default to what he is every time! Never fails!

Let's talk about family. You hang out with this family member who likes to gossip. But, she loves to come around you and sit with you at family outings, so you think she won't gossip about you. Could it be that she has 'dirt' on everyone else, but she's allowing you to spill all of your issues, fears and challenges before she builds her campaign against you?

GOD shows us who people are, but we choose to believe otherwise. Because we, as human beings, want to believe that the next person is just as faithful and loyal as we are. But, people aren't who they are; they are what they are. What they are identifies who they REALLY are. A gossip is a gossip. A liar is a liar. An adulterer is an adulterer. A thief is a thief. A killer is a killer. What a man or a woman is labeled by GOD;

that they are, and they can ONLY be that with you until they are delivered! And guess what? You can't deliver them. You can give them 143 sermons a day, sprinkle hot holy oil on their heads, cut out Bible scriptures and stuff it in their mouths, baptize them in the waters of Jerusalem, or declare your undying love and your living pain to them, but....at the end of the day, they are what they are and they will be that until they go to GOD asking HIM to change them.

"We are all pregnant with something. Be careful who you deliver your plans to; they just might kill your baby."

We are women. So, it goes without saying; we like to open our mouths real big and talk about what we plan to do. Especially when the idea is still fresh, and we are boiling over with excitement. But, all too often, we deliver our plans to the people we think are our friends and what they'll do is run off with your baby or attempt to assassinate it. This is because they were not skilled to deliver that baby, yet, you pushed it out in front of them and trusted them with it.

Just imagine that you were Queen and your baby was heir to a multi-billion dollar kingdom, but your best friend was a slave. You went into labor and asked her to come and deliver the baby, who is now heir to this kingdom. Do you believe that she will deliver this baby and give it to you? No. She will either kill the mother and try to run off with her baby (envy), assassinate the baby (hindrance) or hold the baby for ransom (anointing leech.) We bring people into our lives for many reasons. Either they are where we are, and we can relate to them or they are where we want to be and we want to relate to them. But, here's the problem with that. GOD has called you to relationships (friendly and marriage) that match or supersede the height that you are called to. This way, when you grow; there is not a thing nor is there a person that is close enough to you to pull you down. Everyone around you should be pulling you up or when it is time for someone else to be elevated, the LORD will may send them into your life so that you can pull them up.

Don't give your baby to people with no vision.

"Every person you meet is not qualified to be in your life. Some people come to teach a lesson and some people come to be a lesson."

You may hear me talk a lot on this subject because this is one of the babies that GOD has given me. I had to learn to let go of people in certain seasons, and I saw that when I did, the LORD would promote me. This was because there was and is no person that is so important to me that I am willing to throw away my soul, my blessings, my health, my wealth, my ministry or my marriage for. Because in the same way that we believe others can hold us back from arriving at where we are supposed to be, you can too hold a person back from arriving at where they were called to be.

When people come into your life, they come for a reason and a season. If GOD didn't send them, they've come to corrupt you and uproot every seed that the LORD given you to plant. You see, in order for the LORD to call the increase, the seed has to remain in the ground. But, when you have people around you that are not supposed to be around you; you will feel 'pulled' to tell them your plans (or should I say the location of the seeds you're planting.) After this revelation, the enemy will go and try to unearth the seed.

Pay attention to your friends and associates. Someone calls you and tells you all of their plans and their dreams. Then they get silent, waiting on you to tell them yours. But, instead of telling them, try this Praise the LORD for theirs and say that GOD is still building your vision. Every time they call, do this. Never release the whereabouts of your seed. Sometimes people give you a little so that you can give them a lot in return. Let's say Hanna has $50,000,000 and her best friend had only $50,000. Her best friend goes out and buys Hanna a new wardrobe valued at $5,000. She didn't necessarily do this because she loved Hanna. She did this because she knew that this would pull Hanna to do as she did. She spent 10% of what she had on Hanna because she knew 10% of what Hanna has would be $5,000,000. If Hanna went back out there and spent $5,000 on her, her response would be negative. She would say, “You didn't have to do that! You don't have to do something for me just because I did it for you.” Why? Because Hanna spent what she spent and didn't even graze her expectation. But, if Hanna went and spent $5,000,000 on her, she'd call Hanna the greatest friend to ever live.

But, when you bring the wrong people in, a lesson will begin to take shape. When you let GOD send the right people in, a blessing will begin to take form. Even believers. Some people are sent to teach you, others to be taught by you, while GOD may send many to sharpen and be sharpened by you. When we go outside of the parameters of what GOD wants us to do, we walk inside of a trial designed to deliver us from what we've walked into. Always be prayerful about the people that come in, so you don't have to wound up praying that the LORD will send them out.

"Every wife has a price that only her husband can afford to pay."

"And Jacob served seven years for Rachel; and they seemed unto him but a few days, for the love he had for her." (Genesis 29:20)

Your boyfriend did you wrong. That's okay. You called yourself a 'girlfriend' and called him a 'boyfriend' when those words aren't found in the Bible. So, it was a lesson for you. But, did you get the lesson? Are you still silently testing or loudly rebuking the test results?

Your husband did you wrong. That's okay. Because you probably married the man you wanted to marry and not the man GOD called you to marry. All too often, women marry a man who was intended to be their lesson. Well, he wounds up being a repeat course for years and years until he either gives himself to the LORD, or he gives up on the marriage. A man that is not in CHRIST will give up on the marriage before he would even consider trying on GOD to see how HE fits into his life. Because he has lived before without you, so he knows that he can go on without you, but he has never lived before in the shadows of the MOST HIGH. It is easier for a man to do what they are familiar with than for them to walk into the unknown and be led by faith. That's why they have to come to CHRIST and walk in the light before they are presented with a wife to lead.

The reason so many men do you wrong is because they have not paid the price for you, therefore, they cannot value you. They don't know your value. No matter how much you've done, you can't open a man's spiritual eyes so that he can see you sparkle. You can complain until he comes to church with you, weigh on him to read the Bible, but in the end, we all have a 'default' button. If he is a sinner, he will return to his sin, like a dog returns to his vomit. So, whatever he is, he will default to. If you want to be loved, valued and treasured...then don't step from behind the glass and mix in with the costume jewelry. The expensive jewelry stays behind the counter and only the people that can afford it will get it. But, when you call yourself a diamond, yet you mix with the costume jewelry, you can't get mad if a man doesn't treat you the way you deserve to be treated. You didn't even treat yourself the way you deserve to be treated! And he didn't have to pay much for you.

Let the man go through his tests, trials and promotions and be led to you. Often times, the man you hope to marry isn't the man you're called to marry. You only like the man of today because you are passing through today trying to get to tomorrow. But, when you arrive there, he'll pull you back and hold you there because he wasn't called to walk into today with you. But, the husband, that was called by GOD will not only lead you through, but he'll carry you to some of the best and most blessed times and places because you loved GOD so much that you were willing to stay in HIM and trust HIM. And for that, HE will bless you.

What's Your Story?

There are many of you who have learned a thing or two through your fair dealing of the hand that life has played with you. If you'd like your story to be shared in 'Wise Her Still II,' be sure to email us your story under one of the quotes above or below that fits it best. Or if there is no quote that relates to your story, just share the story and I'll let the LORD give me the quote. Please do not share a story that is not your own. In addition, please indicate if you want your actual name to be listed or if you'd like me to change your name for privacy purposes.

I do believe that GOD speaks to us through situations as well. Sometimes, we are able to help another woman out by sharing our stories and the lessons that came with it. I hope you enjoyed 'Wise Her Still' and I do believe you have grown wiser from reading this book, if even by an inch.

"A treasure isn't valuable because it's pretty. It's valuable because it's rare."
What's your story?

"The future of someone that lives in the past is to be presently dead."
What's your story?

"Some lessons are earned, not learned."

What's your story?

"Seed it. Don't need it."
What's your story?

"Sometimes we outgrow our friends. It's okay. They'll find new ones that they can fit."
What's your story?

"A man may treat you good, but the husband will always treat you better."
What's your story?

"A loser is someone who tries to outrun themselves. Even when they win; they lose."
What's your story?

"A wife that is humble enough to trust her husband with the lead is the same as a wife who is wise enough to trust CHRIST JESUS with her husband."
What's your story?

"Satan has a dating website. Unfortunately, many believers have profiles set up on it."
What's your story?

"Sometimes we have to lose something good to arrive at something better."
What's your story?

"You cannot marry the Devil and expect the LORD to give you away."
What's your story?

"If you want to be a wife, you have to be faithful to your husband. Starting now."
What's your story?

"When you know who you are, no one can tell you who you should be."
What's your story?

"No one can make straight what the LORD has called crooked."
What's your story?

"One of the symptoms of poverty is when a person cannot afford to be themselves."
What's your story?

"Every level has a devil that's fit for a rebel."
What's your story?

"An immoral woman is like a perfume tester in a store. She is always tried, but never bought."
What's your story?

"A man that will hit you is a man that will kill you. The only difference is....you didn't die last time. "
What's your story?

"Satan can only break into your heart when you leave it open."
What's your story?

"A rubber band, when stretched will pop and hurt whomever is holding onto it. If someone is pulling on a person in your life and they are stretched out between you two; let go. Whoever is still holding on when that rubber band is released is the one that will get hurt the most."

What's your story?

“Some people are your friends not because they want to see you do well, but because they want to see what you're doing.”
What's your story?

“Every thing new that we come into, we start off in it as a baby. Grow up; don't give up.”
What's your story?

“No one can stop what GOD has put into motion.”
What's your story?

“GOD always responds to our 'wrong things' in the right way. When people don't like HIS response, they stop listening to HIM and start answering themselves. ”
What's your story?

Made in the USA
Coppell, TX
24 April 2020